A SECRET
I CAN'T TELL

The First Generation of Children

from Openly Gay and Lesbian Homes

JOE GANTZ

Buzz for A Secret I Can't Tell

"A moving testimony to the courage, determination and inventiveness of same-sex parents who battled against all odds to create loving happy families. A Secret I Can't Tell shows how the families Joe Gantz first met four decades ago have gone from being rare and frowned upon to becoming an increasingly common, accepted and successful facet of family diversity in modern America. Bravo!"
-Peter Tatchell, human rights campaigner and gay-rights activist

"As the song says, "Sons of the thief, sons of the saint, who is the child with no complaint" -- and it turns out that four decades ago, as now, the kids of pioneering gay parents had their share of complaints, too, alongside joys, triumphs, and love. All are skillfully rendered in the family vignettes that make up the bulk of A Secret I Can't Tell. Joe Gantz's original interviews and later updates confirm what the evidence, expertise, and experience of the intervening years have shown: despite discrimination, gay parents are doing a great job, their kids are okay, and families are, well, families. All deserve love, respect, and support."
-Evan Wolfson, internationally recognized civil rights lawyer and strategist. He was the founder and president of Freedom to Marry, the pioneering campaign which drove the successful strategy that won same-sex couples the right to marry throughout the United States.

"It is fascinating to read these testimonies of historical pioneers who paved the way for the extraordinary changes which have taken place in my lifetime. Like many in the LGBTQ+ community, I am deeply grateful for those who took the risk for us all. A Secret I Can't Tell recounts the starting point for our journey toward being an open and unashamed secret! Thank you, Joe Gantz for reminding us of whence we came."
-Vaughan Jones, is the minister of Union Chapel in London, and was the founding CEO of Praxis, a voluntary organization supporting refugees and migrants. He has been active in human rights,

homelessness and migrant rights throughout his long career.

"Although our planet continues to progress each year towards a state of greater sexual toleration and respect, we must remember that, back in the 1970s and 1980s, lesbian and gay mothers and fathers suffered tremendous shame for having challenged the traditional model of heterosexual parenting. In this gripping book, Joe Gantz has chronicled his pioneering research work, providing us with a detailed portrait of the lives and minds of those who challenged the unquestioned standards of yesteryear. As both a psychotherapist and a sexologist, I hold this iconic book in very high regard indeed."

-Professor Brett Kahr, Senior Fellow at the Tavistock Institute of Medical Psychology in London, and Visiting Professor of Psychoanalysis and Mental Health at Regent's University London, and author of Who's Been Sleeping in Your Head?: The Secret World of Sexual Fantasies.

"When you open "A Secret I Can't Tell" you step into an American time machine, nervously set the dial for the year 1983, hit go and whoosh, you're suddenly at the kitchen tables, in the dens or riding along in cars with a brave collection of parents with their teenagers who all have something in common, but, because it's 1983, they barely have the vocabulary or the confidence to tell you what it is. With his remarkable 40-year long, three-generation portrait of gay families, Joe Gantz has found a profoundly moving way of moving back and forth between 1983 and today and showing us that, despite momentary setbacks in human and civil rights, we do live in a culture that can evolve for the better."

-John Hoffman, six-time Emmy Award winning documentary filmmaker whose work includes FAUCI for National Geographic, OUT OF MANY ONE for Netflix, RANCHER, FARMER, FISHERMAN for Discovery and THE WEIGHT OF THE NATION for HBO.

To my father

For years of support and advice on this book,
as well as on previous projects. Thanks, Dad!

Contents

Foreword

By Scott Gatz

Scott Gatz is Founder & CEO of Q.Digital

and Board Member of Family Equality

When my son was in kindergarten, the children took turns teaching their classmates about their life outside the classroom. The kids learned a bit about each other's day-to-day lives, what they liked to do for fun, and all about their pets and family members. Toward the end of the year the class read Todd Parr's The Family Book, a brightly hued book that celebrates all different kinds of families through fun illustrations and humor. Taking inspiration from The Family Book, the kindergartners drew their own pages for a book with two captions that included "All families have_____" and "Some families have_____." The answers reflected their age: "Some families have dogs," "Some families have cats," "All families have love," and "All families have toys." And most importantly for my family: "Some families have two dads," and "Some families have two moms."

That kindergarten exercise probably could never have been imagined by the families interviewed in A Secret I Can't Tell. In the 40 years since this book was originally published, we have come a very, very long way. Unlike the era in which marriage was not available to people like my husband and me, today, LGBTQ people in the United States (and in 29 countries) enjoy equal marriage—and, according to a Family Equality Council survey, 63% of millennial LGBTQ people want to start a family, or grow theirs. Marriage isn't just a ceremony or a piece of paper, either. According to the United States Government Accountability Office (GAO), there are 1,138 statutory provisions in which marital status is a factor in determining benefits, rights, and privileges.

The kids Joe Gantz interviewed between 1979–1983 were being raised by same-sex couples who did not have the right to exist in the way they do today. These families were not supported by the law or their communities, and the children frequently expressed the view that no one else their age would be understanding of their family structure. That came with a grave cost: keeping their home life concealed.

Unfathomable to those young people is the kind of world my son is now growing up in. It's a world where he can see many families just like his, and it's a world in which young people feel much safer coming out, and are doing so in record numbers. Each summer, Family Week in Provincetown, Massachusetts, brings together hundreds of LGBTQ-parented families for a week of connection, activities, and fun. It's truly awe-inspiring to look across a beach of thousands of people all from LGBTQ families. Today we have organizations support us like those that run Family Week. Family Equality is the organization advocating for and connecting LGBTQ Parents, and COLAGE is the organization dedicated to connecting children of LGBTQ people. These organizations help families find each other—even in isolated places with very few LGBTQ people. I treasure that my son gets to grow up knowing that he's supported by a community of people, and that his family isn't something he needs to keep secret.

Chapter 1's Selena sums it up best in her 2022 update: "I think it is going to be really hard for anyone who is being raised in a gay family now to understand what it was like to be a part of that forty years ago. Because it was a completely different world…[The change has] felt like the speed of light!"

The stories you will read in these chapters contain pain, love, dysfunction, and joy. Any family has a mix of all of these things in different measures. But these families had more than their fair share of pain, dysfunction, and difficulty as they held tightly onto their secret. They feared being ostracized or losing their jobs, but more frighteningly feared their families being split up. Some lesbian and gay parents were stripped of their parental rights on the grounds that being in a same-sex relationship meant they were violating state sodomy laws, or they were viewed as "deviants" by family court judges. With distance, we can see that these fears led to anguish, anger, poor behavior, dysfunction and a lot of pain. The pressure to keep a secret likely exacerbated normal teenage angst and added stress to already stressful parenting situations. This pain was caused by a society that forced these families to hide in fear. As you read these interviews, I encourage you to remember the prevailing societal force that shaped so many of these moments.

By returning to his subjects in 2022, Joe shows their stories in true context. Time heals many wounds and as we grow older we remember the good times and gain perspective on the bad times. These families were full of love, and they wanted to be the best they could be for each other. Some of the kids are now parents, some are married, and some divorced, creating new chapters in their lives undoubtedly marked—but not always limited by—the secrecy they were forced to maintain growing up. I delight in reading their stories of their own kids knowing LGBTQ kids and families, and how their grandparents were LGBTQ. In just one generation, their families are in a whole new world.

Our society is a much better one today now that families like ours can live free and openly. The unfair pressure on parents and kids to keep a secret is devastating to witness and I'm glad that for many families this is in the past.

Sadly, we are at real risk of returning to some of those days.

We are living in a time of societal backlash that seeks to force our families back into the closet. Laws in multiple states (most infamously Florida's "Don't Say Gay or Trans" bill) are shutting down all discussion or mention of LGBTQ people and our families in schools. Todd Parr's The Family Book has become one of the most banned books in U.S. schools and libraries. Teachers and students are forcing themselves and the story of their families back into the closet, once again making their lives a secret they can't tell. And several justices on the Supreme Court have signaled their interest in overturning the Obergefell decision that made marriage equality the law of the land. And the Equality Act has yet to pass, meaning there is no federal law protecting equal marriage and the many family rights that come with it.

I recently met a young transgender girl in Texas, roughly the same age as many of the children in A Secret I Can't Tell. She kept her gender identity a secret from her classmates until someone found out and told everyone. Her family was forced to pull her out of school and has since moved to another state after Texas enacted a law criminalizing parents who provide gender affirming care to their children. It is unfair and unacceptable to put this burden on our children, and yet here we are again.

It's been 40 years since Joe Gantz interviewed these families. Even today, the love and laughs and struggles are something we can all relate to. The forced secrecy and pressure these kids and parents felt are foreign to most people today, and that's a testament to how far we really have come. I hope that we can all read these stories, the 1983 interviews and the 2022 updates, and see a fully rounded picture of how alike we all are and how unique their challenges were. I hope that these stories teach us what once was and could be again if we don't course correct.

These stories, rich and complex, are not just a view into another era. They are a time capsule. Let's act to ensure that they do not also contain an urgent warning for our future.

—Scott Gatz

Introduction to the 2022 edition of

A Secret I Can't Tell

In 1977 a law was passed in Florida which banned discrimination in housing, employment, and public accommodation based on sexuality. This law was an important step towards respecting gay and lesbian civil rights. However, immediately after it was passed, Anita Bryant, a former beauty queen and a born-again Christian, started a group called Save Our Children to overturn the law. This group based their campaign on the slogan, "Homosexuals cannot reproduce, so they must recruit". They claimed that the bill would allow gay teachers into schools creating dangerous role models for kids. The Save Our Children campaign stirred up so much fear that six months later they were able to repeal the gay-rights ordinance by a vote of more than 2 to 1. This led to a wave of repeals and gay-rights defeats in other states.

The blatant fear mongering and cruelty of the Save Our Children campaign incensed me. I wanted to do something to show the false logic of their campaign. It occurred to me that if people were afraid of the effect of having a gay role model influencing a child as a teacher, then there couldn't be a more important gay role model than having a gay parent. So, in 1979 I decided to show realistic and positive gay role models by finding families raising children in openly gay homes and asking them to tell their story.

In the late 70's there weren't a lot of families raising children in openly gay homes. There was so much hostility, as well as legal issues to consider, that very few families were brave enough to take the risk of openly raising their kids as gay parents. But I managed to find some, and *A Secret I Can't Tell* follows five families raising children in homes where one or both parents were not hiding their homosexuality. This book was first published in 1983, but the publisher went bankrupt six months later and the book was only briefly distributed. I am republishing the book now in 2022, with an update from many of the children, because these heartfelt stories give insight into the intense pressures and prejudice that gay and lesbian families were subjected to at that time.

Perhaps people assume that because I wrote this book I must be gay or the child of a gay parent. That's not the case. I grew up in a reform Jewish family in a very diverse neighborhood in Cincinnati, Ohio. I find prejudice and injustice deeply disturbing, whether that has to do with race, religion, sexuality, or any other unreasonable bias. And this country has a long tradition, still going on today, of vilifying those people who don't fit the norm. The culture wars have shifted somewhat, but it seems that it is still easy to generate fear and hate using the touchstones of race, religion or sexuality.

A lot has been written recently about White privilege. That's the idea that White people have no concept of the difficulties that Black people have to deal with, because they are afforded such a different, much more privileged experience throughout their life. But there is also something that I would call heterosexual privilege. In 1979 I went into this project with good intentions, however I had not experienced anything like what gays and lesbians dealt with every day. I knew that there was tremendous prejudice towards gays and lesbians in the U.S.; that was the reason I decided to write this book. But I couldn't fully understand the impact of this prejudice because I didn't grow up experiencing the constant insults and ridicule, or threats and potential violence, that nearly every gay, lesbian and trans person from that era experienced. So, of course, I could not fully understand how this relentless prejudice would affect someone as they were growing up gay or with gay parents.

I think it was somewhat naïve of me to think that I could go inside these families and show the effect of a parent as a gay role model on their kids, as if you could isolate that one issue in these families. There was so much going on in each of these five families as these gay parents courageously took the risk to be one of the first families raising their kids without hiding the fact that they were gay. As I interviewed each family it became clear that there were many issues affecting the kids, some of which were connected to having a gay parent and others not at all.

To find the families I advertised in gay periodicals and was able to locate and interview 23 families across the U.S. and Canada. From that group of 23, I chose 5 families that I lived with for a week at a time and interviewed, several times over the next few years. This book is written from the tape recordings that I made with these families. Once I turned on the tape recorder I would ask a question to start the conversation, and then I would try to fade into the background and let the person or the family take the conversation in whatever direction they wanted. My goal was to have the kids and the parents talk about whatever they felt was important. So, I would interject as little as possible, while at the same time trying to help each person find what it was that they really wanted to express.

These families were living in Milwaukee, Toronto, Rapid City South Dakota, and Seattle. All of these five families had started out as a heterosexual family where the gay parent had tried to tell themselves that they were straight, or had tried to fit in as heterosexual, before admitting to their spouse and kids that they were gay. And at that point, the family either separated or divorced with the gay parent retaining custody or co-custody.

All of these families had gone through a separation, and several had experienced a divorce. In many of these families the kids also had a step-parent to deal with. In most of the families the parent or parents had been living as heterosexual until recently. And when those parents finally admitted to themselves and the family that they were gay, suddenly the kids had to adjust to this new image of their parent. And that was a big adjustment for the kids to suddenly wrap their mind around. Also, when some of the parents finally came out as gay, they went through something like a second adolescence. They had denied their sexuality for their whole lives, and now they were anxious to act on their sexuality that had been repressed for so long. And their desire to find a new partner often took time and attention away from the family.

My goal in writing this book was to show that gay and lesbian parents are most often loving and supportive parents and good role models, and in that regard are no different than straight parents. Indeed, the gay parents in this book are loving parents and good role models. However, as I interviewed the parents and the kids, I let them talk about everything that was going on in their lives. It quickly became apparent that there were a lot of pressures on these families and that the family life could at times be difficult and confusing. Which of course is not unique to gay families, but nonetheless the situations they described were not always easy for the kids to navigate.

In the 1960's and 1970's the level of hostility coming from our homophobic society, as well as from their own families and communities, certainly had an impact on whether or not someone who was gay or lesbian chose to come out and reveal their sexuality. In addition, in the 60's and 70's there were laws making it illegal for a man or a woman to be dressed in clothes not belonging to his or her sex. States also wielded their liquor laws to arrest gay patrons and shutter gay bars, which were the only place where gay people could be themselves. In 1979, when I began writing this book, there were sodomy laws against "perverted sexual practice" in almost every state. In fact, these laws are still on the books in sixteen states. And it wasn't until 1973 that the American Psychiatric Association issued a resolution stating that homosexuality was not a mental illness.

I came to this project expecting to write a story with a clear and straight forward conclusion. However, the stories that I was being told by these five families were full of complicated emotions. Both the parents and the children were giving me honest and heartfelt accounts of their experiences. Life is messy at times and there are difficulties in the most loving and well-meaning families, regardless of the sexuality of the parents. As I was writing the book I didn't want to whitewash these families' stories. But at the same time, I worried that someone looking for a reason to be negative about gay parents raising children could point to one of the issues in the book, issues that can also be found in heterosexual households, and say this is not optimal.

This book, *A Secret I Can't Tell*, was originally titled *Whose Child Cries*, after a Scottish proverb that goes, "He cares not whose child cries, so his laughs." It was published in 1983 and then I was sent on a publicity tour. I did a lot of interviews with the press, and the book seemed to be selling well. And then six months later my publisher suddenly went bankrupt and the book was no longer being distributed. It took about five years before I was able to regain the rights to my book. By then I was focusing on my career as a documentary filmmaker. (I produced Taxicab Confessions and other TV series, as well as the documentary films American Winter, Ending Disease, and The Race to Save the World.)

When I finally got back the rights to my book, I decided not to republish it. I had this nagging feeling that with all the anger and hostility directed towards gay families in those early days of the gay rights movement, that some readers might not be able to see past the difficulties in these families to notice the love. Forty years ago, there was an avalanche of prejudice directed towards gay and lesbian parents, and I worried that the message of this book might be too nuanced for those hostile times. So, I kept the copies of the book that had been returned to me in my garage, and I didn't republish it.

In the 40 years since this book was first published there has been an incredible amount of change in the way the public sees and treats gay people. These days, gay couples raising children hardly raise an eyebrow. And marriage equality is the law of the land. I feel that now the time is right to put this book out again. *A Secret I Can't Tell* is a time capsule which can give insight into the intense stress and uncommon bravery that gay and lesbian couples and their children had to go through as pioneers in this movement. The stories told by these kids and their parents can help us appreciate the many challenges that gay families had to deal with as the first wave of families living in openly gay homes.

The children in this book ranged from age 7 to 17. Not surprisingly, when the parents came out to the younger kids, some of them weren't even sure what the word gay meant. However, they quickly understood the hostility that their friends and their neighbors felt about their parent's lifestyle. Over the course of three years I visited these five families many times and I would listen to and tape record the children and their parents as they discussed their lives. At first, some of the children weren't very enthusiastic about the project. Typically, the parents had volunteered the family for the interviews, and the kids would find themselves in front of the tape recorder before they were sure this was all such a great idea. And in some of these families, although the parents were open about being gay, at least inside the family, the discussion of what gay was and what it meant was talked about very little, if at all, with their children.

If I were to make one generalization, I would say that pretty much across the board all the children in the book felt that if the secret of their gay parent's sexuality were to be exposed at their school, they would be doomed to a school life of teasing and bullying. These kids felt that they could not invite friends over to their house, or get too close to other kids, because none of their "friends" would ever truly understand their situation. This engendered a sense of isolation. The children in this book also understood that if the wrong person found out about their parent's sexuality, that there was a real danger that they could be taken from their parents by social services. Keeping a secret of that magnitude is quite a burden for an 8, 13 or 16 year old child to have to carry.

It can be said that the gay parents in this book had the choice to be "closeted" or to "come out" and be open about their homosexuality. All of the parents had some friends who knew about and accepted their situation. However, most of the children in these families felt they couldn't trust any kid their own age not to tell anyone. And since the consequences of telling were so great, the kids felt they had no choice but to keep their family's life a secret. At the same time, the children in this book were hyper-sensitive to the way their community thought about and treated gay people. When a friend on the playground yells, "Queer!"—whether innocently or not—that word is full of meaning to the child from a gay home.

Here's Annie, age eight, from my interview with her 42 years ago.

Annie is sitting on the floor in front of her bed. She wears a serious expression as she offers this opinion. "I don't like calling people gay. I don't think it's fair," she says. "People who don't even know what gay feels like get mad about it. Some people think it's wrong, and the people who think it's right, probably are. And some people don't even have a choice. 'Cause when you're it, you don't even know what it feels like when you're not it. So if you're not it and you get to be it—you'll probably like it."

The children in this book are doing their best to understand and appreciate their parent's need to be open about being gay. At the same time, they are trying to reconcile the negative messages they receive from their community with what they feel to be true inside their homes.

Eric, age eight, says, "I think gay people are fairly new. I think people are used to having plain husbands and wives doing their own thing without any gay people around them. When someone says faggot, homosexual, and all that stuff...well, faggot means gay to all those people who don't like it. The word is different. It's sort of different because it means that gay people CANNOT be allowed to live." Eric thinks for a moment. "It's not that they should die. Like they should not EXIST."

All the kids in this book love their parents. As they fiercely guard the secret of their family's situation, they are extremely sensitive to their peers' perceived disapproval, even if they never quite give their peers a chance to disapprove. Some of the kids even reject their friends before the friends get a chance to reject them.

"People are weird," says Selena, age thirteen. "Like they say, we have the gift of reason but I wonder how often we use it. Maybe that's a cynical outlook, but I've seen how people are. They're all for themselves. I shouldn't generalize, but more than half of them are just plain mean. Just sit down and read the paper. The kids in any home, they don't care what's going on. But what they don't realize is that this is what they will grow up into."

When I first showed up at their homes, some of the children were not so sure about participating in this project. But their reticence to talk with me didn't last long. Most of the kids had never even mentioned to a friend that their parents were gay, and that information was ready to burst out. So, when the children and I got over the initial hump, and "What are you going to ask me?" changed to "I can talk about whatever I want?", years of stored-away feelings came pouring out.

About eleven years after publishing this book, my brother and I made the first episode of Taxicab Confessions. I think Taxicab Confessions was the first television show that authentically showed the issues and struggles of the LGBT community as they navigated their lives. For sixteen years, from 1995 to 2011, my brother and I made the series, and over the course of those many years we had numerous taxicab rides where the person in the backseat powerfully and emotionally gave insight into the issues and hurdles facing the LGBT community. However, by the end of that sixteen-year run, most of the gay, lesbian, and transgender people in the back of the cab went from expressing how they were misunderstood by their family and their community, to telling how their family and friends accepted them. That was a huge and very positive transition in these very personal stories, told without knowing that they were being recorded, and I feel fortunate that I was able to witness these profound changes in the way our society was dealing with the LGBT community.

I would like to thank all the courageous parents in *A Secret I Can't Tell* for inviting me into their homes and for sharing their stories about the love and the disputes and the confusion that went on in their families as they navigated being "out" about their sexuality while raising their kids. But I would like to give a special thanks to the children. The trust, openness and honesty of the kids, who represent the first generation of children growing up in openly gay families, is what made A Secret I Can't Tell possible. Lastly, it is heartwarming and gratifying to look back on these stories forty years later and see the progress that has been made for LGBT rights. And let's hope that that progress continues.

Joe Gantz

All names and locations have been changed to maintain each family's privacy.

CHAPTER 1

The Angellini Family

Selena, age 13
Dan (Selena's father)
Andrew (Dan's partner)

"Some things have been harder growing up here and some things have been easier," Selena says. She looks down at her books spread out in front of her on the kitchen table. She has been working on a history paper. "Actually, I can't recall anything that was easier," she says with a laugh.

Selena is thirteen years old with dark brown curly hair, braces, and an embarrassed smile. She also has drooping eyebrows that give her large brown eyes a continually worried expression. Selena is at that gangly, in-between age. She has a pretty face and a budding figure, but at thirteen Selena is anything but the giggling teenager one might expect. She's studious, articulate, and very disciplined. Selena gets home from school at three-thirty every day, and she does her homework until her father and Andrew get home at five-thirty or six.

"I haven't told any of my peers that my father is gay. But it's hard to know what to say about why two men live here. It's a little difficult to explain, not that I really try to.

"People have not said, 'Selena, is your father gay?' They have not asked. If they did, unless they were very close, a very close friend, I don't think I would tell them. It's not that I want to hide from it. It's just..." Selena stops to think. She pushes her lips together and brings her eyebrows down the way she does when she's worried. "Well, they'd make quite a thing out of it at school. Not to mention that my dad and Andrew could get fired from their jobs if people found out."

The kitchen is very clean and orderly. A set of copper pots hang on one wall, a large antique china closet rests against another. Through the window Selena looks out on the street and a large farm beyond. The Angellinis live in a suburb forty minutes drive from Montreal. All the houses here were built in the last ten years and each sits on a third of an acre. The Angellinis' street is at the northern end of the area zoned residential, so they are lucky enough to be able to look out on rolling fields and cows instead of a grid of ranch-style homes. It won't be too long, though, before this farmland also is developed.

"The whole town knows. They haven't come out and said it, but they've put two and two together. They all know. Like the teachers at school, they treat me differently. They might be nicer to me, they might be more strict with me, but they don't treat me like the other kids.

"One important thing I've learned is how to be myself. I've learned not to go along with everybody else." Selena bites on the end of her pen as she stares across the table. "This might be naive terminology," she says, "but who's going to notice you in a crowd of five hundred people who all are wearing mink coats, when you're wearing a mink coat too. No one will. I mean, I'm not being different for the sake of being different. I'm just being myself— which happens to be different.

"I don't think I ever want to be normal. I'm just not normal. And I don't mean that I'm gay. I'm just not a normal child. I don't think it's because—," Selena leans on the table. Her hands are balled up tight. "—Well, partly it's because of the way I've been raised. We do things differently here. We have antiques, instead of regular furniture. We don't eat at the regular, quote, unquote, hours. But I don't think that's totally the cause of it. I'm just me. I'm not part of the crowd.

"Most people are not going to go their own way. They're not going to do a thing that they think is right, that they think is a better thing to do. They're going to follow everybody else. Well, personally, I'm not a follower. I'm not exactly a leader. I'm by myself." Selena closes her books and stacks them in a pile. She puts her papers on top. A car comes up the street, and Selena turns to see if it might be theirs. It's not. Selena looks at the clock; it's almost six. She's anxious for her father and Andrew to get home so she can stop talking about all this.

"Basically, the kids at school do not tangle with me," Selena says. She sits up straight and pushes her hair back from her face. "I don't know. They're not rude. They're also not friendly. They leave me alone because they know who I am. And they know I'm not one of them.

"When I first came to this school I was very shy. The kids made fun of me behind my back. I know it because other kids have told me, and I have good reason to believe them. Basically, they didn't like me because I was what they call a 'suck.' Because I was very sensitive and if anyone did something that I didn't like I'd go bawl my eyes out to the teacher."

Selena has her arms crossed as she thinks for a moment. "I don't have any reason to be like that anymore. The kids don't give me any reason. I don't think I've made myself a snob, although they'll call me that. They'll call me anything. I learned the hard way. Now if they try to hurt me, I get up there and I tell them that they're all wrong. I don't take it anymore."

Selena goes to the refrigerator and pours a glass of milk. She is nervous. She leans against the sink and looks out toward the street. The sun has dropped below the horizon. The cars passing by the end of her street have turned on their headlights. Selena watches them pass. "I'm not one of the crowd, not in my school life or my home life. It's just that you really notice it at school, your differences really stand out." Selena clears her throat. "I don't act like they do. I care about my schoolwork. I care about the way I look, the way I act. I'm not going to go around smoking because it's the thing to do." Her voice is high, and shrill. "They're snobs. They laugh when they get in trouble. If I got in trouble I wouldn't laugh.

"I'm just different. And it's not because of the school I'm in. It's because of me. I'm an only child and I've grown up differently." A smile quickly passes across Selena's face. "More differently than they know, than they will ever know." She laughs suddenly, a sad laugh. She shakes her head. "I can't be like them. I can't be two-faced. I'm just not like that."

A small green car pulls into the driveway. "They're home!" Selena yells excitedly. She runs down the steps and grabs her coat. She steps into a pair of her father's boots and runs outside without lacing them. Dan and Andrew are just getting out of the car. Each man is wearing a dark suit and carrying a briefcase. The light on the garage bathes the driveway in an electric glow.

Selena comes bursting out the door and runs to her father. He catches her as she runs into his arms. "Boy, this is some greeting," he says, smiling and enjoying it.

"I knew we were late, but I didn't think we were that late," Andrew jokes.

Selena hugs her father. She doesn't say anything. She has her head against his chest and he has his arm over her shoulder. Together they walk into the house.

****

"Can I give this to Sandy?" Selena asks her father. Dinner is over. Dan is rinsing off the dishes and putting them in the dishwasher. Andrew is wiping off the table, and Selena is putting the leftovers away.

"Go ahead," Dan says. Sandy is an affectionate and over-weight golden retriever. Selena wants to give him the leftovers from everyone's plate. Before Selena even moves, Sandy starts wagging his tail and heads for his bowl.

"Did you see that!" Selena shouts. "He understands English!"

"I've been saying that for a long time," Andrew tells her.

Selena scoops the leftovers into Sandy's bowl and in one second he gobbles them up. He looks to Selena for more. She shakes her head.

Dan does almost all the cooking. Tonight, he made a chicken casserole for dinner. Andrew is the one who makes sure the kitchen is always clean and orderly for Dan to cook in.

Dan fits the last of the silverware into the dishwasher and sits down. Andrew puts the sponge in the sink and joins him. The bottle of wine is still on the table from dinner and Andrew pours them each a glass.

"I met Andrew in February, 1974," Dan says leaning back in his chair.

"We'd only known each other a couple of months when we decided to live together," Andrew adds.

"We gambled. We both took a gamble," Dan continues. "You have to take risks periodically in your life." There is a plate of cookies on the table, and a pitcher of milk. Selena helps herself to both of them. "I was always very candid. I said, 'you know, I'm not an easy person to live with. I'm very demanding—' "

"I've got a kid," Selena chimes in.

"Well, yes, I said I had a child who was coming back shortly. Selena was staying with her grandparents while I finished my Ph.D. in Adult Education. But really, things in our relationship happened very fast. I remember on our second date, Andrew turned to me on his little stool and he said," Dan mimics a high, pleading voice, " 'may I come home with you tonight?' "

"Dad!" Selena protests.

Dan cocks one eyebrow. "I said, 'we might be able to make some arrangements. ' "

"Listen to this magnanimous—"

"How could I say no," Dan says, interrupting Andrew's protests. He goes into his high voice again. " 'Do you think I could come home with you tonight?' "

Andrew shrugs. "I asked if I could go home with him. He wasn't making any offers."

Dan and Andrew are very different. They both have beards, but that's where their similarity ends. Dan is shorter at 5'9". He has light brown hair combed back, and a strong straight nose. He talks fast and is quick to show his anger. Andrew is 6'2", with short black hair combed forward and a bald spot at the back of his head. He's a slower-paced, more patient person than Dan. If something disturbs him, he is more apt to react with a quip than he is to blow up.

Andrew is a designer by profession. He wears his clothes like he designs his interiors, smart, neat, just the right colors. In fact, each morning Andrew sets out Dan's clothes as well as his own. He even ties Dan's tie and hangs it up for him to grab on his way out the door. Selena describes her father by saying, "He comes home at night and tells me, 'Selena, hang up your coat.' In the meantime he undresses and drapes his suit all over the bed, waiting for Andrew to pick it up." And Selena is right. Dan does have a habit of demanding special attention.

"So, we scrambled around like crazy," Dan says, "looking for a place because Selena was coming back very soon. Andrew had a condominium, which he sold, and I had some property which I got rid of. We pooled our resources and we bought this place." Andrew pours himself another glass of wine. He asks if Dan would care for another. Dan nods and Andrew fills his glass. "Andrew was so afraid of meeting you," Dan says to Selena. "He was sure you were going to say, 'you're living with him?' "

"She said something to that effect the very first night," Andrew reminds them. Everyone laughs.

"She learns very quickly. I told you," Dan says, his left eyebrow raised again. Selena laughs. She covers her mouth to hide her braces. Andrew is smiling. Everyone is in a good mood.

Andrew is wearing a brown wrap-around sweater tied with a sash. He is wearing sandals with brown socks on underneath. Each day when he gets home from work Andrew changes into something more comfortable. Even when he's relaxing, Andrew's well-dressed.

"Unlike Dan," Andrew says, "I never thought I would have a child. I had already accepted my situation. I was homosexual, and homosexuals don't have children." Andrew sits back in his chair. He looks at Selena for a moment without speaking. "Sometimes I get upset because Selena says, 'you're not my natural parent.' So I tell her, 'you're not my natural child.' That's the conflict, and it goes both ways."

Andrew takes a sip of his wine. He puts the glass gently back on the table. "But having a child is a very enriching experience. Beyond the loving aspect, and those little touches, is the fact that your life becomes much larger. To raise a child takes a lot more, but it gives you more." Selena smiles. She covers her mouth. Andrew is embarrassed too. He's looking down at the table.

"They fight like cats and dogs," Dan says, "the two of them. But deep down there's a genuine caring relationship. If something happens to him or he's sick, she's very empathetic and supportive. And the same goes for Andrew. But fight—God, do they fight. I have to put my foot down and say, 'All right, no more!' "

Dan suddenly changes to a kidding tone. He has a smug look on his face. "I become the mediator. Believe it or not, I have to be the calming influence here. Did you ever think you'd hear me say that?"

"No, I didn't!" Selena yells, and she laughs out loud.

"With some of the ideas you have spun around this place," Andrew says, speaking slowly and evenly, "I would say you ought to be a calming influence now and then." Andrew pauses a moment as he stares at Dan, "after all the disruptive suggestions you've made over the years."

Andrew and Selena both laugh at that. Dan lowers his head and scowls at them. That makes them laugh even harder.

****

"I would always have a problem when friends came over, because they would want to see the house." Selena is in her bedroom, sitting on her bed. Her books and papers are spread across her desk. "We'd go up to my dad's and Andrew's room and there'd be this big king-size bed. It got a little complicated.

"I always got the feeling that the kids felt intimidated by them. They both have beards. They both, you know, are strict. Things like that. And then when I had someone sleep over they'd both come in and kiss me goodnight, 'Well, we're going to bed,' and they'd disappear into that room." Selena takes a strand of her curly hair and winds it around her finger. She has a wide-eyed look on her face. "What do you say? When I was younger my friends didn't really know what was going on anyway. They didn't understand. But now we're older. Now, I think they would."

Selena's room has two single beds, one against the wall on either side. They have yellow-flowered bedspreads and there's a yellow-flowered arched canopy over each one. Selena sleeps in the bed furthest from the door. The nearer bed is inhabited by a dozen or so stuffed animals. Her desk is in between the two beds, against the far wall. Above the desk is a window which looks out on the front yard.

Selena has finished her homework. There is a book lying open on the bed next to her. It's one of those sappy paperback novels she likes to read. The picture on the front is of a young girl running. The title of the book reads, Lost Horizon, Terry Comes Home. The girl on the cover is crying.

"I lived with my grandmother from age five to age seven in California," Selena says. "She was very protective. When I came here I didn't know anything about anything. Kids my age, eight years old, believe it or not, were very interested in boys already. They knew about sex, they knew everything about boy-girl relationships. Of which I knew nothing. They really got on me on that score.

"In grade four it hurt me. By grade five I was completely oblivious to them. And then in grade six I got up on top. I said, 'Good-by to you. Make fun of me as much as you like, that's it.'" Selena shakes her head. She is sitting up very straight on her bed. "On top isn't the right way to say it. I just became myself. I said, 'If you don't like it, it's your own fault, you have to accept me as I am. Accept me as I am or you don't accept me at all.'"

The bedroom and study part of the house is separated from the living room, kitchen and basement by a doorway. It's as if there are two very separate sections, the family area, and the public area. The door which separates the two parts is an antique door which Andrew found, stripped, and hung. It's made of old oak and has exquisite carved detail. If a visitor comes by they are entertained graciously in the front of the house. But only the most trusted of friends does Selena, or her parents, invite past the antique door to see the living area.

"There are still a lot of things that hurt, and there will always be those things. Everybody has that as far as I know. I just became tougher." Selena bites her lower lip. "Not tough exactly. Like this type of thing." She holds her head up and adopts an indifferent look. "I'm still vulnerable in my own way. I just have a shell that covers up some of the things that I don't want other people to know about. And until I know that people are going to be understanding, they're not going to know about them."

This is Selena's last year in the Catholic school she attends. It only goes up to the eighth grade. Selena refuses to go to the local high school next year. She refuses to be with the same kids for four more years. Her father understands. Together they have decided that Selena will transfer to a prestigious private school in Montreal proper. In fact, the whole family plans to find an apartment there to stay in during the week, because it would be too hard to correlate three schedules of driving back and forth from their house to the city each day. That's a big commitment for everyone to make. But Selena wanted a new school, with new friends, and Dan and Andrew felt that it was important.

"By switching schools next year I'm sure that some people have got the impression that I'm trying to run away from things that are bothering me. That I'm running away from the life that—I shouldn't say the life—the situation here that I dislike." Selena is fooling with her hair as she stares across the room. She has a worried look on her face.

"I suppose it's true in some ways. But I'm not really running away. I just don't like the people in our town. Everybody knows everybody else's business. And that would be fine if people were nice about it, or something like that. But they're not. They're going around adding things, and twisting the story, and talking behind your back. And I can't take that. It just seems to me that they're not nice people."

****

"When you're working in a conventional situation and you're a member of a minority group, such as a homosexual," Dan says, "you wear a mask. And if someone cracks a queer joke, which they're always doing, you laugh or you don't. For a long time I laughed. I don't laugh anymore."

Dan and Andrew are in the downstairs family room. Andrew started a fire in the fireplace which is just beginning to catch. This was a pretty ordinary ranch-style house when they bought it. However, Andrew has done much to change the feel of the interior. The room they're in now has been decorated to have an "old cabin" feel to it. Except for a big overstuffed chair, all the furniture pieces are restored early American. The mantle around the fireplace was replaced by an antique wooden mantle. And the walls of the room, originally ordinary wallboard, are covered with wide pine planks. An old yoke, as well as a wooden pitchfork, are hung up for the effect.

Dan continues, "There's a certain degree of duplicity. On the one hand you have to make a living, and in so doing you have to play the game and play by someone else's rules. For a good third of your day you're wearing the mask. For the other two thirds, if you're lucky, you're able to be what you genuinely are.

"That, in itself, is difficult. It creates stress. Particularly when you are at work and some macho S.O.B. decides to preen his feathers and in so doing thinks a good fag joke is appropriate." Dan is gearing up to be angry.

"These people are just doing their little performances," Andrew says indifferently. "I feel like, 'fine, as far as I'm concerned you're just one step lower on the ladder of humanity.' They're trying to prove something, and it's a very weak way in which to prove it."

The fire is burning well now behind the glass doors of the fireplace. It's throwing a pattern of orange light against the far wall. On the couch Dan is sitting very straight. His arms are crossed in front of him. Andrew is next to him, sitting on one leg and resting against the arm of the couch.

"I think wearing a mask is difficult because you can never wear it all the time," Dan says. "It's just a matter of time before the mask slips—it's like a hairpiece or something like that." Andrew laughs, Dan doesn't. "And if it slips people see those little idiosyncrasies, or mannerisms, or what have you, that tend to give you away."

"You have to be on your guard," Andrew offers. "Sometimes you might be with someone who knows, but you're still out in a public place so you can only semi-relax. And all the people you see each day are kept in different compartments, they don't ever meet each other."

Dan turns to Andrew and smiles. "I think this is all part of the reason we yell and argue a lot," he says. "It's symptomatic of the tension. I think we get it off our chest. We don't throw things like some people do. We don't throw objects, we throw words. They hurt sometimes. I think the cliche, 'You always hurt the ones you love', is very true. Your loved ones see all the unpleasant parts of you. But one has to get rid of that frustration.

"Sandy! Sit down!" Dan yells at the dog. His voice is a startling command. The dog has been leaning against the couch, which, because he sheds, is not allowed. Sandy lies back down. Dan's voice goes back to normal. Neither he nor Andrew pays the outburst any mind.

"The frustration builds up. If you can't get rid of it, what happens? It keeps piling up and piling up and piling up. If you don't dump it, you just break, you crack. If you get rid of it, it's gone. And you carry on." Dan takes a deep breath and lets it out slowly in a heavy sigh. "So, I get rid of it. I yell a lot at home."

The room becomes quiet. One can hear the air being sucked into the fire through the vents underneath the glass doors. The room has gotten very warm. Andrew undoes his sweater and takes it off. He folds it carefully over the arm of the couch.

"I don't really bring things home that much," Andrew says, "not in a direct way. I never express any of that directly because it just means he will get angrier. So I don't really—"

Dan doesn't accept that answer. "I'm an angry person, about a lot of things," he says. "And I suggest that Andrew is angry too. However, his anger manifests itself in a nagging way." Dan looks at Andrew. He makes a face to try to show that he didn't mean that as an insult.

Dan goes on. "We all have to watch what we say, what we do, to whom we are talking. Even Selena does." Dan's voice softens as he speaks of Selena. "Even she's learned to edit, to think about who she's speaking to. She's learned to ask herself if what she's saying is likely to alienate that person."

"She's very protective," Andrew explains. "She's very protective of what goes on in this house. And she's become more mature in certain aspects than her peers. Because she's had to look at them, and what she sees she doesn't always like. She's not quite like them."

Sandy gets up and walks around in a circle. He walks around in a circle a second time, and then lies back down. Andrew has his arm over the back of the couch. He's watching Dan who's about to say something.

"There's one quality about Selena that disturbs me. It's that she's too aware of what other people feel." Dan adjusts himself on the couch. He can't seem to get comfortable. "Like when we're out in public, if I feel like behaving a little loony, you know, I'll do it. For example, if we're at the supermarket and I feel like skipping down the aisle, in order to inject some levity into a depressing situation, I'll just do it. I may do some childish thing, any crazy thing. Like trying on stupid hats. And Selena will go, 'Dad, will you stop it!' " Dan mimics someone whispering furiously.

"That's just what all kids go through," Andrew tries to explain, "being embarrassed by their parents. I think that's part of exposure to her peers. Parents just don't do those things."

"Well, I'm not! I'm not—" Dan is shouting again, groping for what he's trying to say. "—I wouldn't be a typical parent if I were straight. Dan is shaking his head. His eyes are darting back and forth. "She gets that embarrassment from the kids at school, who get it from their parents. It's that stupid, narrow-minded, myopic view of life that everyone has to conform!" Dan is fairly spitting out the words. "And if you don't conform to a predetermined norm, or if you deviate from that norm, they will make things very hard for you."

Dan clenches his teeth together. He is scowling. "Like today at the market, those three slobs in front of us in line. They were making cutesy little comments in reference to Andrew, joking and giggling. They couldn't stop staring." Dan looks at Andrew. Andrew shrugs as if he doesn't care.

"They were three pigs. That's what they were. They were dressed like pigs, they looked like pigs, they probably eat like pigs." Dan breathes in quickly through his nose. He's staring straight ahead. "Those kinds of things don't bother me any longer," Dan says in a low voice. His eyes are furious.

****

"There was this one week when I went bananas," Selena says. "See, Thursday I went to the mall and there was this guy there that I knew. And he kept looking at me. I couldn't stand it. I was going scarlet, just red. So I walked away and went into Radio Shack. But there were two guys there and they kept staring at me.

"It was so strange because I had always been turned down by guys at school. Well, not turned down," Selena shrugs her shoulders, "because they had nothing to turn down. But they had always tried to upset me, it seemed. Then all of a sudden that one day, I got all the attention. And the day after that, Friday, I was getting a lot from the boys at school as well. I was going, 'I can't believe it.' I mean Monday and Tuesday they were just saying 'get lost, kid,' and then on Thursday—everything changed. Suddenly everybody was giving me all the attention and all at the same time. I was going so fast. It was like I was a top that never stops."

Selena is wearing a long, blue and white nightgown with blue flowers on it. She's sitting on her bed with her legs folded to the side. Her weight rests on one arm. She is sleepy, and her body is relaxed. She looks very graceful. Sitting on the bed as she is, with her braces, her worried brown eyes, and her in-between figure, Selena is very much a mixture of a young girl and a woman.

"My father asked me once what I was going to tell boys when they start coming over and they ask what's going on. I said, 'it depends on the guy.' It would have to be a steady boyfriend before I would tell him. I certainly wouldn't tell someone I was just double dating for the evening."

Selena stops. She gives a big, gaping yawn. When she opens her eyes again they are teary. She smiles and blinks back the tears. Looking around her room she thinks about what it was she was saying. Her smile slowly fades and she becomes intent again.

"I was at school not too long ago, and these kids were saying things about gays, negative things. So I said, 'I know a couple, a gay couple, and they are very nice people.'" Selena's voice is soft and apologizing. "I felt I was backing out by not saying parents, by not telling them that they were my parents. I don't know." Selena considers it again. Her hand is over her mouth. "When I think of that, it makes me feel like I'm a follower and not a leader. I feel like I'm succumbing to everyone else and letting them put down the rules."

The wind, blowing across the field, rattles Selena's window. She turns toward the sound. A car drives by on the street. Selena takes a breath, and sighs.

"I've imagined conversations with boys, telling them the way my father is. I know if I ever—," Selena makes a face "—I mean, here I am getting far-fetched again. But if I ever get a steady boyfriend, and if we were planning to get married or something, he would have to know. And then I would have to look at his reaction to see if he'd, you know, accept it.

"I've thought, 'what if I fell in love with someone and they didn't accept my parents.' I mean that can't stop any person from falling in love with another person." Selena's voice becomes emphatic. "I mean I can accept a person for what he is, for his likes and dislikes. I would hope that person could accept my parents. I would hope that he wouldn't say rude things about them. And if he didn't understand it but he really loved me, he might change a little bit. I mean, he might not just be totally revolted by the idea that I have been raised by gays.'

The sound of Dan and Andrew coming up the stairs interrupts Selena. As Dan passes by her doorway he looks into her room. "You're still up?" he says in disbelief.

"Yes, I'm talking on tape."

"Go to bed. Go to bed." Dan turns off her light.

"Dad!"

"There is always tomorrow." He comes over to her bed and puts his hand on her head. He picks up the edge of her covers. "Come on, get under here. You should have been in bed long ago."

"I am in bed."

"Asleep! You should have been asleep long ago." Selena laughs. She gets under the covers and he pulls them over her. "Goodnight," he says, and kisses her. Andrew comes into her room and kisses her goodnight as well.

Dan sits down on her bed. "Are you ready for your test tomorrow?" he asks.

"Yes."

"Good." He kisses her again and Selena hugs him. "Sweet dreams, pumpkin," he says. He gets up to go.

"Don't shut the door all the way," Selena calls out to him.

Dan leaves the door open a foot. "Goodnight," he whispers. He walks down the hall to his room.

****

Dan and Andrew have just gotten home from work. Everyone is in the living room. No one is talking.

"We had an argument on the way home from work tonight," Dan says. He takes a sip of his drink. "It seems we're always arguing about one thing or another."

Selena shakes her head. "I'm glad you said that and not me."

Andrew makes an attempt at a joke. "Well, you must admit, our communications are not broken down."

The living room is beautifully designed. It has a thick blue rug and white walls. It has Victorian furniture, a marble mantle, and several large paintings in the formal tradition of the nineteenth century. Selena is sitting on the couch. The couch is cream colored, with a curved, wooden three-leaf clover back. Dan and Andrew are across the round coffee table from Selena, in two matching oak chairs.

"Well, we are always arguing," Dan says, "I'm a very difficult person to live with and Andrew isn't easy either. So, between the two of us, there are bound to be volatile moments. Hopefully, they erupt, we argue them out, and we move on." Dan looks at Andrew and then he looks at Selena. He shakes his head. "We're in a gay fathers group," he says. "Most of the other fathers look at us in amazement, like, 'how do you two stay together, you're always arguing?' "

"We're both opinionated people," Andrew says, trying to give some explanation.

"And it's always so much fun to make up, too," Dan offers. Andrew laughs. Everyone seems to be relaxing a bit. Andrew takes a sip from his drink. He leans back in his chair.

"Go lie down!" Dan's voice is a loud command. Sandy has come over to be petted. "Lie down!" Sandy walks back to the doorway. He's not allowed in the living room. "Down...down!" In slow motion the dog goes down to the floor. He looks over at Dan. Dan stares back at him. "He just gets his hair over everything," Dan explains. Andrew is looking through the paper. Selena is resting on the couch.

"You left your coat on the chair in the kitchen," Andrew tells Selena, "and your books are all over the table."

"I'll get them Andrew."

"If you would 'get them' before we got home, you wouldn't have to be reminded," Andrew tells her.

Selena makes an exasperated face. "I'm sorry," she says, "but I cannot stand his nagging. Andrew is—he's even admitted it—a nag. He comes in the door, I haven't seen him all day, and the first thing he does is complain. Either I forgot to bring the garbage cans in, or my school work was left on the table. Or he walks down the hall and my door is open, and I happen to have a sock on the floor." Selena looks at Andrew. Andrew isn't looking at her. "It's not so much anymore. He has learned to say good evening and then goes into it." Selena laughs, a nervous laugh. "He complains a lot. I mean, he's one person you can never please."

Dan butts in, "Tensions, there are all sorts of tensions which contribute to that—"

"Andrew and I got along really well at the beginning," Selena continues, "at the initial beginning. Then we had a pretty bad experience with the truck one night when we were moving, and I began to see him more as a person. I'd never seen anyone react that way. It was pouring rain and the truck lights weren't working. Andrew was so angry—"

Andrew very calmly stands up.

"What's the problem?" Dan asks.

"I'm going in the other room," Andrew says in a soft voice.

"Do you see this as getting negative?" Selena whines.

"I feel it's getting very negative. I'm sorry, I am personally feeling very negative."

"Because of what I have said, Andrew? You're feeling negative because of what I have said?"

Andrew addresses Selena, "I have never said anything that—" he pauses looking for the right word. He becomes impatient. "Never mind," he says, dismissing it all with a wave of the hand.

"What did I say that was so bad?" Selena's voice is high and loud. "Didn't I say we got along really well in the beginning? Didn't I say I began to see you more as a human being?"

"Yes, but you work yourself right up again to the fact that things aren't very good." Andrew is standing next to the door. He has his arms folded across his chest. He looks very uncomfortable. "There hasn't been anything good?" Andrew asks Selena. "Really? Not even lately? Not in-between?"

****

Dan is lying on the bed in his blue terrycloth bathrobe and socks. He has just come back from checking on Selena, she's already asleep. The TV is on without the sound. Andrew is reading the TV guide aloud. He is wearing a brown and orange plaid bathrobe and brown pajamas. There's nothing on tonight which interests either of them. Andrew turns to the next page and reads the shows for tomorrow night. On the TV, three people are running around a sofa chasing each other, and yelling, silently. Dan sits up and props the pillows behind him.

"When we first moved in," Dan says, "one of our neighbors down the street brought by this basket of tomatoes. It was harvesting season." Dan stretches, and yawns. "As it turned out that was just an excuse to get into the house, an offering that opened the door.

"Remember, we were in the backyard the next time she came by," Dan asks Andrew. "She pointed to different parts of the house and said to me, 'Oh, there's the living room, there's the bedroom.' She already knew the house somewhat from the last family that lived here. 'Is that where Selena is going to sleep?' she asked.

" 'No,' I said, 'that's Andrew's study.'

" 'Oh, well where's Selena going to sleep?'

" 'Well, Selena's going to sleep on the other side.'

"She said, 'aren't there two bedrooms upstairs?'

"I said, 'yes. I'm going to have one as a study.'

" 'Oh, then who's going to sleep in this bedroom?' And she pointed to our bedroom.

" 'We are.'

" 'Oh. Ohhhhhh.' " Dan says. He has his eyes opened very wide, as the neighbor woman must have. Andrew laughs, Dan doesn't.

"When the people moved in next door," Andrew explains, "she could hardly wait for them to get their first box out of the truck before she ran over there to tell them about the strange situation they'd moved next door to."

"She's a bitch," Dan fumes, setting his jaw in anger. "She gets a sadistic pleasure out of destroying something." Dan looks at Andrew. Andrew simply lifts his eyebrows as if to say, 'what can you do.'

Andrew gets up and changes the channel on the TV. He flips from one show to the next. After he's gone through them all he gives up and lies back down. A different show is playing silently now. There's a man and a woman, and they're having a serious conversation at an outdoor cafe. Andrew watches it as Dan is lost in thought.

"Our primary goal as parents," Dan says finally, rubbing his eyes with the palms of his hands, "is to insure as best we can that Selena escapes as unscathed as possible. We don't want our homosexuality to disorient her, to cause her frustration, embarrassment, alienation, hostilities—" Dan shakes his head slowly. "She knows the situation isn't going to be easy. She's already been exposed to that."

Andrew watches Dan as he talks. His face is sympathetic, and also a little afraid. "We're not into drugs, our lifestyle is very conventional in many respects," Dan continues. "We're trying to expose Selena to different alternatives, without placing value judgments on them. I think she eventually has to make those decisions for herself. For instance. I'm an atheist, but Selena has attended several different Sunday schools. I don't know whether she'll become religious or not. It's hard to say. We just want to give her a foundation upon which she can build a reasonably happy, meaningful life."

Andrew gets up. "I'm going to get us a drink. What would you like?"

"Drinks? We're about to go to bed."

"I'll make hot milk, or cocoa."

"You don't want to talk about this anymore do you? It's making you nervous."

"No, I don't care," Andrew says. "Wouldn't you like something to drink?"

"Just lie down," Dan tells him. "We'll go to bed in five minutes." Andrew sits back down. The dog walks over to Andrew. Andrew pets him.

"We're not gay activists," Dan says. "We don't really interact with the gay community much. If we go into Montreal, it's usually to visit friends, most of whom, interestingly enough, are straight. We do almost everything together as a family. Whether it's visiting friends, going to movies, plays, vacations. It's always been like that."

The wind can be heard blowing the spruce trees out front and in the bones of the house.

When he speaks again, Dan's voice is softer, gentler. "All I want," he says, "is to be left alone." He runs his hand back through his hair as he stares across the room. "I'm not going to do anything that would embarrass people, or offend them. When you know that people feel uncomfortable in the presence of overt homosexuals, what justification does one have in being overt? To see them squirm? That doesn't make any sense to me."

Dan pauses. He turns and looks across the room into the darkness of the hallway. "I feel there's never any justification for rudeness," he says. "In fact, it's much more difficult and challenging to make someone feel comfortable. But I expect the same kind of respect in return. And unfortunately, that reciprocity doesn't exist."

The windows tremble again. "Is it going to storm?" Dan asks Andrew.

"Feels like it," Andrew answers.

They both look at each other and give tired smiles. Andrew scoots over until he's leaning against Dan's side. Dan puts his arm around Andrew. They lie like that, listening to the wind and watching the television. Andrew brings up one hand and rubs Dan's beard. Dan closes his eyes.

"When Selena was younger," Andrew says, "each morning I would get her dressed, brush her hair, and send her off to school. She thought it was marvelous, all the attention. In addition to that, I was sewing most of her clothes because she was an odd size." Andrew smiles.

"Selena's teacher, Mrs. Bowen, came up to me one time at a school picnic. She said, 'We feel so sorry for Selena. She doesn't have a mother to do things for her.' "

Suddenly Dan is wide awake again, his voice already angry. "I've felt for a long time that there was this feeling of sympathy for Selena. 'She's been raised by these two queers, you know, and probably has had an unhappy childhood. Therefore, we better compensate for that.'" Dan focuses his stare on Andrew. "Even some of our friends," Dan says, "they mean well but they think, 'Oh my God, poor Selena. She has that father who's a raving maniac, and that stepfather who's a nag.' But God, she's a pretty together kid, despite those severe handicaps."

****

Andrew is next to the door, on the brink of leaving. His voice is quiet, but firm. "I'm feeling very negative. I cannot explain it when I feel like this."

"You cannot look at yourself objectively and laugh," Dan tells him.

"No, wait a minute," Selena says, pleading, "is it something I said?"

Andrew is wearing his dark-blue suit pants, and a white shirt. He hung up his coat and tie first thing when he came in this evening. "Very much so. And every time I go to say something, I've been interrupted and—"

Dan explodes. "SAY IT THEN!" Everyone is startled by the suddenness of Dan's anger. Andrew is the most confused. He drops down in the chair next to the door. With a numb expression he starts to talk.

"I just feel—as though I'm always at the very, very bottom end of this, OK? As though I've got nothing that is really worth a lot." Andrew is sitting very straight in the chair. His voice is soft and distant. "Every time I'm asked to do something I try to do it. And I also expect a little back. But every time I ask for that, and especially lately, I'm told that I shouldn't be asking."

Selena tries to speak. "But Andrew what does that have to do with—"

"You know, Andrew," Dan interrupts, "you have a way of expressing yourself in such a vague, obtuse," Dan is measuring his words, accenting each one, "nebulous, obscure way that no one can attach concrete meaning to what you're trying to say." Dan pauses and then repeats himself. "Now again, what is bothering you?"

"Dad, I understand what Andrew's trying to say."

"Well, he's talking to me!" Dan snaps. "And I can't. Are you talking to me?" he asks Andrew.

"I was just—it was in reference to—"

Dan interrupts again. "Are you talking to the tape recorder?"

"No," Andrew insists. "I was asked why I felt so negative and that's the best I can say it." Andrew is sitting next to the door. His shoulders are hunched up. He is staring vaguely in front of him. Selena is on the couch, and Dan is in one of the wooden chairs.

"I have repeatedly said to you that Selena should be able to articulate her feelings," Dan says. "And once she's finished, then you can articulate yours. But you can't close off her feelings and deny them! And that's how she perceives it."

"I'm not denying them—"

"But you take everything as a personal affront, and you've done it all your damn life!

"Dan, don't psychoanalyze me." Andrew's voice is suddenly firm.

"That's what you always do, and I'm tired of that."

"Just wait a minute, can I say something?" Selena pleads. "May I say something, Andrew?" Andrew doesn't acknowledge her, neither does Dan. Selena speaks anyway.

"You said I largely contributed to your negative feelings, correct? Okay, can I just state one incident where you didn't do such a great job, and where I think I disappointed you. But where it clashed." Selena is speaking nervously. Her eyebrows are knit together in that concerned expression of hers. "How old was I? I was in grade five or six, and I had long hair. Andrew always put my hair in a ponytail. I hated it that way, and I was angry at him, so the minute I got to school I would take it out." Selena gives a nervous smile. She brushes her hair back from her face. "Well one day Andrew came home from work early and drove past the school while I was at recess. I was right next to the road with my hair down. I just kept going, 'Oh my God, oh my God, I don't want to go home.'

"Andrew was in the kitchen when I got home. I walked in—silence. I was angry at him, and he was angry at me. I thought, and I still do think, that he had no right to say, 'you have to wear your hair in a ponytail.' "

"It was the beginning of your pimples."

"Well, so what."

"It was cleanliness."

"Andrew, I washed my hair every other day. You should have said, 'listen, don't complain about your skin if you're not going to put your hair up.' "

"Well, I have said many times Selena, you have to express some positive. You never remember the positive."

"You're the one that's abused all the time!" Dan shouts at Andrew. "No positive statements, no strokes. We always put you down at the bottom." Dan bangs his hand on the table with each phrase. The table sways. "You are the chief cook, the bottle washer, the maid."

"That's not what I was saying," Andrew is flustered. He looks completely confused. "I was just pointing out," he says, his voice distant again, "that she seems to remember all the bad moments and she never seems to remember—"

"She's expressing how she feels. I'm expressing how I feel—"

Selena tries to get a word in. "I can state more than five instances today where you've been perceived in a positive way, Andrew. And I cannot, except since we sat down by this tape recorder, say where you've been perceived in a negative way. There are many positive things, and I can list them."

"It's a chronic problem, a chronic problem," Dan mutters.

Selena laughs. "And it's symptomatic of a very serious situation," she says, mocking her father.

"Yes," Dan agrees. "It's symptomatic of a very serious situation."

Selena laughs again and rolls her eyes. "Dad, you should really change. Like, you say you always know how a program is going to end, because once you've written one script you've written them all."

"That's true."

"Well, you ought to rewrite your lines Dad, because I can say your next line for you." Selena repeats it again. "It's symptomatic of a very serious situation."

Andrew smiles, "I wish you had finished your psychology courses, Dan," he says, "or never taken any." Andrew chuckles softly. "Now if you'd finished those courses," he tells Dan with a serious expression on his face, "you'd be able to come up with the solution." The serious expression dissolves and a slow, deep laugh rolls out of him. Andrew gets up and leaves the room.

****

"The only time I can remember that they spelled it out for me," Selena says, "was when I was about seven." Selena is sitting on the big overstuffed chair in the downstairs family room. The cushion is very soft, and Selena has sunk down into it. "There was this little mobile that Dad had in his study. It had cards that came down with words on them, heterosexual, homosexual, and a few others. One day I asked my father what each of them meant. When I got to homosexual Dad said, 'that's what we are.'

"I remember that I continued playing on the floor of his study. It didn't seem unusual to me at all. I'd never known my father to live with a woman. My mother left when I was a year old." Selena gives an uncomfortable smile when she mentions her mother. She shrugs her shoulders. "I don't know why it didn't strike me as strange, but it was just as if he'd said I'm 37 or something like that. I went, 'oh, okay.'"

Selena hears arguing coming from upstairs. She makes a face. Dan and Andrew went back to their bedroom after dinner, after a dinner without much in the way of conversation. It's always hard for Selena to say how long they are going to stay mad after an argument— sometimes it's an hour, sometimes it's a week. And Selena worries about that. Tonight, though, she decided she wasn't going to worry. At least that's what she told herself.

"My father and I overheard a conversation on the bus," Selena says. "These people were talking about the families that lived on our road, 'the blanks, the blanks, the homosexuals, the blanks, the blanks.'" Until that happened I never thought much about my father being gay. But after that, I started noticing adult attitudes had changed towards me. I even know some parents who have told their kids," Selena switches into a sing-songy voice, "'do not go near Selena Angellini.'"

Selena is wearing a blue dress, something like a frock, with a white turtleneck underneath. She has on knee sox and no shoes. Her legs are pulled up on the chair beside her. She's holding her ankle in one hand.

"People can't accept people who are different than they are. I can't sometimes," Selena says. "Like when I go to an old age home, or to a place where they have people who are retarded. I get frightened. I see those people look at me with a strange look in their eyes. They might be drooling, you know.

"And when I think that people can't accept us I think, 'well, I can't accept some people.' I mean, I can accept them, but I'm still scared of them sometimes. I tell myself, 'they're just normal people, they're not—' " Selena stops to think. Her hair is pulled back and clipped in a barrette. She runs her hand absently along the side of her hair.— "Maybe not normal, but they're still people."

As Selena changes her position, the chair makes all sorts of creaking noises. She is sitting cross legged now. The big leather chair rises up behind her making her look tiny. She leans back against the soft cushion.

"I was in a school play once and we were supposed to form a circle. This black girl, who was one of the first blacks that came to our school, was next to me. I was supposed to hold hands with her. At first I was a little skeptical. But she just held out her hand and smiled and I said, 'fine.' Then the girl on the other side goes, 'Nooooo, I'm not holding hands with her!'"

"I was very young at the time and I was hurt by that. The black girl, she was hurt too, to think that someone would be like that, so cruel. I don't like the way God made some that are so much more giving," Selena says, "so much nicer than us."

Selena's lips are pursed. Her eyes look very hard. "People are weird," she says. "Like they say, we have the gift of reason but I wonder how often we use it. Maybe that's a cynical outlook, but I've seen how people are. They're all for themselves. I shouldn't generalize, but more than half of them are just plain mean. Sit down and read the paper. The kids in any home, they don't care what's going on. But what they don't realize, is that that stuff in the paper is what they will grow up into."

Selena looks disgusted. She sniffles and rubs her nose with the back of her hand.

Dan and Andrew come down the steps. They open the door to the family room and they're all smiles, arm in arm. "Are we interrupting?" Dan asks.

"I thought you two were fighting?" Selena's face immediately begins to relax. She smiles.

"Let's not call it a fight," Andrew says. "Let's call it an argument."

"Just a few tears shed," Dan adds. "No harm done."

Smiling, Selena holds her finger up to her lips. Dan and Andrew quietly walk over to the couch and sit down. Selena continues with what she was saying. As she does, her eyes are on her father and

Andrew. She is checking to make sure that they are really getting along.

"Even if I'd been raised differently, even if he was still my father and he was living by himself or with a woman, I still think he would have raised me with a good attitude towards gays," Selena says. "I get the feeling that he would have. He's just that type of person. He doesn't resent, really, any other type of human being."

"Thank you, thank you," Dan says. Dan is leaning on Andrew's shoulder, a big smile on his face. He seems giddy.

"But still I'll say one thing. Even though I'm living with my father who's a homosexual, and the ever growing—I'm not sure it's really growing, but they seem to be coming out of the woodwork." Selena laughs. Dan and Andrew laugh too. "I guess they're just facing up to it or something," Selena says. "But even though I've been exposed to gays and live with them, it's still difficult to—I don't know whether the word is accept, but it's difficult to think of it.

"I'm not uncomfortable with my father and Andrew. But even though I know my father is homosexual," Selena smiles nervously, she giggles, "it's still hard to imagine. Getting down to the bare fact that he is, it's hard to admit it to myself." Selena looks at her father as she talks. She's embarrassed. Dan and Andrew listen quietly. Neither seems defensive or hurt by what she is saying. "I mean, I accept him the way he is. But even though I do, I go, 'forget that.' In a way it's just hard to imagine."

Dan lies down on the couch with his head in Andrew's lap. Andrew smiles and puts his hand on Dan's chest. Selena is thinking. She's biting her nail. Dan starts to say something but Andrew shushes him with a finger over his lips.

"It's just the fact that, you know, you hear so many things about gays. Even I, sometimes, almost believe it. I mean, there are weirdos who are heterosexual but you don't seem to hear about them as much.

"It reminds me of something I read in a history book, this relates to it in a way." Selena is looking at her father. "When the Indians killed the settlers it was called a massacre, but when the settlers killed the Indians it was called a victory. It's the same relationship. When a man who's heterosexual does something, they don't make such a big deal out of it. And I get very upset about that."

Selena stops talking. Her father is lying in Andrew's lap with his eyes closed. "Are you listening. Dad?" Selena asks.

"Yes, very much so. I thought that was an interesting example, a good example." Dan opens his eyes. "I've had a couple of drinks and I'm finding myself very sleepy," he says. "But here, let me sit up and then you'll know I'm listening." Dan sits up next to Andrew. He rests his arms on the back of the couch.

Selena uncrosses her legs. She looks tired herself. Her eyelids are heavy and she leans with her weight on the arm of the chair.

"The question has arisen, in fact several people have asked—I mean implied—'are you?' They want to know if I'm gay, or if I think I'm gay. And I would like to say, 'I am not.' I can't really say that yet. But I don't think I am. And by saying, 'I'm not,' it's not that I'm against it.

"I think it was Anita Bryant who said something like, 'if a child is raised by a homosexual, that child will grow up to be homosexual.' And I don't believe that." Selena leans back in the big chair.

Dan shakes his head, disgusted. "She started her campaign by saying homosexuals are out to seduce the kids. She wanted to frighten people. These people are ignorant—uninformed I should say, not ignorant." No matter how tired Dan is, he is always able to summon the requisite anger. "She did it deliberately to scare them. You know? It's as if Orson Wells said, 'the Martians have landed, everyone jump out your windows.'"

"And it worked," Andrew adds.

"Yeah, it worked. Because they don't know any different."

Selena covers her mouth as she's overcome with a big yawn. She blinks several times. "I'm heterosexual all the waaayyy," she says. "If you have a stunning-looking woman walking down the street, and a stunning-looking man, I can tell you which way I'm going to head." Selena covers her mouth again as she laughs. "I've always been interested in boys."

"You see," Dan pipes in, "it's great that she can talk about that. I've always been interested in the male physique. Like we have Playgirl—"

Selena interrupts. "Not physique, Dad. It's the male person."

"Oh, the male person," Andrew says, smiling. "Like when we were watching that television commercial with all those guys running around in cut-offs." Andrew starts to laugh. "The milk ad where you said, 'that's the one I want. Which one do you guys like?' " They all burst out laughing, Selena, too.

"It was a beer ad," Dan says.

"Beer-milk, milk-beer," Andrew shakes his head. Everyone can't stop laughing. Selena's eyes are tearing. "I still think it was the funniest moment."

****

This morning, being Saturday, Dan padded around the kitchen in his slippers and robe and put together a huge plateful of banana pancakes. He topped them with real maple syrup and everyone ate big stacks. After breakfast the dishes were put in the dishwasher, the kitchen was cleaned, and the whole family headed for the mall.

The Angellinis enjoy the weekly grocery hunt. The three of them push one cart, they check prices, plan meals, argue about what they should get. It's an unhurried weekly ritual. It's more expensive than a movie, but also more tangible. Both Dan and Andrew make a good income; although they aren't extravagant, they can afford to buy what pleases them.

At the check-out counter there's a long line. While Dan and Andrew talk, Selena looks through the different magazines on the rack, Seventeen, Mademoiselle, Vogue. She looks through all the pictures of the women and the latest fashions. Selena is dressed in jeans and a pink sweater. Her hair is pulled back and tied with a piece of ribbon. Selena is in agreement with Andrew, that expensive clothes should wait until she stops growing. She still likes looking, though. She gets more and more interested in clothes every day.

As they go outside to load the groceries, the day has turned cloudy. It feels like it may snow. Dan brings the car around and they put everything in the trunk. There's one more stop to make on the way home, and that's the liquor store. Dan pulls into the parking lot and Andrew gets out of the car. He is halfway to the door when he realizes he doesn't have his wallet with him. Dan and Andrew each carry a leather bag with their wallets and whatever else they need. Andrew comes back to the car. He takes his wallet from his bag and slams the door.

Selena is incredulous. "Did you see what he did!" she says to her father as she watches Andrew enter the store.

"What?" Dan asks, confused.

"He took his wallet and not his bag. I can't believe it!"

"What?"

"If I did that he'd have a fit." Selena is looking in the direction of the doorway where Andrew disappeared. She is angry and excited at the same time. Her face is nearly pressed against the backseat window.

"He's just getting a bottle of wine."

"Remember when I took my wallet instead of my purse, that time we went to the movie?" Selena says. "Remember how much flack Andrew gave me? He went on and on about how wrong it was." Selena is incensed. She can't believe it. And she doesn't want to let this opportunity pass, either.

"Now let's not get into a big thing here over his wallet." Dan is asking Selena in an appeasing tone. It's as close to pleading as Dan gets.

Selena nods her head. "Okay," she agrees reluctantly, "I won't say a thing." Selena has a smug look on her face. "But the next time he tells me that I'm doing something wrong, I'm going to remind him about this. Huh!" Selena is watching the door for Andrew to reappear. She has the same intent stare a cat wears when it is waiting for a mouse to leave its hole. "After all the trouble he gave me, he just takes his wallet out of his bag. I can't believe it!"

Andrew comes out of the store and gets back in the car. He has a bottle of wine in a paper bag. He sets it on the seat next to him.

"Hello, Andrew," Selena says sweetly.

****

"I learned not to tell anybody anything," Selena says. "Like any person my age. I've found that after I've told somebody something, I always wish I hadn't." Selena is in her bedroom, on her bed. In her hand is a book she's reading. There is a box of Kleenex on the corner of her desk. Selena pulls one out and blows her nose. "I'm getting a cold," she says softly.

Through the window the sky is a still, grey-blue, and the wind has stopped blowing. The world outside has become quiet. The brown grass can still be seen in the front yard and on the hills beyond. That's very unusual. In Montreal, it's uncommon for the frozen ground not to be covered by a blanket of snow in mid-December.

"I found friends—well, quote, unquote, friends. And I made the mistake of confiding in them at the beginning. Just about things that were special to me, just little things. Things that I told them and I didn't want to tell somebody else." She frowns. "They went and told everybody."

Selena is sniffling. Her cold seemed to start just when they got home from shopping. Selena was in the backyard playing with Sandy, and her nose started running. Her voice is slightly nasal anyway. Now, with the cold, it sounds even more so.

"I don't feel lonely," Selena says. "I quite like being alone. When I was younger I invited friends over, and we never thought much of two men sleeping in the same room. However, now it's different. Now I'm at an age where my friends would know exactly what it means."

Out of the corner of her eye Selena sees Andrew through the window. He is marching across the lawn, strings of lights under one arm, extension cords under the other. Selena watches him. He stretches out the extension cords in three parallel lines on the lawn. He lays out the rows of light bulbs. Andrew picks up one of the strings of lights and wraps it carefully around a tree. If the string doesn't go over just the branch he is aiming for Andrew will shake it down and keep trying until it does. Selena watches him make a couple trips around one tree and then she turns back to her room. She pulls a Kleenex out of the box and blows her nose.

"A lot of the kids at school know that I don't have a mother and that I live with my father. If they were to ask the question, 'does anyone else live with you?' I would answer it. But I'm not close enough to any of them to invite them over. So, it never comes up." Selena clears her throat.

"At this new school I'm going to next year, I doubt I will ever bring a friend home who will eventually talk. I just wouldn't have friends like that. It's like at the school I'm at now, the kids who would have laughed at it, or found it offensive, or whatever, they belong to that group I never associate with anyway. The immature group. So, we never would be friends in the first place."

Andrew is starting to wrap the second tree. He tosses the end of the string of lights up to the top of the spruce. He pulls it back out because it doesn't lie just right. This happens several times. Each time he throws it, he patiently pulls it back and throws it again. Finally, it stays where he wants it. He walks around the tree adjusting the lights, branch by branch.

"Like one time I had this girl over who I didn't really feel that comfortable with. We were going to the school dance and we had to come here to change first. But see, she didn't have time to assess the situation. We just came in, changed, and left. If she asked any questions

I just switched the subject. In my new school friends might come over, but it would be like that. They wouldn't have time to figure out what is going on."

Selena pushes her pillows up against the wall. She scoots back and leans against them. Her feet, in her white socks, stick out over the edge of the bed. "Eventually it will probably come out," Selena says, opening her brown eyes wide. "My father always carries this leather bag, and if he ever comes to a function at my next school—" Selena's voice trails off. She stares sadly in front of her.

"It doesn't bother me that much, and it's getting to bother me less because it's becoming more common. But if he comes to my next school, I'm not going to say a damn thing. Let them think whatever they want to think. I'm positive that they're going to say something about it. They'll probably ridicule me for the rest of my school life, until I leave that school. I just think people are like that."

It starts to snow outside. First a few flakes fall lazily from the sky, then more. Andrew has finished wrapping the trees. By the time Andrew walks with the end of the cords to the garage, to plug them in, snowflakes are filling the air. They are falling lightly on the grass, on the trees, on the driveway. Andrew plugs in the strings of lights.

Selena sits up and sneezes suddenly. She sneezes again. She takes a tissue out of the box and wipes her nose. "Sometimes I wonder if I'll ever find someone that I can talk to about these things," Selena says. "It's impossible in my school, but I know it's not impossible. Then again, maybe I'm not looking for that person. I don't know."

Andrew is out in the yard surveying his work. He's facing Selena, but the light in her room is not on and he doesn't see her inside. He's walking this way and that way, making sure the lights are sitting just right. He will adjust them once, and then adjust them back the way they were. The snow is settling in his hair, on his coat. Selena smiles as she watches him.

****

"We've, in fact, been put down innumerable times by homosexuals," Dan says, "because we are, quote, 'the married couple trying to emulate the heterosexual status quo.' " Dan clears his throat. He crosses his arms. "That's a crock of it," he says.

Everyone is in the living room. Dan and Andrew have spent the afternoon doing projects, and now it's time to relax. Andrew has fixed everyone a drink and given them a coaster to set it on. The problem is that Dan, Andrew, and Selena are not very good at relaxing. They're more comfortable working on some task around the house than they are just sitting about.

"A commitment is something that necessitates work," Dan says. "Ours is not a relationship that was made in heaven. We fight—"

"And how," Andrew chimes in.

"—we don't physically fight, we argue. We argue to get things off our chest. But I care very much for Andrew, and I think he cares very much for me." Dan pauses with his hand over his mouth. He is talking softly. There's none of the usual anger in his voice. He looks at Selena, then back at Andrew.

"There was a period there where it seemed like every week Andrew or I was going to break because of the tension. You know? Andrew was never satisfied with anything Selena would do. Selena would try to please him, and the more she tried, the less he was pleased. Those are just classic behavior manifestations of stress. I don't think they're attributable at all to homosexuality. It has to do with very mundane kinds of reasons, one of which was economic."

"That's why I don't believe that saying that money does not buy happiness. I think that's false," Selena says.

"There's a cute little expression," Andrew tells her. "If you're going to be unhappy, you might as well be rich and unhappy."

Dan and Selena laugh. Dan takes a sip of his drink. He puts the glass back on the coaster. The snow is still coming down outside. A fragile white layer covers the bushes outside the window. The one leafless tree in the backyard has neat little mounds of snow balanced on every branch.

"But I will state," Selena says with a wave of her hand, "that Andrew, you are a nag. God, you are a nag." Selena starts to giggle.

"Well, you don't remember too well," Andrew snaps. He sits straight up in his chair. Dan sees this and tries to smooth things.

"Well, you are Andrew. You're a nag in the sense that you're a perfectionist. You want things done one way and one way only. And you can drive someone to distraction with that." Andrew doesn't look at Dan. He is looking into his glass. "I can drive someone to distraction because I'm very logical. I will focus in on someone and keep probing and probing and probing," Dan makes circling motions with both hands, "until they answer my question and answer it the way it should be answered. And until such time as they do, they're not going to escape my net."

"OK, so what am I?" Selena asks.

"You're distracted," Andrew says sarcastically.

"No," Selena says, "I'm live and let live. I've picked up a lot of nagging from Andrew. However, if somebody did not clean up after themselves, if I cared enough for them, I would pick up after them without saying anything. I cannot wait until I get a chance to prove it."

Andrew raises his eyebrows and rolls his eyes. Selena watches this and then mimics him. Andrew stiffens.

"When Andrew has a problem," Dan says, "he can't laugh at himself. I can laugh at myself, after a certain point. After it reaches the absurd, really the absurd, I can laugh."

"Four drinks later," Andrew offers.

"No, I can really laugh, but you can't. You take yourself much too seriously. But there are more similarities between Andrew and I than there are differences. We have similar tastes in things. We have a similar value system."

"You're both crazy," Selena adds.

"We're both a little crazy, yeah," Dan agrees. "But I don't retain things. I don't hold a grudge for days, that kind of nonsense. We have a fight, the feeling may go on for one or two days, but by and large I'll get it off my chest and put it behind me. Andrew retains it in the recesses of his mind. All of a sudden I'll say something and he'll go, 'yeah, just like three years ago when blank, blank, blank.'"

Andrew is sitting with his arms folded. Selena swings her leg back and forth, nervously. She is watching Andrew to make sure he isn't getting too upset.

The blustery wind outside picks up the snow from the bushes and throws it against the window. The wind will gust for a moment and then it will be perfectly still, and the snow will drift lazily down from the sky. Again the wind will pick up and scatter the snowflakes before it. As the snowflakes hit the window they appear to be running from the wind in panic.

"There is only one hostile one in this house," Andrew says. He is speaking softly and slowly. "Dan gets very hostile on many occasions to those around him. And he turns them off. However, he doesn't direct that, for the most part, towards Selena."

"So, you're going to hold it against me, because he's like that?" Selena's voice is very high. It's piercing.

"Selena, he is very protective of you. There is nothing he wouldn't do to protect you. Including venting any outbursts so they go everywhere else and around you. When he's angry with you, it's very, very short lived."

Dan shouts, "I can forgive and forget—can you!"

"I think I can," Andrew maintains an unruffled tone, "on occasion. I'm not nearly as good at that."

Sandy, who has been sleeping next to the door, comes over and puts his chin on Andrew's knee. Andrew snaps his fingers and points at the floor. Sandy sits down. Andrew snaps again and Sandy slowly, very slowly, lies down. He puts his head on his front paws.

"I get very angry," Dan says, "and it will take maybe forty-eight hours, or seventy-two hours, and then I'm over it. I don't bring it back. You fight dirty," Dan tells Andrew. "There's a dirty way of fighting and that's where you bring incidents that have occurred previously and you contaminate the whole argument."

Selena waves her hand to get attention. "You can bring incidents back if someone says, 'I'm not like that,' and you can state five instances where they were."

No one answers her comment. The room becomes quiet. Both men are absorbed in their own thoughts. Selena looks from her father to Andrew and then back to her father. She starts giggling for no reason.

Andrew clears his throat. "It's just a matter that my values are different," he says with a kind of hopeless wave of his hand. "I can in a logical way understand that. I was brought up in Europe. When I was a kid I helped my parents, and then if I had time after that to be sociable, terrific. That is, if I didn't have other responsibilities, e.g., my homework." Andrew looks at Selena. His voice is very calm. "When the work's all over, then you come down and enjoy yourself. When I grew up that's how it was."

"When you grew up!" Selena repeats. "That's all you ever talk about, when you grew up!"

"What I'm feeling, Selena, is that I haven't changed my role in life. I'm still doing what I was doing as a kid. The only time I really enjoyed a party was the one where you ran around out there like an idiot—"

"And you sat down."

"Well, it was his birthday party," Dan says with a laugh.

"I don't think it was so bad that I sat down and enjoyed my own party.

There's an uneasy silence. Selena blows her nose. Andrew watches her, waiting for her to finish. She puts the tissue back in her pants and he begins again.

"On the average day, Selena, you're supposed to do certain things. Often I do them because you're busy with homework. But you'll go into the kitchen, have a little snack—"

"And I clean up!"

"I'm afraid, Selena, that's where you're wrong." Andrew's voice is soft and even. "You do not always clean up after yourself."

"Neither one of you cleans up on Sunday mornings," Dan says in a joking way, trying to lighten the conversation. "On Sundays when I walk into the kitchen—"

"Fine," Andrew interrupts. "Then why don't you make us breakfast in bed."

Dan is suddenly furious. "You see how you contaminate an argument!", he yells.

"I think that would be a super idea," Andrew says, calmly laughing to himself.

"Screw the breakfast in bed!" Dan shouts. "That's totally irrelevant to the argument. We're talking about cleaning up afterwards!"

****

"He's my father, right? And I treat him as a father, usually. But there are some times when I wish he would just BUG OFF." Selena is in her room, on her bed. She takes a deep breath and lets out a sigh. "I don't need both of them saying, 'clean up your room,' 'get this done,' 'get that done.' There are some times when I get very upset and I just want to say, 'Get Lost—Go!'"

Dan and Andrew are in the kitchen. They're working on dinner. On Saturday nights the two of them usually put together something elaborate. They put in hours of preparation, and they set the table with the fine china and silverware. It's a weekly ritual that grew out of the fact that they have few friends whom they feel close enough to invite to their home. This is one way to make an evening special, just among the family.

Selena sits quietly. It's already dark outside. She looks out the window but sees instead the reflection of her closet and her other bed. The stuffed animals sitting on the other bed appear to be looking in through the window from outside. They're all in a row, watching her. Selena yawns.

"We have arguments because of our differences of opinion. Like my father said earlier, if he's had a bad day he'll take it out on Andrew. Then Andrew will take it out on me. In most families the child is at the end, you know, that's it. But not in this one. I bounce the ball right back." Selena is talking softly. She's very tired. It's an effort to keep her eyes open. Perhaps it's the cold coming on. She takes the quilt off the edge of the bed and covers herself. Only her head and feet stick out.

"You know the expression, 'you hurt the ones you love the most'? It's true. The only ones you feel comfortable with, you take everything out on them." Selena's expressive eyes look out from underneath the quilt. Her curly hair is uncombed and sticking up on one side. "But like I said, I do hit back. I mean, I won't take it. That might sound like I'm a snob. But it's not that. I just don't think that it's fair at all.

"There have been times when I've been in the wrong. Everybody gets in the wrong sometimes. I was last night. I was upset about something at school. Dad came home from work in a good mood, and I was in a snappy mood. But the same thing happens when he or Andrew comes home and they're boiling over with something from work. It just erupts."

The uniform Selena wears to school is hanging on her closet door. It's a simple blue skirt and white blouse. There is also a blue jacket in the closet. Selena's room is neat. She straightened and vacuumed it this afternoon.

Sandy looks into Selena's room. He sees Selena and, in his lumbering walk, comes over to her. He puts his chin up on her bed. "Hi," Selena says. Her arms are under the quilt. She takes her foot and pets him on the head. Sandy stands there looking up at her with his big brown eyes. Selena moves her foot and rubs him under the ear.

"I can't say I love my mother," Selena says, pulling the quilt up to her chin. "I can't say I love her because I don't know her. She left when I was a year old. And I've only seen her three times since then." Selena yawns, then continues, "I don't know why, but I don't hold it against her that she couldn't relate to children and she couldn't act as a mother to me. I mean, that's the way she is. I'll have to accept her for that. I'm who I am, and she'll have to accept me for that also. That is, if she wants to accept me." Selena's voice trails off. Her eyes are very heavy, she keeps blinking.

"I don't really miss my mother. Although there are times when I wonder what she's doing and what it would be like to have a mother. Because the older you get, when you're going through adolescence, even though you can talk to your father about everything, you can't. Even though he says you can talk to him about everything, you really can't. I talk about virtually, almost everything with him. But there are some things—" Selena looks out the window. She sees the row of stuffed animals staring at her from her other bed. "There are just some things that I would rather talk about to my mother, or to another female."

Sandy scratches at Selena's bed. Selena pets him on the head with her foot again. He sits very still as she does. "Good dog," she coos to him. "Very, good, dog." Sandy has his eyes closed. He has a look of reverence on his face, as if he were being knighted or something.

"I find there's only one thing that's really important that I lack," Selena says, biting on her bottom lip. "However, if my mother lived here I wouldn't have it either. And that's a role model." Selena laughs a nervous laugh. "So, what I do is I look at our friends, and I take bits and pieces of each one. Which is probably what a lot of kids do anyway, despite having two parents."

Sandy puts his big head down on Selena's foot. She smiles a tired smile. "You big dummy," she tells him. Sandy lies there with his eyes closed, hoping that Selena will pet him some more. She doesn't, though. She just watches him. And then she closes her eyes.

****

The kitchen is full of smells, Cornish hen smells, chestnut stuffing smells. Dan and Andrew work as a team. Dan runs around the kitchen, chopping and mixing and cooking, and Andrew runs around after him, cleaning up the mess. Dan is at the counter cutting carrots. The kitchen is full of the motions and industry of two men furiously preparing dinner.

"If it hadn't been for Andrew these last seven years," Dan says as he cuts, "Selena would probably not be the feminine little child that she is. I have no ability in terms of telling her how she should wear her clothes, or her hair." Dan mimics Selena's voice, "Andrew, does this blouse go with this skirt? How does my hair look? What do you think of these shoes?' She always goes to him."

Andrew smiles. He dries his hands on a towel and takes the Cornish hens out of the oven. A wave of rich, warm smells fill the room. Andrew retrieves the juices from the bottom of the pan and dribbles them over the light brown back of each bird, making them glisten. He does this to each one twice. Andrew puts the pan back into the oven.

"Of course, Selena doesn't always take his advice and that hurts his feelings," Dan says. "Andrew will tell Selena, 'why should I give you my opinion, you don't care what I say.' But she does care. She's always asking him what he thinks."

Andrew puts some water and the vegetable steamer in a pan. He puts it on the stove and turns the burner on. "I had never thought about parenting before I moved in here," he says. "I had never gone through the bit with combing hair, making sure all the clothes were clean, of looking after everyone on a day-to-day basis.

"You had to look after me on a day-to-day basis," Dan says without stopping his slicing.

Andrew laughs. "I'm still looking after you. She, at least, has learned." Andrew comes up behind Dan and puts his arms around him.

"I know a good thing when I see it," Dan says. He slides the carrots over the edge of the cutting board, into the bowl with the broccoli. "Could you start the water, Andrew?"

"I already have."

Dan checks the stove. "You're way ahead of me."

"As usual," Andrew tells him.

The vegetables are put into the steamer and the lid is returned. Everything is cooking now. There are stuffed Cornish hens in the bottom oven, and Yorkshire pudding in the top oven. There are carrots and broccoli cooking on the stove. The kitchen smells wonderful. Dan puts the bowl and the knife in the sink for Andrew, and he wipes off the cutting board.

Outside the snow has stopped, finally. There looks to be three or four inches in the front yard. The Christmas tree lights wind through the branches of the spruce trees and shine into the night.

"Selena has become very defensive," Andrew says. "I don't really mean defensive. I should say defending of us, very protective. Like if her friends get a little too close—" Andrew holds his hand out as if to say, 'that's far enough.' Dan and Andrew are both leaning up against the counter. The steam is beginning to rise from the vegetable pan with a soft hiss. "It's partly her own embarrassment and partly, well, she understands that the situation is not publicly acceptable."

"We're just two people," Dan says, "two people trying to raise a child. We're trying to give her a halfway decent start in life, despite the handicaps that we present for her. I think as she gets older and becomes more secure there will be less tension. She won't be so reluctant to speak for fear she'll let the cat out of the bag."

Andrew nods his head in agreement. "I remember we were watching a gay rights march on the news one night. I asked Selena what she would think about Dan and I marching in one of those parades."

"It was just a question," Dan says very definitely. "We're not the type to do that. I don't think you were asking it as a serious question."

"No, I was just curious to see what she thought. And what she said was, 'well, it would really show who my friends are. But I think I'm going to end up with no friends.' "

Andrew goes over and peeks in the oven. The Yorkshire pudding is done. He turns the temperature way down. Dan stares out the window. He rubs the bridge of his nose. There's worry in his eyes.

"We're a close-knit family, I would say." Dan looks over at Andrew. He is speaking slowly, and he seems confused. It's as if he is thinking about one thing while talking about another. "We argue and we fight but we still care a great deal about each other." Dan looks out the window again. "What we do," he says, staring at the lights shining on the three trees in the front yard, "is we try to protect each other as much as we can."

****

The dining room table has such a shine, you can see yourself in it. Andrew has put out candles and turned down the lights on the chandelier. He has set the table using a beautiful set of pink and white china and sterling silverware. Andrew lights the candles.

Dan comes in carrying a platter with the three Cornish hens. "Selena was fast asleep," Dan says. "She was a little curled-up lump in her bed." He puts the platter down in the center of the table.

"Did you wake her?"

"As gently as possible."

Dan goes back into the kitchen and brings out the Yorkshire pudding. It worked perfectly. It rose a good eight inches in a graceful arch above the glass pan. He sets that down as well. There is a large plant in-between the table and the sliding glass doors. Crouching down to avoid the branches, Andrew grabs the base of the plant and pulls it away from the table.

Selena pats into the room in her big fluffy slippers. She's yawning. She drops into her chair and rests her head on her hand. Selena closes her eyes.

"How was your nap?" Andrew asks.

"I don't remember," Selena says.

Dan brings in the bottle of wine. "Well, look who's made it to the table." He pours a glass for Andrew and one for himself. Andrew begins serving and Dan sits down.

"Can I have your plate, Selena?"

Barely looking up, Selena hands him her plate. Andrew serves her one of the birds, a helping of pudding, and some vegetables. He gives it back to her and she puts it down. She's still resting on her hand. Selena closes her eyes again. Andrew stares at her miffed. Dan waves to him not to pay attention to it. Andrew takes Dan's plate.

"Tomorrow, I was thinking," Dan says, "that we could go to that movie in the afternoon. The one at the mall. What's it called?"

"Yeah, I know which one you mean," Andrew answers. "Isn't that a war movie?"

"No, it's not a war movie, it just takes place during the war. It's supposed to be very touching." Dan has his eyes closed, and a look of concentration on his face. "I can't remember the name of it right now. That's aggravating."

"You know," Selena says, "it doesn't hurt me that I don't belong to 'the group' at school. If anyone ever asked me, 'aren't you upset that you don't belong?' I'd say, 'No, because they're not the kind of people that I'd want to be friends with, from what I've seen.'" She looks up at her father.

Dan blinks several times trying to orient himself. He smiles at Selena. She's pushing her food around on her plate with her fork. She takes a small piece of broccoli and puts it in her mouth. "It's difficult," he says. "I think one needs friends. You need people you can talk with."

"It bothers me," Selena says, "that 99% of the kids in that school are so narrow-minded they cannot realize that the people who talk behind my back, talk behind their backs as well. I don't need that. I'd prefer to stand alone. This group of kids wants to be in so much that they'll laugh at their own expense. Or a person will walk all over them but they'll still go back and follow that person. They're so stupid."

Selena is speaking into her plate. She has her fork in her hand. She moves a carrot into the gravy and then pulls it back out again.

"I think you're like me," Dan says. "I'd rather have a few very, very dependable friends, as opposed to having a lot of superficial acquaintances." Selena doesn't look up. "People who would walk the last mile with me, that's very important. I think if you have five or six good friends in your lifetime you're doing well, very well."

"We've got—" Selena is counting on her fingers, "we've got five—no, we've got six."

Andrew laughs. "Selena, dear, you don't need to actually count them. It's not the exact number that matters."

Selena doesn't seem to hear that. "We have more friends than the average person—who are genuine," she says. "Okay, so a lot of heterosexual couples have a lot of friends. But how many would still be there, you know, if something was different."

Andrew pours himself another glass of wine and fills Dan's glass. He continues eating. The candles flicker on the table. Dan is watching Selena. "It makes for a lonely existence at times," Dan says. "I won't deny that. I remember as a kid I always read a lot. Reading was my way of fantasizing and escaping from the loneliness."

"Well, I don't read to escape from loneliness," Selena says sharply, looking up at her father. "I read because it's interesting. And at times I would much prefer to read than to be with some people."

"I know," Dan says in a soothing way, "and you'll excuse yourself."

"Yeah."

Dan looks down at his plate. He picks up his fork and starts eating. Andrew serves himself more pudding. He asks anyone else if they'd care for some. The table is quiet of conversation. There are just the sounds of forks against plates and the ting of a glass set back down on the table. Selena is ignoring her food. She is sitting, staring in front of her. Suddenly she puts her fork down. It drops with a "clang" onto her plate.

"What's wrong?" Dan asks her.

Selena puts her head on her hand. "I don't know," she says.

Andrew looks at Dan. Dan puts his knife and fork down. "Come on, tell me what's wrong, Selena," he asks again.

Selena clears her throat. Her voice is shaky. "There's just a lot of pressure, you know?" She rubs her eyes with her fingertips.

"I don't know what you mean," her father says.

Selena shrugs her shoulders, as if she's not going to answer. She covers her eyes with her hand. "I'm not doing that well in school," she says, talking slowly. "The kids are getting on me in one corner, the teachers are getting on me in another corner, my grades are trapping me from the other corner." Selena's voice is wavering. "There's pressure around the house. Andrew thinks he's chief cook and bottle washer, as he likes to put it. He's depressed. Dad, you're depressed. You don't like your job. I'm getting pressure dumped on me—" Selena's voice cracks. She stops herself before she starts to cry.

Dan takes her hand which is on the table. As soon as he does her body begins to shake. Tears fall from her eyes. Dan pulls her to him and she sits down on his lap. She buries her head in his chest and she cries and cries. The room is filled with the muffled sound of her sobbing.

"It's going to get better," Dan tells her. He holds her head in his arms. "It will get better, Selena."

"How do you know?" Selena struggles to get the words out.

Dan doesn't answer right away. "I don't know," he says finally. "I just think it will."

Selena cries for a long time. At first, she's lost in the sobs. Then, gradually, they become softer. Dan is holding her, while Andrew watches them, a worried look on his face.

When Selena finally stops, her face looks sad. At the same time, though, it looks completely relaxed now. Her eyes are red and her curly hair is sticking up where it was pressed against her father's chest. She sniffles.

Andrew gets up. He picks up his plate and takes it into the kitchen. Selena moves back into her seat and sits hunched over in her chair. She wipes her eyes and her nose with the back of her hand. Dan takes a handkerchief out of his pocket and gives it to her.

Andrew brings in two cups of coffee. He puts cream and sugar in Dan's. The room is quiet. Wax is running down the side of the candles onto the glass holders, and onto the table. If Andrew saw that he would be very upset. Selena pokes at the wax with her finger.

"We have a lot of arguments," Selena says softly, breaking the silence.

"Yes, we do," Dan agrees.

Selena's plate is pushed to the side. She's leaning on her arm, which is leaning on the table. She looks up at her father and her bottom lip is trembling. "Remember," she says, "a couple of weeks ago after we had a bad argument, we decided that that would be the last one. And we invented the word goosefeathers. We said that when we start an argument, if one person wants to quit, they could just say goosefeathers and walk away." Selena looks like she might cry again. Her eyes are filling up with tears. Dan takes her hand. "Every family has arguments," he tells her.

"Every family has arguments but I think we have more than the average amount. I know that we'll never get rid of them completely."

"No," Dan says, "probably not."

"But there's only one wish that I have." Selena sniffles, she clears her throat. "I only wish that we could have an argument, clear the air, hug each other, and have it be over with."

"I think that's what is supposed to happen," Dan says.

Andrew's eyes are also filling with tears. He blinks them back. "Selena, I think that's a wonderful suggestion," he says. "I think we can all try it. We can try it again."

Selena starts to cry, softly this time. One tear spills down her cheek, then another. "That's what I'm hoping for," she says. "That's my only wish." Her father takes her hand and pulls her back onto his lap. She hides her face in his chest again and she cries. Andrew smiles at Dan. He picks up his napkin and wipes tears from his eyes. Dan looks confused, he's not sure what to do. He closes his eyes and holds her.

Update:

Selena Angellini

Summer, 1983

Dear Joe,

Were you beginning to think you'd never receive this? Actually, I've been feeling kind of guilty that I haven't written sooner so I thought it was time I put pen to paper. However, I should forewarn you that I just got in from work, so please ignore the fact that my train of thought is not in any particular order.

To begin with. I've just completed my junior year in high school (successfully to my surprise). My school "life" is improving steadily, with this past year being one of the best. I've developed my own circle of friends outside of school, and I hardly have any problem with the "kids" in my classes. In other words, we co-exist without much friction. I think part of the reason for my "expanding" popularity is that we're all growing up and slowly learning to accept each other's individuality and idiosyncrasies that make life so much more interesting.

However, the majority of people I socialize with are of university age. In other words, between twenty and thirty—which is a considerable age difference. But despite the age difference we share a lot of interests and pursuits. I think one of the reasons my friends are older is that I've experienced a lot more of life than most of my sixteen-year-old peers. I've been exposed to a wide variety of interesting people and I've gained something from that which usually only comes with age. I'm not saying that I know everything. It's far from that, actually. However, I do find I'm more on the same "wavelength" with older adults.

Well, enough of that. How about some information on my family? We're all still here, complete with our lovable dog, and it seems that family life has quieted down somewhat. We still have occasional "spats" to clear the air. But I think that, because I'm grown up, I am able to more easily see their point of view and empathize with them to a certain degree. Anyway, we're all pretty happy and I think another contributing factor is that we all have our time to ourselves.

My parents (that's how I've always referred to my dad and his lover—because they both are my parents) usually go up to the house on the weekend. I usually stay in the city at the apartment, to see my friends, or babysit, or whatever. It's very relaxing to have the place all to myself, and in this way we can all have time on our own to wind down after a busy week. By doing this we find that we don't get on each other's nerves as much because we aren't always in each other's back pockets.

I'm extremely grateful to my parents for their understanding and support in the fact that they realize I need to have some time by myself. It also displays their trust in me and their knowledge that I'm sensible and won't do anything stupid or foolish. As a matter of fact, if I decide to go out I phone them up and tell them where and with whom I'll be. I call again to let them know I'm back safely. I love the arrangement. I don't feel suffocated and therefore don't have a reason to be rebellious like so many other teenagers who are consequently very unhappy.

Anyway, to change the subject, I'll just drop in a little line about a few of my accomplishments this past year. I managed to get on the honor roll at school, which, needless to say, I was very pleased about. Also, I took a course and received my certificate that qualified me as a lifeguard. I was a swimming instructor of little children, and I had a great time teaching all the little kids how to swim. Also, I spent some time as a volunteer in a group that works with mentally and physically handicapped teenagers. But my major accomplishment was that I got a summer job. I'm very fortunate to have found summer employment because I'm constantly reading about all the university students who are unable to get jobs.

Anyway, now that my life has been pulled together, I've decided to do the same to my body. So, I've joined a gym and I'm taking some self-improvement courses as well. They include etiquette, grooming, diction, walking, wardrobe planning, etc. Life is getting to be more and more exciting and interesting.

Anyway—gotta rush and go strain my muscles.

Take Care,
Selena

2022 Update to the Angellini Family

Joe – Hello.

Selena - Hello, long time no see.

Joe - It has been a very long time. It's been a very, very long time. I mean, about 40 years.

Selena - When did we first meet?

Joe - Well, you are 13 in the book, but I worked on this book for four years.

Selena - Given that I was in eighth grade going into high school, that seems right. Except I'm going to be 55 this year. So, that'd be 42 years. I'm sure I look exactly like my 13 year old self.

Joe – There are some subtle changes.

Selena - Stepping back into my 13 year old self, your chapter on our family does take me right back to the bedroom you describe, and the family room downstairs that you describe. And that dinner at the end, in the dining room. I mean, it's like I'm transported right back there.

Joe - I think I told you that I'm now going to call this book, A Secret I Can't Tell. And I think that keeping the secret affected your whole family. It affected pretty much every family in this book.

Selena - Yes, I recently read the original foreword. Which totally and completely unexpectedly made me cry. And then I read your introduction, which I don't think I've ever read before, and that also made me cry. Yes, much of my waking life was really navigating how difficult the world made it for us, not how difficult having two gay parents was. It was no different than having any other two adults in your house that occasionally fight and argue and cry and have good days and bad days and lose jobs and just live their lives. But it was the intensity and the pressure of the secrecy and the potential consequences that was overwhelming. And I don't think I understood how overwhelming it was until I happened to pick up this book again on August 17. The same day you emailed me to tell me you were republishing the book after all these years! But I had never before really given that constant stress any thought. It was our everyday reality. It was simply what we had to deal with.

Joe – Yeah, that was a hell of a coincidence that you reread the book right before I emailed you… But you did say, early on in the chapter, "if I ever told this to anybody, no one in school would be able to deal with it. They would all reject me." And you also said about your father and Andrew, "if any word came out about it, they could lose their jobs?" I mean, that's a lot of pressure on a 13 year old to keep a secret.

Selena – Yes, I was very aware of that. I was also very aware that I could be taken away from our home. I knew that my whole world could come crashing down. We didn't have any legal protection. If the government wanted to come in and say, "two men are not supposed to be raising this kid"-- well, that was it. I knew it was a constant risk.

Joe - And looking back on it, how much did that weigh on you psychically, the pressure of having to keep that secret at all costs?

Selena - I talked about that in the book. My desire was to get the hell out of that small town and into the city as soon as possible. Because I got more anonymity by doing that. And I got to start over. Once we moved, people didn't know what my living situation was so I didn't have to worry about people whispering in the hallways or anything like that.

Joe - But you still had a secret to keep. In the book you say, "I'm going to have to tell a boyfriend one day, and what happens if he doesn't accept my father? I mean, you could still love someone who didn't understand." When did you tell a boyfriend for the first time?

Selena - I have to laugh at my 13 year old self in the book. But yes, the first boy, not technically a boyfriend, was a wonderful person that I met on a school trip when I was 15. He went to a different school, and he was the first person that I shared my unusual home life with and remains one of my dearest friends. But I never sat down and told him. I did to him what I ended up doing to my first serious boyfriend, and similar to what I ended up doing with my husband. Which is, I talked around the issue, I never explicitly stated it, and then I just had them meet my father like they would any other Dad. This high school friend came up to our cottage for a week and got the full view of life with my dad and Andrew. And when they eventually left to return to work we remained longer, and yet we never particularly talked about it directly. But it was clearly evident that I had a gay father and I live with two men.

Joe - But why couldn't you bring yourself to just say what the situation was, explicitly.

Selena - I don't know. I think because what was important to me was that people got to know my father and Andrew as people first, and not have this preconceived stereotypical notion of them as gay men. And it was unfortunate, but my husband did not meet my father until my father was already diagnosed with a brain tumor and was dying. However, had my father not been sick, I would have done the same thing with my husband that I did with everybody else. Which is, bring them cautiously into my life to get to know the situation. I wanted people to get to know my father, without coming to our home focused on the fact that he was a gay dad or a gay man.

Joe - So how long had you known your husband when you told him?

Selena - I had known him for a few years, but we hadn't been dating all that long. He's not a very emotive person. He is actually the antithesis of my father in terms of being willing and able to talk about feelings and fears, and he's not physically demonstrative. I mean, I feel that he loves me, and I love him, and I'm very happy, but he's certainly a very different human being than my father.

Joe - So, did you finally have a talk with your husband about your father being gay, and did he accept it right off the bat, or did it take him a while.

Selena - He didn't appear to have any problem with it. But I think at that time it was still relatively new to him. And over time it has absolutely evolved into a non-event. Like most people, we have good friends and family members on both sides who have come out. But 25 years ago, that was not the case. I really thought it was my father's grave illness that would get in the way and not him being gay. His diagnosis was out of the blue and he died a horrible death within 10 months. Clearly I was a wreck and I wasn't a whole lot of fun to be with. And who wants to grow a relationship under those circumstances? Right?

Joe - What about your son? When did you tell your son? How old was he?

Selena - He was super young. I think it was just always part of the of the discussion. Now that being said, when I came into my husband's family, I did not share with my in-laws, or any family members, that my dad was gay. I didn't start sharing that, actually, until another family member came out. And that was about five years ago. My husband's family are lovely, lovely people. But they are not a-- let's talk family, let's dig into this and see what it means for you and how it makes you feel, and what was growing up like that like. I mean, there is little if any introspection and examination of feelings, etc.

Joe - That's very different from how you grew up.

Selena - It is the antithesis of how I grew up.

Joe - Yeah, that family of yours was always ready to examine everything and always ready to get into it.

Selena - My father had a big burlap wall-hanging that said, "The unexamined life is not worth living". It really was his mantra.

Joe - In the book, you said, "I'm not a follower. I'm not exactly a leader, I'm by myself." You also said, "I'm just different. And it's not just because of the school I'm in, it's just me. I'm an only child, I've grown up differently, more differently than they know, than they will ever know." So, tell me about that.

Selena - Yes. But that statement, "more differently than they will ever know", is loaded. And only one piece of it is the gay parents. There's a whole lot more. I showed up to live with my dad and Andrew at age seven. And my first seven years had nothing to do with homosexuality. But they had a lot to do with the child that I was, and the person that I became.

Joe - Tell me a little bit about those seven years. I know you were raised by your grandmother. And your mother left at age one?

Selena – I believe my mother actually left at six months. My mom and I have a relationship now that started when I was 17. She called me on my 17th birthday. It's not a mother daughter relationship, but it's a relationship. And she and my son have become really close, which I'm thrilled about, as is my husband. But in my first seven years of life I lived with six or seven different sets of adults in six or seven different family environments. To be clear, at no time was I the victim of neglect or abuse of any kind. I was fed, housed and sent to school, often haphazardly clothed, but I was ok. It was clearly a stressful existence. And what's the word I'm looking for? Just the upheaval, right? Every time I turned around, it was like, well, where am I living now, and who's taking care of me now? And the situations that precipitated many of those living changes were abrupt and somewhat dramatic, some of them were very dramatic.

Joe - I didn't know about any of that.

Selena - My mother leaves when I'm six months old, and I'm living peacefully as a child with my father, just the two of us in this tiny apartment. By the way, both my father and my mother have said that neither of them was actually aware that my father was gay at that time in their lives. My mother left because she wanted to pursue a career in New York City and parenthood wasn't her thing, whereas it had always been a dream of my father. At some point in there, my dad figures out that he's gay. But that aside, the phone rings one day, and it's his mother in law, saying that my uncle has been shot and killed in his home.

Joe - Oh my God.

Selena – My aunt and uncle had two young kids, one was about two years older than I am, and the other was about six months older than me, I think. For reasons that would necessitate a separate book, my maternal grandmother won't take in her grandkids. And so my father, who has no biological relationship to this family, right, and his mother in law hates him with a passion, ends up with custody of all three of us. Three kids under the age of five, two who just lost their father and are not related to him in any way. My mother is not maternal. My aunt is going to prison. So here's my father, a single, gay man, completely alone in a new country , Canada, now responsible for all of us. So the four of us are a family for two years. And then, suddenly, the children's mother is released from prison and my dad has to give the kids back. He didn't want to, but he didn't have a legal leg to stand on. So, those two kids fly home, and I am also sent to a separate city to now live with my father's parents while my dad does to graduate school, and now I'm four.

Joe – And there's more?

Selena – Yes. His parents aren't looking to raise a four year old. So I move again, and this time I move in with a couple who are college friends of my dad. But then that family has marital problems and I am sent back to live with my Grandparents. Finally, at age seven, I go to Canada to live with my dad and Andrew. Obviously, by that point in my life, a lot has gone on, right? The irony here is that the world would have been aghast that a 7 year old was sent to live with two gay men, but, in hindsight, the 10 years that I spent with my dad and Andrew were the most consistent time period I had ever spent in one home

Joe - It was a pretty traditional life with your dad and Andrew. They happened to be gay, but everything about your life was predictable. You ate at the same time, you always did everything together on weekends. You must have welcomed that.

Selena – Yes, I did. But then of course there were the fights. I still remember my father would slam open the door in the middle of night when they had a fight and say, we're getting a divorce! And I'd think, well now what's going to happen to me? There was this level of potential upheaval that was always just below the surface. And it may have looked to you like they had their finances in order, but they didn't.

Joe - So there was also stress around money?

Selena - There was enormous stress around money. To the point of potential foreclosures, repossession, etc. There was huge stress around money, and that pervaded all aspects of my upbringing, from age 7 forward. At the age of seven I was part of all of those conversations and aware of all that stuff. I was an adult at a pretty young age.

Joe - Was that a positive or a negative, mainly?

Selena - I think everything ends up ultimately being a positive, but it's difficult to go through at the time. That's how you learn and how you grow. I mean, I went and saw my mother a couple times when I was about 8 and 10 perhaps. I saw her very infrequently, but when I did visit her, she was, as I now realize, borderline homeless. A tiny living space with no possessions and no furniture. Just a mattress on the floor and a small fridge with orange juice and muenster cheese in it? So, between my first seven years, and my life with my father, I had the whole spectrum of choices you could make in life, and ways you could live your life, kind of laid out on a platter for me.

Joe - Most people learn about all those different options from TV shows or books. You got a first-person trip through all of those possibilities, it seems.

Selena – Yes. I had a friend of mine in eighth grade, who shared with me that she was sexually abused by her father and her brother. So, I was fully aware that things could have been a lot worse. A lot worse. In some ways my upbringing was crazy. But like I said, I was never physically or sexually abused. Yes, I knew too much too soon, and was expected to understand things that were probably age inappropriate. But in the grand scheme of the number of kids who have been abused and even destroyed by their family members, my upbringing wasn't so bad.

Joe - There seemed to be a tremendous amount of love in your home with your father and Andrew. It was maybe mixed up with a lot of arguments and confusion and whatever else. Also, you had step parent issues and Andrew was a big nag. But all of you were so protective of each other. And it seemed to show how much love there was in the family.

Selena - Yeah, when my father and Andrew broke up, that was actually pretty hard on me. Andrew did not take the breakup well, at all. I continued to keep in touch with him for many, many years, I still sent him Birthday and Father's Day cards. He'd been part of my life for 14 years even though I'd only lived with them for those 10 years, before I was off to college. But those 14 Christmases, that was the longest span I'd ever had any adult continuity. But he was such an angry person after that break up. There were endless diatribes of "your father this and your father that". It just became so exhausting and toxic that I just couldn't deal with it anymore. So our contact tapered off and ultimately ceased.

Joe - You were protective of the secret because you didn't think your friends would understand and be able to treat you right after learning the truth. However, you also saw the way the world was looking at your father and Andrew. If you went to a grocery store and people were giving sideways glances, or whispering something, you were very protective of them. The whole family was very aware of being slighted. And then you had the nosy neighbors.

Selena - We had to be hyper aware. But we did have one set of neighbors that were just a godsend, our immediate neighbors were from Germany. They had no issues with it and were so welcoming. And it was so wonderful to be warmly accepted by another family. We were this little party of three in this tiny little town and we stuck out like Rudolph the reindeer. About 6 years ago I got back in touch with a girl who had lived down the street. And she shared that, "my parents told me not to come to your house anymore." I was mostly aware that kids were told that, but she was the first person who revealed that her parents told her not to come over. However to her credit, she still came to our house.

Joe - And did her parents say why she couldn't come?

Selena - I mean, you're in a small town with one stoplight. You get two men living in a house. They carry purses in this almost entirely Catholic agricultural town, and have a seven year old girl. We were given a wide berth.

Joe - It's really interesting how prevalent the prejudice was at that time. It was horrible. And here we are now. Yes, it's 40 years later, but it's so different.

Selena – Yes, and it is so very sad that my father never lived to see any of that.

Joe - How long ago did he die

Selena - 24 years ago. That's before Ellen was on TV, before you had Anderson Cooper on TV, and Don Lemon on TV. And now lots of gay people are adopting kids, and gay couples are getting married. Every time I turn around, I'm meeting same sex couples who have multiple kids. I mean, it's a different planet than the one I grew up on.

Joe - Most of the other kids in the book had been raised in a family where their parents were together for many years and they thought their parents were heterosexual. Then suddenly, one or both of their parents come out as gay or lesbian, and they have to adjust to that. You had a different situation, in that you really never saw your father with a woman. So you didn't have to make that mental adjustment.

Selena - I didn't. I really can't remember back to a time when I lived with both my biological parents. Right? So I didn't have the upheaval, if you will, where life for a certain period of years looks one way, and then the next day, the rug is pulled out from underneath you.

Joe - How soon after you moved in with your dad and Andrew did they kind of sit you down and say, this is the situation.

Selena - There was a mobile in my dad's office with all these words on it: Heterosexual, Homosexual, Asexual, etc. And because I loved words, I asked my dad and he just explained what every word was. And when he got to the word, homosexual, I was seven or eight, sitting on the floor playing. And I said, Oh, so is that what you are? And he said, yes. And I'm like, okay, what does that word mean? And he told me something like, it means two people of the same sex who love each other, and that was that. I mean, when things are presented as facts they don't become a big deal. They just are facts.

Joe - Since you had been in so many homes before living with you father and Andrew, the concept that you could be taken out of your father's home, against your will, against his will, must have been kind of overwhelming in the back of your mind.

Selena - Yes, it really, really was. Because it had happened to me before, right? I mean, my grandparents showed up one day unannounced, picked me up from school and when I came home all my things were packed and I was put in the car and taken to my next home. And that was that.

Joe - So the idea of that happening again, in a home that suddenly you're pretty comfortable in, that must have been hard for you.

Selena - Especially when the door would slam open and dad would say, "we might get divorced?" I remember he actually asked me, he said, "well, if we break up, which one would you live with?" And I, at that moment in time, answered Andrew, because he was quieter. I think I was nine or something at the time. I still wince when I remember that conversation. I can't imagine how hurtful that must have been for my father even though I didn't really mean it.

Joe - Well, I guess you had to deal with a lot of arguments in your family.

Selena - Yeah. And I think it is going to be really hard for anyone who is being raised in a gay family now to understand what it was like to be a part of that forty years ago. Because it was a completely different world. It was a *completely* different world. And I don't think it changed dramatically for 20 years after that time. But then the last 20 years-- it's felt like, the speed of light!

Joe - It's been pretty amazing.

Selena - I picture it like an egg hatching. There's just this little crack here, and then another crackle there. And then eventually enough people are in the public eye that people know and respect, and that seem otherwise "normal", right? And it's like suddenly that egg cracks wide open. And it seems like it happens overnight, but it's been cracking for a very long time. Having people with a high profile speak up and live their lives makes a difference. I am not a Kardashian follower, but I remember when Jenner was on the Wheaties box. When it became clear that it wasn't a stunt and she really was coming out as trans, I thought, how great is that? She was an Olympic athlete, no less.

Joe - It is wonderful how much easier it is for kids growing up. Middle schoolers are coming out as gay. Whereas, 40 years ago they'd be afraid to come out as adults.

Selena - You know, a child that I've known since birth announced last year that they are "non-binary". And I think it is beyond wonderful that they can admit that before they've gone through destructive years of keeping a secret and being criticized and hearing insults behind their back. If we get to a point where people can just live who they are and feel confident and feel appreciated for who they are, that would be a wonderful situation and make for a very different world. I mean, I look back at my father, he was such an angry man. Oh my God, was he an angry man. But he'd spent his whole life hiding something that was fundamental to who he was. I can't even imagine what it's like to exist like that. And my grandfather really had difficulty with his son being gay. But he did try, from a distance.

Joe - Over time, did your dad's parents accept his homosexuality.

Selena - His mother did, eventually, although it was never once talked about openly. His father died too young for it to be an issue. So, no, my father never had a close relationship with his parents.

Joe - Well, you have lived through a transformation in this country and seen it close up. I think the pressure that society put on your family… nobody could live through that pressure without some serious ramifications.

Selena - We were pretty isolated, we only had each other for the most part. In the scene at the end where I burst into tears when we're in the dining room. I don't remember that exactly. But reading it took me right back to that hallway and I felt exactly how tired I was padding down the hall. I could still see where I was sitting at the table and I could practically smell the food. I mean, you just made it come alive for me. I had this flood of images from all those dinners that I'd forgotten. And from my vantage point now, I understand how flippin hard it is to be a parent. I look back at my dad and he was 25 when he became a dad and I can recognize that he really was doing the best he could under extraordinarily difficult circumstances. I really wish he could have seen that everything turned out okay for me.

Joe - Yeah?

Selena - He got to see me get my law degree and start work, and he did meet my husband. But he loved kids and he never got to meet his grandson And my son would have benefited so much from knowing his grandfather. There's a piece that's missing from our life, which is the emotive piece, and the digging into feelings and learning how to express them in a healthy manner. Understanding why you feel the way you do, what might be motivating you, etc. All of that can be messy, complicated and emotional. But because my husband and son are so different from my father, the apple doesn't fall far from the tree, my son doesn't have any exposure to anything like that. My husband's family are good people, great people. Way better people than my biological families of origin. That being said, my father's side does a handful of good folks, and the two cousins that I lived with from my mother's side way back when are solid folks as well.

Joe - Well, I guess your son can get that emotional side from you.

Selena – Maybe, but it would have been neat if he'd had my dad to learn from. And my son likes to be in the kitchen. If he could have seen my father in the kitchen doing those elaborate meals, you know, using every pot in the kitchen. They would have had a great time together.

Joe - It's amazing, all the things that go on into each person's life. Thank you again for being a part of this, and for being who you are, and for filling me in on what's been going on over the last 40 years.

Selena - I'm still freaked out by the fact that your email showed up the day that I received the book, after I finally found it on the Internet. I'd been meaning to order the book to re-read it for years but had trouble finding it. And then the day the book arrived, I'd started reading our chapter and then I cried telling my husband and son what I was reading over dinner, and that was really only the second time my son has seen me cry. My husband wondered what might have happened to 'the author', and I said, "I have no idea but I'll see if I can look him up after dinner." And then, I return to my computer after dinner, open my email and there is a message from you after 40 odd years telling me that you are re-publishing the book. That was crazy! I shrieked and my husband came running. We were both speechless.

Joe - That's truly amazing.

Selena - Well, I think it's fate saying your timing is on point.

CHAPTER 2

The Weston/Roberts Family

Annie, age 8
Peter, age 13
Lynn, age 7
Margie (Annie's mother)
Lois (Peter & Lynn's mother; Margie's partner)

"When I was about three or four years old they started fighting a lot. They fought almost every day," Annie speaks slowly. She's eight years old and very serious when she talks. "I can't remember what they were fighting about but it was about me, and their relationship, and if they ever got divorced who would have me the most."

Annie is sitting on the floor in her room, the room she shares with Lynn. She has brown hair to her shoulders, parted on the side, and bangs. She shrugs and says, "When I was three or four my dad would just plan something and my mom would plan something and they both—first my dad would pull my arm out, and then my mom would. And I didn't know where to go.

"One day they got into a big fight and I didn't want to hear it, so I went in my room and hid someplace. I could still hear it so I put my fingers in my ears." Annie rests her chin on her knee. She pushes her fingers through the carpet. "They said, 'I want to get a divorce!' 'Yeah me too!' That just made me feel sad," Annie says, looking up. "I wanted to get them back together, but I didn't have time. Because the next day they got divorced."

****

Peter's keeps blinking his eyes. He has big brown eyes that look even bigger through the lenses of his tortoise-shell glasses. He's nervous. "I don't think it was right, you know. See, Margie was already divorced and all."

Peter, his sister, Lynn, and their mother, Lois, live with Annie and her mother, Margie. Peter is thirteen and Lynn is seven. The two families have been living together for three years now. After living in a succession of apartments, Lois and Margie bought a house six months ago. It's part of a new sub-division being built right outside of Aberdeen, South Dakota. On one side of them is a house which has just been completed. It's without grass or shrubbery, and no one has moved in yet. On the other side is an empty lot. Behind their house are hills covered with tall grass and rocks. They stretch for a couple miles to a road. Beyond the road is the army base. Peter and Lynn's father, and Annie's father, both used to be stationed at the base.

"We were a happy family. Then different people came—Margie

came along, and all that. And the family started to go to nothing. I'm not saying it was their fault—."

Peter's voice is strained, and he keeps blinking. He pushes his glasses up onto his nose and runs his hand back through his curly hair. "Before they were divorced Margie would, like, come by every day for about five hours. My mom was spending more time with Margie than she was with my dad. My parents used to spend a lot of time with each other. They used to go out to eat a lot and all that. Then it just started to wear off. By that time I knew they didn't like each other too much."

Peter holds his lips together tightly. He is sitting straight up in his chair. Peter is very polite, and the way he speaks is almost formal. There is little of the joking around one finds with other kids his age.

"I was younger and I didn't really know what was going on. When I started to know what was happening, I didn't like it. They started sleeping together and kissing each other and all that. This was around the divorce—a little before. I didn't really know, it sort of seemed like friends kissing. I'd seen friends kiss a lot, but not every day. You know, not come along every day.

"I thought I should make my dad aware it was happening. If I did he'd thank me, but they'd be mad at me. If I didn't tell him and he found out, he'd get mad at me and they'd be glad I didn't do it." Peter looks down at the floor and shakes his head. "I'd lose either way."

****

"I would read books about women together, and I would have fantasies," Margie says. Margie has light brown hair cut in much the same style as her daughter's, down to the shoulders and parted on the side. She's wearing a white sweater, jeans, and gym shoes. "It was only when I actually found myself in love with another woman that I panicked. I thought, 'Oh my God!' I started labeling myself and feeling terrible. Before that, I was married and I loved my husband. Sexually it was a drag, but I loved Joe. He was a good person. And he was great with Annie. So, it was just my little secret and I went about my life with Joe.

"When we got back from Guam where Joe had been assigned," Margie says, "I got into selling Shaklee products. I found out that I could deliver fine talks, that I could really sell. And I got very involved in the business. Joe had a route sales job and he wouldn't get back til eight at night. He'd spend maybe an hour with Annie and then be in front of the TV until he fell asleep on the couch. That's how our marriage was. We weren't divorced until after Lois and I met. But for a long time before that there wasn't much there."

Margie and Lois's house is on the circle at the end of a dead-end road. The few cars that pass by the house are just pulling into or out of driveways. There couldn't be a safer street for kids to play on. As Margie sits beneath the kitchen window, the light from the cloudy afternoon sky shines on the side of her face.

"Lois and I met at a Shaklee meeting, five years ago. I was immediately taken by her, and we became close friends. Shortly after that, Lois's husband, Sam, joined her selling the products and then the two of them talked me into all three of us forming a partnership." Margie takes her glasses off and rubs the bridge of her nose. The lenses of her glasses are tinted a rose color. "I know Sam wanted me around because I could motivate him, and vice versa. We had the same way of looking at the business. But on the other hand, I think he liked me, and at the same time I liked him. We had a good relationship. That's why it was becoming so strained, my falling in love with Lois."

Margie sits back on the couch, lost in thought for a moment. She crosses one arm over her chest and rests her chin in her hand.

"I had imagined it would be possible for me to fall in love with a woman," Margie says, "I should say. I'd imagined it possible for me to have sex with a woman. But I always figured it would be in another city where no one knew me. I never thought it would be like this, having Sam as a good friend." Margie shakes her head slowly from side to side. She puts one fingernail between her teeth and bites on it. "It just seemed like a situation that was going to be painful, for me and for everyone else. I was afraid it would go nowhere. I kept saying to myself, 'What the heck am I doing?', you know? 'Why am I doing this? What am I getting myself into?' "

Margie picks up her coffee cup. She blows softly across the top. "You know," Margie says after a long pause, "I had thought about being with Lois a lot. But that wasn't acceptable. In the context of the way I was brought up, it was wrong. I can still remember the first time something happened between any of us. Lois was there, and I went and laid down in Sam's arms. He was the one who held me, for the longest time. Because that was more acceptable.

"It began as a threesome, but pretty soon it got to be where it was just Lois and I. We never purposely excluded Sam." Margie thinks for a moment. "I take that back. I don't think Lois liked him there because their sexual relationship wasn't too hot. And oftentimes Sam would exclude himself. He had to know what was happening. He would discover the two of us together and say, 'You guys go ahead, I don't feel like it tonight.'

"I tried to keep things going smoothly," Margie says. "There were times when Sam and I would go into the bedroom alone and I was literally just being polite. There was just no way I could be honest about it. In order to be honest I would have to admit to myself that I wanted to be with a woman, rather than a man. And that was just too hard for me to admit."

****

"I knew my marriage was hurting. I knew it wasn't going right," Lois says. "I knew something needed to be done, but I wasn't ready to let go. Here's something that's falling apart and here's something that seems to be coming together. How do you cope with both? I felt really torn."

Lois is a short woman with curly brown hair. She is very personable and talks easily with people. She has a high voice, a staccato laugh, and she speaks fast. The face Lois shows to the world is of a person with boundless energy and enthusiasm.

"Margie and I were spending a lot of time together, but at first it was just friendly and it was all very confusing to me," Lois says. "I wasn't sure what I wanted," she says. "Did I want him? Did I want her? Did I want anyone? Margie felt like she didn't want our marriage to break up. She was frightened that she would be the cause of it. So, we ended up staying together, the three of us, much longer than we should have.

"At one point, Margie talked about moving out of town. She couldn't handle it any more. I was in the middle trying to hang on to her and figure out what to do with him. I think I spent an hour convincing her, giving her every disadvantage of moving without once saying, 'I need you to stay. I need you to stay for me.'"

Lois laughs, her quick, high-pitched laugh. "I couldn't say that. At the time I just couldn't say it. I'd never done anything like this before, and I didn't have the energy to spend thinking about what it all would mean. But I wouldn't let her go."

The kids are upstairs. Margie is working the evening shift and won't be home for hours. Lois has just gotten home from work herself. She is wearing a brown skirt, a vest, and a yellow blouse. Her shoes were discarded as soon as she walked in the door.

"As time went on and Margie and I became closer, Sam started getting very strange," Lois says. "He was getting to the point where you couldn't reason with him at all. He was really scary." Lois is staring across the room. "He was withdrawing. He's a silent person anyway, and he was getting much more silent. He would talk about a person outside himself, and he would talk about being inside this wall." Lois sighs as she shakes her head from side to side. "He wasn't eating. He was depressed one minute and high the next. I was afraid of him. I was afraid of his anger."

The sound of the girls arguing can be heard coming from upstairs. Then it stops. "One night he exploded. It happened to be the night before Easter. He had me up against the wall by my throat, my feet weren't touching the ground. All this stuff was just erupting, and what he was saying wasn't important." Lois grimaces. "Then he passed out, or played possum that he passed out. It scared the hell out of me," Lois says. "It was really a heavy, heavy night."

****

Lynn is sitting on her bed. She's smiling. Lynn runs her fingertips along her eyebrows and pushes her hair to the side just above her eyes. She giggles.

"I remember when my dad left," she says. "He left without saying goodbye. 'Cause he left early in the morning."

Lynn has a high, childish voice. And when she's nervous she smiles a lot. She is waiting, as if she's said all that she remembers, or all she has to say.

Then she starts again. "Peter made a plane and he tore it all up. Peter tore the plane up when our dad left."

Lynn smiles. Her eyes are squinting, and her eyebrows are low over her eyes. She waits. While she's waiting the smile slowly disappears.

"I remember him calling us about two hours later. He said that he was sorry he left without saying goodbye." Lynn thinks for a minute. "It made us feel a little better after he said that." Lynn stops talking.

Her hair falls over her eyes and she pushes it to the side. She smiles. "That's about all."

****

Peter is sitting on Margie and Lois's waterbed. He's sitting on the corner of the frame. Their room has the large bed, a dresser, the one window, and a closet with a sliding door. There are no pictures on the wall. They haven't gotten around to decorating their room yet.

Peter pushes his glasses back up on his nose. He's very upset. "OK, see, one Easter night we were coloring eggs and my parents were having a fight." Peter is blinking. He's talking in bursts. He will stop in the middle of a sentence and take a breath or two, and then go on. "So, umm," breath, "as they were fighting he, my dad, bumped his head on," breath, "you know, a shelf, and almost knocked himself out," breath, "and all that."

Peter is blinking and sniffling. It seems like he doesn't have enough air inside him to finish even half a sentence. "See it was on Easter night," breath, "he was almost knocked out so we had to call an ambulance." Breath. "They came and they were going to make him stay at the hospital, but he didn't want to." Breath, breath. "He wanted to spend Easter with us. And then they, after that," breath, "that next day after Easter, he went to work, he said goodbye, and he never came back." Peter hugs himself. He's on the verge of tears. He takes his glasses off, rubs his eyes, then puts them back on.

"The next time he came to see us I was in the fourth grade. He lived in a motel." Peter's voice starts to crack. "He went to see my sister first. And then they told me to come out in the hall. I was in school." Peter stops. He breathes in gulps of air. "He said he was leaving, that he wouldn't see me for a while. And then the whole rest of the school day I didn't do a thing—"

Peter starts to cry silently. His body is shaking. Tears roll slowly down his face. He wipes them away with the back of his hand. "I walked back in the room as he was walking out—and then I started to go back out to the hallway, because I missed him—just for that short time. But he was already gone."

****

"Peter and Lynn were—" Annie stops to think. "Well, I thought the two kids were lucky 'cause they got a father and mother and I don't, not that's living together." Annie is in her and Lynn's bedroom, sitting on the floor in front of the bed. She's wearing blue pants and a peach-colored t-shirt. Annie is concentrating very hard. She looks very serious. Annie is speaking slowly, searching to find just the right words for what she's trying to say.

"I got a bit jealous and I wouldn't speak to Peter and Lynn. I wouldn't speak to nobody. I would sit by my mom and just listen, and wish that my mom and dad were like Sam and Lois, instead of being divorced."

Annie's and Lynn's room has two single beds, one in each corner against the far wall. There are two white dressers in the room, and a large doll house. There are lots of stuffed animals. The girls' beds are made but their toys and animals are lying scattered about on the floor.

"So, one day Sam and Lois divorced," Annie says, "and Sam just left. Peter and Lynn didn't know it till the next morning. They were sad and I felt like I had done something." Annie thinks for a moment. "I felt like I did something, you know, by not talking to them. I thought that it was, um, my mom's—my mom's and my fault that Sam left. And I felt, 'Ohhh boyyy, was I really dumb to be jealous.'"

"Ever since we met Lois, my mom and her were going out together. My mom started taking Lois out to fantastic places that Sam couldn't take her to. They were going someplace and Sam was just there to take care of us. He was getting mad that my mom was taking his place. So I felt that my being jealous made my mom take—made my mom feel that—." Annie shakes her head, confused. She wrinkles up her forehead thinking as she puts her chin on her knee.

"One time I told my mom that I was jealous about them two, Peter and Lynn, and she goes, 'Well, don't try to do anything.' Then one day I think I did something that made Sam mad, and after that he and Lois started having fights. So, he got mad and he left one night. That really made me upset at myself. I felt Peter and Lynn would be sad like I was. But in my mind I'd go, 'Now we're even.' So I started talking to them. We started being friends."

****

"Lynn and Peter had been visiting their father," Lois says. "The divorce was final. I'd been given custody of the kids. Summer was over. It was time for them to come back, and Sam didn't send them. I let another week pass before I confronted him, but I already knew what the answer was going to be. Sam said he wasn't sending them back, he was going to keep them. He said they were already enrolled in school in Milwaukee and that's where they were going to stay." Lois shakes her head, remembering. Her voice is emphatic. "I talked to the lawyer from the American Civil Liberties Union. I explained we didn't have much money. First bit of advice, 'Kidnap them back.' He said, 'If it doesn't work you'll probably have to go to court, and if that happens the odds are against you.' 'I know,' I told him. 'You don't have to make me aware of that.' "

The lamp on the table next to the couch is the only light on in the room. It casts a circle of light across half the couch and the drapes covering the window. The house is quiet.

"We made this big elaborate plan. The way we had it laid out, it was like a James Bond movie. We had to get them out of Wisconsin as fast as we could in order not to have to worry about custody papers. Because if we were stopped in Wisconsin we could be charged with kidnapping.

"We drove to my brother's house, got his car, and parked ours just outside the state line. We didn't want to take the chance that someone would recognize our car." Lois puts her hand over her eyes. She takes a deep breath and lets out a long sigh. "As we drove to their school Margie and I got down on the floor of the car. It was really strange— cloak and dagger. You pick up a criminal feeling. It was so weird They're your own kids, but legally you're kidnapping!"

Lois lets out another sigh. "My brother and sister got out and waited for Peter and Lynn to get off the bus. While they were standing there the principal came over and asked them, 'Who are you?' They said they were Peter and Lynn's aunt and uncle. Apparently, Sam had warned the principal that something like this might happen. It was illegal for the principal to involve himself, but he did. He went in and called Sam

"There was a line of about five buses and Peter and Lynn were on one of them. Another sister of mine in the car goes, 'I see them, they're on the bus!' I started to cry. I was so excited. All of a sudden my brother shouted, 'There he is!' My brother and sister ran to the car, and the next thing I know we're speeding down the road without the kids I didn't have time to understand what was happening. I didn't have time to think. And then I realized, Sam had showed up at school."

Lois's voice suddenly becomes weak. She closes her eyes for a moment before she begins again. "At first I wanted to go back so I could confront Sam. But then I didn't know if that was what I wanted to do at all. There wasn't time to think about it. It had happened so quickly. I was so tight. I was lost."

****

Lynn is talking softly, in a nonchalant voice. "I like the last family better," she says. She pauses. She is swinging her legs against the side of the bed, first one leg and then the other. "One reason is that it was with our dad." Lynn smiles and lifts her eyebrows. "And another one, I guess, is Peter would have been nicer if Annie wouldn'ta come along. I'm not saying that it's Annie's fault. I guess it's just the way he's been trying to make Annie like his best friend, trying to make her laugh."

It's almost Lynn's bedtime. Annie and Peter are already in pajamas, downstairs watching TV. Lynn has on white pants and a pink turtleneck and snoopy socks. She puts her hands underneath her legs, tucks her heels in between the boxspring and the mattress, and leans forward.

"In court we had to go in a private room and these two guys asked questions. I only remember one thing that they asked." She smiles. "If we wanted our dad to come back to our mom. I said, 'yes' "

There's a knock on the door, and Lois calls out that it's time for bed. Lynn stares in the direction of the knock. She looks tired, her eyes are puffy. "It's a little hard to remember all that stuff. I don't talk about it very much. And when I think about it, I feel sad." Lynn is speaking in a tiny voice. She swings her legs against the side of the bed. "That's mostly the way I feel."

****

Margie and Lois's house is a split-level, ranch-style home. From the garage one walks into the living room-dining room-kitchen area. In the back of the living room there's a stairway. It leads upstairs to two bedrooms, Margie and Lois's, and Lynn and Annie's. The stairway also leads downstairs to the TV room and Peter's bedroom. Lois and Margie are in the TV room, sitting on the couch. The TV is dark. It's been off since the kids went to bed.

"The things those kids were saying to us were frightening," Margie says. She is sitting at the other end of the couch from Lois. She has a lot of energy from just getting off work. "It was unbelievable. We'd talk to Peter and Lynn on the phone. The longer they were with their father the more impossible it was to reason with them.

"For example, they would both say to Lois, 'You are going to come live in Milwaukee.' Lois would say, 'No, I'm not. This is my home, this is where I want to stay.' Their reply would be, 'We know that if we pray to Jehovah, you will be here, you will come live with Daddy. Daddy has told us this. It says in the Bible...'

"It was so frustrating to hear that and not be able to reason with them," Margie says. "Sam told them that if they prayed enough to Jehovah, that Mommy and Daddy would live together in Milwaukee. It was really sad. I don't think anything brought us to tears quicker than to realize they were still hanging onto that."

Lois is smoking a cigarette with one hand. In the other hand she is holding a Kleenex. Margie looks over at Lois and they exchange sad smiles.

"While we were waiting for the hearing," Lois says, "we were standing outside the courtroom and the kids got off the elevator with their attorney." Lois's eyes are teary. She wipes at them with her tissue. "It was the first time I had seen the kids in two months.

"They were nervous and tight, and so was I. I walked over to them, said hello, and then I walked back. I didn't hug them, I didn't want to touch them. I was holding myself together with everything I had. I was trying to keep from saying, 'Oh my god! What's going to happen to us?' I didn't want to say that to the kids. I couldn't do that."

Lois is sniffling. She takes another tissue from the box and blows her nose. "After the first hearing," she says, "when we knew we were going to go into a custody thing, we asked the kids, 'Do you understand why this is happening, do you understand what the issue is?' That's when we brought up being gay. But they didn't want to hear anything about that. It wasn't that they didn't want to hear that we were gay. It's like they were saying, 'We can't afford to feel, we can't afford to let our feelings go.' "

Lois looks over at Margie, who nods in agreement. "We took the kids out to lunch one day, and they were both very distant. They said, 'We know what you're going to do. You're going to try and talk us into coming and living with you.' " Lois's voice is subdued. She has none of her usual enthusiasm. "It wasn't them I was hearing. I heard their dad speaking and the word of Jehovah. It was painful. The brainwashing... I really felt like I was dealing with brainwashed children."

Margie's eyes are wet with tears. She scoots over closer to Lois. "They told us several times," Margie says, "that we wouldn't inherit the kingdom of the earth because of the way we lived, the way we were." Margie looks over at Lois. Lois nods as she wipes her eyes. "And they kept telling us that Sam still loved Lois and that if they would move back together, and she would become a Jehovah's Witness, then they could all live together again in this world."

****

"After that we went to court." Peter has a worried look on his face. "You see, we went to visit him for a summer, and after that—so one day he kept us—" Peter is so nervous he can't finish his sentences. "According to the school you're in—well, anyway, they went to court. They went to court and all that."

Peter is wearing brown Levi's jeans and a yellow button-down shirt. He's not wearing shoes because he's supposed to leave them at the door when he comes in the house. Peter is gripping the frame of the waterbed with both hands. "We couldn't—we couldn't be in there. We couldn't be in the real court. We were in—up in another room with another one of our lawyers." Peter is blinking back tears. When he pauses, his lips purse as he attempts to keep himself from crying.

"So then we went to the—down into the waiting room. The trial went on for about a week, and we were down in the waiting room doing nothing, just waiting around. I don't know how I felt, you know." Peter's voice cracks. "'Cause I loved them both." He shakes his head. "I felt sad."

****

"The minute the judge realized what was involved," Margie says, leaning forward as she talks, "he turned to Lois. She was on the stand. He said, 'What is your relationship with Margie?'"

Tears well up in Margie's eyes as she describes it. She can't keep from smiling. "Lois was spectacular," Margie says. "She simply said, 'I'm in love with her.' I was so proud to hear her say it that way up there on the stand.

"Then all of a sudden I realized, 'My god, I'm surrounded by her family.' She's got nine brothers and sisters. I figured the entire group had gotten up and left. I put my head down and just looked at the floor. I was scared to death to look from side to side. I had her two sisters on one side of me, and her mom and dad were down a ways. It was coming out about the threesome, it was coming out about being gay. I was feeling guilty. I felt like a home wrecker. I just couldn't look at anybody at that point."

Margie leans back. "Finally, the judge took a recess and I had to stand up. I turned around and everybody was still there, the whole crew. I was surprised. Her dad had a faraway look though, he and Jim. They were the ones that were hurting. Jim is her oldest brother. He's the one that had sat in that bar and said to Sam, 'Sam, you're a damn liar—she's not a queer.' He defended her to the end, and it really hurt him."

Margie and Lois have moved over next to each other on the couch. They are holding hands, and each has a Kleenex in her free hand. The sound of a car passing by can be heard outside the window.

Both women look exhausted. Their eyes are puffy and there is a slackness in their faces. Margie goes upstairs to pour herself another cup of coffee. Lois picks up her pack of cigarettes, takes one out, and lights it. The clock on top of the TV says five minutes to one.

"Sam was not a Jehovah's Witness when he left South Dakota," Lois says. "His brother had been one for years, and Sam always disliked his brother's religion. Dislike isn't even a strong enough word for the way he felt about it."

Margie comes back and sits down next to Lois. She takes Lois's hand again. "Sam came in during the writ, and he brought his bible with him," Lois says. "The writ comes before the trial. During the proceedings Sam kept wanting to read out of his bible while our lawyer was questioning him. But our lawyer didn't want that, not yet. She wanted to save that for the trial."

Margie interrupts. "We had been told by our lawyer not to show very much emotion if we could possibly help it. But when Lois was on the stand, Sam would laugh, he would sneer, he would shake his head, talk to his attorney, and he was continually opening his bible and thumbing through it. It was bizarre. I thought, 'This is good, because it's not appropriate behavior.'"

Margie and Lois look at each other, and then Lois continues. "As the process went on, Sam went into this thing with his bible. Each time he moved his chair he would re-position his hand on it. There were three attorneys, we had one, Sam had one, and there was one appointed for the kids. I think the kids' attorney was becoming more and more uncomfortable with Sam. When it came his turn to question Sam, he said something about Sam not believing in furthering the education of the children. The Jehovah's Witness' belief is that there's no need for college. There's a need to learn a craft so you can exist, but your real purpose for being here is to spread the Word.

"Mr. Gimbel, the kids' attorney, said to Sam, 'Do you mean to tell me that you don't think the children should go to college if they want to be doctors or whatever?' Sam started to quote some scripture to answer what Mr. Gimbel had just asked. Mr. Gimbel said, 'I want to know what your opinion is of that.' Sam pointed to the bible and said, 'This is my opinion.' And Gimbel says, 'You mean to tell me you don't have an opinion of your own?'

"Sam grabbed the bible and he shook it at the lawyer. He yelled, he actually yelled in the courtroom. 'This is my opinion!' he screamed. He totally lost his cool. Mr. Gimbel said, 'Thank you, no further questions,' and he sat down."

Lois closes her eyes for a moment. She takes a deep breath and lets it out. "I know in the beginning both the social workers were recommending that Sam get the kids," Lois says. "But as the trial went on they ended up changing their recommendations. When it came right down to it the judge had to decide whether to give the kids to two homosexuals, or to give them to a religious fanatic. He gave the kids to us."

****

After school, first Peter comes home from junior high, then Lynn and Annie from elementary. There are rotating chores which all the kids have to do every afternoon. One vacuums and dusts the living room, one vacuums and dusts the television room, and one cleans the kitchen. Chores are done first thing after school, every day. The kids are very good about doing their chores. They come home from school, take some fruit out of the refrigerator, and get right to work.

Behind the house there are rolling hills covered with tall waving grass, except at the steepest part where the sand and stones are bare. Someday this will be part of the development, more streets, more houses. Now it forms a huge backyard for sledding in the winter and exploring the rest of the year. After the house is cleaned the kids often go together to the hills. The hills go back for perhaps two miles and then come to a fence. Beyond the fence is a road and beyond the road is the army base. There is always the sound of traffic from the road. Softer, but still constant, is the sound of the wind blowing the grass. And then from time to time there is the roar of a plane coming into or leaving the army base.

The kids have few friends and seem to prefer the company of each other. They wander across the hills, usually just the three of them, playing, arguing, and passing the afternoon. There is a place they call the goldmine, which consists of a U-shaped depression in the ground about three feet deep. The entire bottom and sides of the depression are covered with fist-sized stones, and there's a piece of plywood over the top. There's room to crawl in one side and crawl out the other. The kids found it just the way it is. There's not much to do inside the goldmine except move rocks around, and that's mostly what they do.

Peter is sitting next to the opening. First Annie squeezes out from underneath the plywood and then Lynn does. Annie has two rocks with her which she thinks might have gold in them. She shows them to Peter. He holds the two of them, one in each hand. One, he says "definitely doesn't," but the other one might. Annie puts the "might" one on top of a large pile the kids have accumulated. The girls sit down next to Peter.

"A lot of times me and Annie get into fights," Lynn says "Sometimes, like, it's the way we look at each other that causes a fight If I looked at Annie it would seem like I didn't like her." Annie giggles "And Annie would say, 'I can tell you don't like me,' or something.' Both girls start giggling.

"If Lois and my mom hadn't lived together," Annie says, "I wouldn't have nobody to play with except myself, and that isn't very fun. When I was in kindergarten I lived on Hanes and no one really lived by me. So I was lucky that Lois and my mom met and, um, went with each other."

The girls are both in a very laughing mood. Peter is scratching a the dirt with a rock he's picked up. He looks at it and shows it to Annie. Annie shows it to Lynn. Peter collects rocks, and there's no shortage of them in South Dakota. He takes a minerology course at the junior high school. Lynn hands the rock back to him.

"Before Annie moved in," Lynn says, "Peter and I had a lot of fun. We still do have fun—just not too much." Annie laughs. Peter smiles without looking up. "He's just acting funny," Lynn says. "He used to act nice. Sometimes he acts silly and I don't like it. I start getting a little mad. Sometimes I feel like he's trying to take a friend away from me."

"Which friend?" Peter asks,

"Annie," Lynn says.

Annie laughs.

The sun is going down and it's getting cool out. Lynn is the only one with a warm jacket on. She's wearing her winter coat. The other kids are wearing light, summer jackets. Annie doesn't even have hers zipped up.

Annie is staring straight ahead, thinking. She starts to talk. "When Lynn and him fight, it's like—because I'm around or my mother is around. When they're here, they fight most of the time. But when they're with their dad, they don't fight because I'm not there to be helping anybody."

"Yeah, it's her fault," Lynn says, and she bursts out laughing. Annie laughs too.

"Lynn! You're not talking," Annie shouts. "Now shut your mouth till I'm done." Lynn keeps laughing.

"Let's go back," Peter says. "It's getting late." He takes the rock in his hand and throws it. It disappears silently into a clump of tall grass. He gets up, Lynn does too.

Annie is still thinking. "It's not my fault," she says. Annie sits and watches Peter and Lynn as they walk across the top of the hill. They are silhouetted against an orange sky. Annie watches until they start to disappear over the edge. "Wait up!" she yells. She gets up and runs after them.

****

"We never discussed in detail whether we were going to be affectionate with each other in front of the kids until I got into the alcoholic treatment program." Margie is talking. "We ran into this quack who is a lesbian and gave up her son. She was very adamant, and she said we shouldn't be affectionate in front of the children. But we had been affectionate when Sam was still around, I mean hugs and kisses. It was bad enough hiding from everyone else in the world, let alone three little people that live right in the house with us. It just seemed impossible."

Lois nods in agreement. "I like to hold hands in the car," Lois says. "But if a pick-up comes by, Margie will pull her hand away. She's afraid that the people in the pick-up can see us holding hands on the seat." Margie smiles, embarrassed. Lois continues, "If it's dark out at night I'll move over next to her in the car, especially if we're out on the expressway or coming in from the hills. Then when we get to town, with the street lights, I move away.

"Right now," Lois says, "I do prefer to control who knows. If people find out, okay, I'll deal with that. I won't let it be terribly upsetting. It's bound to happen, people are going to find out about me. But the community we live in, I'm not ready to take them on. I'm content with where I'm at."

****

Annie is sitting on the floor in front of her bed. She's taken her jacket off, and it's lying next to her. Annie's face is flushed from running all the way down from the hills. Her voice is soft as she begins to talk. "At first I didn't know what gay meant," she says. "I had this problem where my mom would tell me, and I would completely forget. My mom told me it meant two women living together. I just said, 'That's right. You two are living together, and I don't think there's nothing wrong with it.'"

Annie is kneeling on the floor, sitting back on her shoes. She has her hands tucked in-between her legs. "Having a friend is just doing things together. Like going to a park and sitting down, or talking about what you did. And loving each other is living in the same—." Annie stops, confused. "Well, let's see. If you were a lesbian and you had someone else, the things you would do are, you'd sleep in the same bed together. You would, you know, like with relatives, you'd hug each other and kiss them. It's just like that."

Annie brings up one knee and hugs it to her chest. Her forehead wrinkles as she stares down at the rug. "I'm understanding it a little bit, but I still haven't come to a point where I understand it completely. So I feel just a teeny—a tiny bit uncomfortable with it. But that was about a week—I mean two months ago. Now I don't feel very uncomfortable when they do that.

"They're kissing more and hugging more than my dad and mom did. 'Cause my dad and mom were barely doing that after I was born." Annie starts picking at the rug with her finger. "I get jealous sometimes, and sometimes afraid. Sometimes I feel that Lois is taking my mom away from me, 'cause I don't have as much time with her as I used to when they weren't living together. Ever since my mom met Lois, my mom's been taking Lois out more than she's been taking me. The only time she's hugging and kissing me is either when Lois is talking to someone else or when she's not with Lois. When Lois is at work and my mom's not."

****

Lynn is sitting on her bed. She is wearing a blue-flowered dress and knee sox. The last traces of sunlight are coming through the two windows above the bed. She smiles and runs her fingers along her eyebrows pushing her bangs to the side.

"The word gay means when two mothers are living together." Lynn thinks for a moment and then adds, "Because they divorced their husbands. They had too many fights."

It was still light in the room when Lynn sat down on the bed. And now the last bit of blue is leaving the sky. The room is becoming quite dark. But Lynn doesn't move to switch on the overhead light. She is sitting very still, with her hands folded in her lap.

"Our dad and our mom divorced. Margie and Mom, they loved each other. So they went together." Lynn smiles. She shrugs her shoulders. "That's all I know."

****

Peter pushes his glasses up on his nose. "The first time I heard that, you know, they were gay," he says, "I didn't know what the word even meant." Peter blinks several times. He is talking quickly. "It's when two people from a different relationship love each other." He clears his throat. "And they're the same, you know, sex."

Peter is short for his age. But his hair forms big curls which stand out from his head about three inches all around. That makes him seem taller. Peter is a helpful and serious thirteen-year-old. He doesn't smile very often. And when he does, the smile breaks through gradually, as if he isn't sure of it.

"I'd heard people use the word gay, and other words for all that. People in school use them. They use them like to pick on people." Peter pushes up his glasses. "I don't like it. Because they don't really know the facts, that people really are or not.

"I wouldn't tell the kids at school about this. Well, some of 'em, some of the other kids' parents might be gay. So, some might not react to it quite—that it was so bad. But some of 'em would start to tease us, you know, throw rocks through the windows probably."

Peter is sitting up very straight. He is staring intently in front of him, thinking. After a while, he says, "I've told one person. His name is Roger Curran." Peter shakes his head. "We'd go do stuff like shoot pool and all that down in his basement. I just told him, you know, that they were gay." Peter breathes in quickly and crosses his arms. "I didn't know how he'd react. He said he'd keep it a secret, so that made me feel a little better." Peter's eyes seem to grow bigger as he talks. "But still, not the greatest," he says.

****

The other kids have gone downstairs. They're playing a game in front of the TV and they're waiting for Annie to come join them. You can hear their voices through the floor. Annie is still sitting in front of her bed. There's a little piece of paper which is on the rug. Annie absently crumbles it between her fingers. She sighs.

"Carrie says, 'you're queer' to everyone. And there's this other girl in my class, Sharon, who goes around and kisses almost every girl she sees. So kids always tell her, 'You're gay!'

"I don't like calling people gay. I don't think it's fair," Annie says. "People who don't even know what gay feels like get mad about it, and they don't like it. Some people think it's wrong, and the people who think it's right, probably are. And some people don't even have a choice. 'Cause when you're it, you don't even know what it feels like when you're not it." Annie takes a big breath and sighs again. "So, if you're not it and you get to be it—you'll probably like it."

Peter yells from downstairs to see if Annie is coming or not. "In a minute," she yells back. Annie takes the crumpled piece of paper sitting next to her and flicks it with her finger. It goes sailing under the table.

"I'd rather have a man as a husband, though," she says. "Not because I'm against it. It's just that I feel like, you know, having a man around the house." Annie pushes her hair behind her ears. She's a year older than Lynn but she's about two inches shorter. Lynn likes to wear dresses and even perfume when her mother lets her. Annie is more into wearing pants and playing kickball. "It's not that being with a man is better than being with a woman. I just think that I'd want to be with a man, like if I ever fell in love with a man."

Annie looks up from the rug where she's been tracing designs with her finger. She smiles. "I already know a man that I'd like to marry but he's too old. He's black, but that doesn't make any difference. He's a singer." Annie smiles, embarrassed. "His name is Charlie Pride."

Lynn and Peter can be heard arguing downstairs. Annie looks in the direction of the noise and listens. The arguing quiets down. Annie continues looking in that direction, thinking.

"If I fell in love with a girl," she says, "I'd just be roommates with her. You know? Sleep in our own beds, in our own bedrooms. Sometimes I think it's not right, and sometimes I think it is. I just wouldn't, you know, sleep in the same bed because I wouldn't like it if anyone found out about it. If it was one of my friends, I just think that they wouldn't like me anymore."

This time it's Lynn who yells for Annie to come downstairs. "OK!", Annie calls back in an exasperated voice. She gets up to go, but stops and sits on the edge of her bed. She has a serious look on her face. As she sits on the bed her feet don't nearly reach the floor. She's eight years old, and she's confused. But she wants very much to explain what's confusing her.

"It's like, sometimes I wet the bed," Annie says, "but I don't want my friends to find out. Because I'm afraid that if they do, they're not going to be my friends anymore. Because even if I have to lie to them, and tell them the cat wet the bed, they laugh. So I don't want to tell them. I don't like telling them things I'm not supposed to tell them." Annie has a very solemn look on her face as she stands up to leave. "I won't tell them the things that I do."

****

Dinner is in the oven. After a long day at work Lois came right in the house and started cooking. Now that everything is organized for dinner she sits down at the kitchen table. This is the first chance she's had to sit down since she got home. "They've had to adjust to a different kind of woman, a different kind of mother," Lois says. "A tired mother. A mom that comes home and says, 'I cannot read you a story tonight, I can't even talk.' "

Margie won't be home until eleven-thirty or so. She's working the late shift again tonight. Lois rubs her eyes. She leans forward with her elbows on the table. "There's sometimes guilt. 'I should be able to do both,' I tell myself. I should be able to be a mother, be a person who manages a home, and then also be a person who's got the energy to do an eight-hour job.

"Before I had to go to work I would be here when the kids came home from school. I'd sit and listen to what kind of day they had. I had time to do that. Nothing had to get done right away. But now when I'm home from work, sometimes I'm not unwound. They want to tell me about their day at school, and it's really very difficult for me to listen."

Lois gets up and checks the stove. She's cooking noodles and carrots. Hamburgers are in a pan ready to start. She turns the burner on. "Margie usually cooks when she's home. I'm perfectly content to clean up afterwards," Lois says. She stirs the noodles and takes a poke at the carrots to see how they're coming along. "As the oldest of nine brothers and sisters, and then having my own kids, I feel like I've cooked enough meals in my life."

Lois takes a peek underneath one of the hamburgers and puts it back down. She pushes the top of each one with the spatula and the pan hisses. "There were a tremendous number of bills left over from the marriage. When Sam left I had no job and no money. I found that I couldn't get a loan based on the fact that we had a joint credit account, but my credit would be damaged if the payments weren't made. It was just a dichotomy.

"I went, 'My God, there's no way we can pay these things.' And if we didn't what would happen to the one vehicle we had? Somebody was going to have to keep their credit in good shape." She turns over the burgers one by one. The pan spits and hisses four times.

"What we tried to do, since the car was in Margie's name, was make sure her bills were paid first. But it didn't work. I got so used to hearing the collection agencies on the phone at work that it was like talking to anyone. I figured, 'What the hell, I'm not going to fight it. There's nothing I can do at this point.' "

"Kids! Come on. Dinner!" Lois calls out. The television set is turned off and the kids come running upstairs. They are all discussing something as they sit down at the table. Lois serves the food onto four plates and puts one plate at each setting. The discussion stops as the children begin to eat.

****

"Most of the time when Lois and my mother fight they make up and they're back together," Annie says. "They just aren't quitting so easy like my mother and father did. So that's one better point." Annie yawns. "The other part is that it's lonely without my dad. That's the bad point. Well, it's sort of nice in some ways. I like it a lot better than having my mother and father living together and being unhappy. It's a lot better than that."

Annie has her blue and yellow striped pajamas on. She is sitting on her bed. The board game that was started in front of the TV was finished in the girls' room. It's still spread out over the floor.

"I'm starting to like Lois more than I used to," Annie says. "When I first met her, you know, I used to hate her guts. I felt she was going to take my mom away, and probably, you know, make me do stuff like cleaning that kids don't have to do. So I used to hate them, her guts I mean. Until one day we had a long talk about it and I started being friends."

Annie pushes her hair back behind her ears. She yawns again and covers her mouth. It's past her bedtime. Annie can hardly keep her eyes open. "The only thing I remember," she says in a soft voice, "was Lois talking to me one day about my mom. And then I was crying and I was answering, you know, my honest words. It's hard after you haven't been friends for about three years, you know, or two years— or one year. I can't remember exactly," Annie says. "But it's been getting better. And I hope it gets better and better still."

****

Peter is lying on his bed. He's got his pillow propped up behind him and his arms folded over his chest. "I don't like Margie and Annie," he says. "And I don't like my mom. I like my sister. I love her but, you know, we don't really get along together. She's picking up from Annie what Annie's picking up from Margie."

Peter's door is closed but the TV can be heard coming from the next room. Lois is watching, trying to wait up until Margie gets home from work. The girls went to bed long ago.

"Like I'm on the bottom of the post. Since they came together, since Margie moved in, I'm like the pit around the family. I'm the worst. Annie's on the top, Lynn's the second, and I'm the bottom."

The headboard Peter is leaning against is also a shelf. There are models on top of it, mostly airplanes. There are also rocks on the shelf. These are the most prized members of Peter's rock collection. Peter has rocks on his dresser and his table as well. They're in a shoe box under his bed and a basket in his closet. Peter is lying on his bed with his shoes off. He has his legs crossed at the ankles.

"See, they listen to Annie mostly, and then they listen to Lynn. If the girls told on me, they'd listen to my mom, then they'd listen to Annie, and then they'd listen to Lynn. By that time my mom and Margie would have decided that it was all my fault before my story was told."

Peter takes off his glasses and puts them on the table next to his bed. His eyes look smaller when not seen through the thick lenses of his glasses. Peter is squinting.

"They sort of make Annie the high authority over me, Lynn too. One time I missed a part of the bathroom and Lynn told me to do it. I was going to do it after a while. Then I forgot about it and she told Margie and Margie got after me for it. So I have to listen to the girls also. I just don't like it, you know. It's like a student having authority over the teacher."

****

"I think there's a problem there for me," Margie says, "having a young boy growing up, finding his own." Margie just got back from work. She's sitting on the couch in the living room. Lois wasn't able to stay awake any longer and she went up to bed. "I don't understand why they have to come into their own in such a cruel, sarcastic way," she says. "I just don't understand why it has to happen.

"I saw it with my brother, and I'm seeing it happen with Peter now—the cockiness, the sarcasm. There's cruelty sometimes in the things he says, all in trying to show his own strength, his own power, his... maturity or whatever."

Margie is wearing jeans, work boots, and a red and white striped shirt. She is one of the few women working at the power company. Her job is in the control room, checking all the dials and gauges to make sure none of the equipment is overloaded. Margie is in her early thirties. She has a gentle face with soft features. She is a healthy-looking, attractive woman, and she's most comfortable in the sort of clothes she wears to work.

"It's the tone of voice, I guess, that bugs me. It's a superior type of thing. You know? I mean, it sounds like the girls are really dumb and he's going to show them how to do things. It's unnecessary as far as I'm concerned. I have a real hard time with that. He'll tell them what to do, how to do it, when to do it. I just get really defensive. I end up stepping in and telling him to leave them alone." It's after midnight, but it always takes Margie a couple hours to wind down after work. The house is dark except for the lamp at the far end of the couch. Margie sits with her coffee cup in her hand.

"I'll tell you, when he gets into that position, Peter reminds me a lot of his father. And his father could be a real drag as far as taking care of these kids went." Margie puts her cup on the circle of wood that's part of the lamp. She leans on the arm of the couch. "Sam babied Lynn, spoiled her. She was Daddy's little girl. He never let her grow up. He made sure she was in a dress and had her hair combed and—he just took care of her constantly. We'd walk through a store and it would be, 'Daddy, will you carry me, Daddy this, Daddy that.' I don't know, it just drove me nuts. I thought, 'Gosh, if he didn't relate to her that way she'd be growing up much faster, and a lot of what I saw in her would be blossoming more.'

"It just bothered me, the way he coddled her all the time. The way he treated her like a little baby. And it's not that Peter coddles the girls at all. It's the tone of voice, I guess, that bugs me. It's a superior type of thing, like he's so much more superior. And he sounds a lot like his dad when he does that."

****

"My dad has these friends," Peter says in a soft voice. He's lying on his bed. "They're a nice family. I'd like to have them for a family. They're usually always smiling, and they don't usually fight. They do a lot of things." Peter's voice starts to crack. He stops and swallows.

"One day the father took me to where he works. See he works with a construction company. He took me there and showed me how to build a house. And also, I wanted to buy some perfume for my sister, a little bottle. It cost like ten dollars and I only had three. It was a nice fragrance for a little girl, and he helped me buy it."

Peter is bumping his legs against each other as he thinks. After a pause he continues. "I don't really like this family that much. It's not the funnest family I've liked," Peter says. "They favor the girls. They like to see the girls doing better than me. Like they're jealous 'cause— I don't know. Because I'm the oldest in the family, the oldest of the kids, and I can do a lot more stuff than the girls. I guess they're jealous for the girls."

The room is bright. The overhead light and the light on the shelf are both on. Peter's glasses are on the table next to his bed. Without them he looks younger. He's short for his age anyway. At thirteen he's not even a head taller than his seven-year-old sister.

"Well usually, you know how men act snotty to women? That's the way Margie acts to me, snotty voice and all that. It's like a strange voice, babyish and superior. It's mixed, you know. She talks to Lynn a little bit like that, but not as much as she does to me. She talks to Lynn like a fourth and me the rest.

"One time I told one of the girls to do their work and they wouldn't do it." Peter starts to sniffle. "I told them to do their work or to stay in their room for the rest of—until mother came home. One of them called Margie, and she called me up and threatened that she'd get me if I didn't leave them alone. Then Margie called my mom."

Peter sits up and swings his feet over the side of the bed. He picks up one of his rocks off the shelf behind his bed and rubs it between his fingers. This rock has been cut in a machine that they have at school. The outside is dark and rough, but the inside is white and smooth and very shiny. Peter is rubbing the smooth side. He's seems to be on the verge of tears.

"I asked my mom one time why she never played games with me. And she said she would, she'd play with me." Peter starts to cry, quietly.

"Then I asked her to one night, and she—right as I asked—she said no. She didn't think of what we had said. And now she doesn't even remember that talk."

Peter drops his head. He wipes his eyes on the sleeve of his shirt. "My mom pays more attention to Margie than she does to me," he says. He sniffles and wipes his hand across his nose.

****

"I just—I don't know," Lois says. "We have a problem putting two families together. There's some dynamics here that put Margie and I against one another. She has a softer approach to the girls, and she'll tell you I have a softer approach to Peter.

"Lynn seems to be absolved from it. It seems to be Peter and Annie. I'm beginning to think it has to do with the first child. I don't know what it means, and I don't know where we're going to end up, you know? It's just something right now that I'm watching."

Lois, as usual, is awake early. Everyone else is still in bed. Lois wakes up early every day. She likes to get going, it's part of her style. She talks fast, she walks fast. It's easier for Lois to be doing something than it is for her to relax. Her job is working for an insurance company, in charge of the telephone customers. She's good at making social conversation. She also has an ability to smile and make someone feel comfortable. Lois plans someday soon to be a saleswoman for the company. She'll probably make a good one.

"Margie became extremely critical, very negative about Peter," Lois says. "She told me she saw a lot of his dad in him. 'That's got to stop,' I said. 'He's a child, he's learning how to be an adult. He's going to be obnoxious, he's going to be rebellious. It's going to take patience.'

"He'll go, 'Oh, god!' when you ask him to do something. It's like you just asked him to do the worst rotten chore in the world. I say, 'Fine, you still have to do it.' I don't demand he not talk to me that way. Margie sees the girls as better behaved than Peter. I tell her, 'Wait a minute. We may not be having a problem with the girls right now, but when the girls are thirteen we may be having our hands full with them.' "

Lois is sitting at the kitchen table, having her usual breakfast of coffee and a cigarette. "Peter and Annie got into a fight a while ago," she says. "Annie had gotten mad and thrown some of Peter's trucks.

Peter couldn't find them, so he hit her. He wouldn't let her go in the house. 'You're going to go find my trucks!' he kept saying to her. I sounded like such a big deal that Margie and I went outside.

"Margie swooped Annie up. I walked over to Peter and asked him what happened. I think it's okay to disagree and argue, but if you take someone else's property and do something with it, then you have to be responsible for going to get it. Margie disagreed totally, absolutely totally.

" 'He had no right hitting her,' she said.

" 'OK, but she should go look for the trucks if she threw them.'

" 'No, no,' Margie said, and Annie never went out. I helped Peter find the trucks. He was upset because they were special to him. He was just really angry and hurt. Margie couldn't see past her daughter being—in Margie's eyes—tormented by Peter."

Lois looks out the window. It's a beautiful day. The sky is blue and cloudless. It feels like it might be cold outside, but it's very sunny. I will warm up later in the day.

"That's when I decided to put Peter in the Big Brother program," Lois says. "I felt, his father has left, and he's in a house with all women I thought it would be good for him to have a male he could confide in Maybe there would be things he would feel more comfortable saying to a man than a woman, or things he'd be more comfortable saying to a male friend than parents. We went down and applied for it. I think it was a good decision. He likes his big brother very much."

****

"One time my mom had been feeling down and she just decided we'd be together for a while," Annie says. "I had a cold, but it wasn't too bad. She bought me some cough drops, and we drove around in the car and went to shopping centers. That made me feel really good."

Annie is in her pajamas, having breakfast. The other kids are watching cartoons downstairs. Every time they laugh at something Annie stops to listen for a moment. Even though she can only pick up a vague hum, Annie seems to have one ear concentrating on the TV.

"When my mom and dad would have real bad fights, my mother would say, 'Annie, put on your shoes, put on your coat, we're leaving.' And we'd go out for a couple hours and drive around. Then one time with Lois she goes, 'Come on, we're leaving,' and Lois said, 'Why don' we talk it out at the table.' My mother said 'No' at first but then Lois talked her into it. From then on that's what they've been doing."

Annie eats a spoonful of cereal and drinks from her glass of milk. "I guess I didn't feel good when they left each other, 'cause that reminded me of my mom and dad. But my mother didn't really want to leave Lois, no matter what. She just wanted to leave and be alone for a while with me. It's not that she talked to me instead of Lois, but—" Annie stops to think. She takes another spoonful of cereal. "She just talked to me when she didn't like Lois very much, and she was feeling bad."

The kids laugh again downstairs. Annie turns towards the noise. It's Saturday morning cartoons. Annie is practically leaning in the direction of the television. Slowly she turns back and continues with her cereal.

"I know my mother and Lois are going to make it," Annie says. "They're not going to leave each other. And even if anyone tried to make them they wouldn't leave each other." Annie finishes her glass of milk. "That's what I feel." Annie takes her bowl and puts it in the sink. She goes back, grabs her glass and puts it in there too. She runs out of the kitchen and down the stairs.

****

"I realized when we first moved together that the relationship between Margie and Annie was very strong, Lois says. "If I wasn't there to meet her needs I saw her go to Annie. Good Lord, Annie's eight now, she was five then."

Lois shakes her head. She takes a cigarette from her pack and lights it. "One time I asked Annie if she wished I would leave so she could have her mom to herself. She said, 'Yes.' She didn't pause, she didn't apologize, simply yes." Lois laughs remembering it. "I told her, Annie, I'm not leaving. I'm not going. You can love your mother your way, I'm going to love her mine.

"When I see Margie trying to have Annie take care of her, then I get angry. She's not letting Annie be a child any more. She's asking her to be something different." Lois crosses her arms and leans back in her chair.

"So, I said all that to Annie. She didn't respond much, but I think she heard me. I could tell she was listening."

****

"I want to stay close to Peter. I don't want him to end up hating me." Margie is in her bathrobe. She has just gotten up. She yawns a big yawn, and stretches. "I've told him, 'Peter, I have a difficult time with you right now. You just get on my nerves.' By spitting out that kind of thing, I think it makes it better. We're telling each other what it is we're feeling.

"I've spent some sleepless nights thinking I should be a better step-parent, that I should like him more. There are lots of times when I get a kick out of the things he says, the way he thinks. And Peter is very kind to his mother. I mean, my brothers were never like that. Peter is so helpful and kind to his mother. It can be very touching. But knowing all that, still, I get up in the morning and things start all over."

Margie grew up in South Dakota. She describes herself in her youth as fairly wild. She partied and drank and was rebellious against the restrictions her family tried to set for her. As a child, she wasn't close to her father, a tight-lipped, closed-off man.

All that has changed now. Her father has changed. He and Margie's mother live on a small farm near Aberdeen. They have a few animals, a cow, some chickens, and geese. Her father takes care of the animals simply because he likes having them around. Both Margie's parents are retired. Margie and Lois frequently bring the kids out to the farm to visit. The kids love it there, and Margie's parents enjoy the kids. There's a stream behind the house where Peter goes fishing with his "grandpa."

The farm itself has a strange beauty to it. The land is flat and dry, and colored a variety of browns and reds. It's a quiet corner of the world with a brick ranch-style house and several home-made barns scattered around. In the evening the wild turkeys, which Margie's father feeds, come and sit in the trees. They are three and four feet tall, and silhouetted against the darkening sky like strange prehistoric birds.

Margie runs her fingers through her hair. She lets out a sigh. "Just the other night Peter hit the little neighbor girl and I freaked out. I saw Tanya bent over with this terrible pain in her stomach. I ran downstairs. I grabbed Peter by the shoulders and I said, 'What the hell did you do!?' I grabbed his shoulders very tightly. He immediately started defending himself. What else do you do when you're pounced on?

"I realized what I was doing and I tried to slow down. I started to explain myself. I told him, 'Do you understand why I don't want you to hit? Do you understand what I'm saying?' Pretty soon, for the first time, I saw him relax a little bit. He said, 'Yeah, I understand.'

"He went upstairs and I was still feeling guilty for grabbing him so hard. You know? In the process of telling him not to hit, I had just hurt him. That doesn't make much sense. So, I went in the bathroom and I said, 'Peter, I really feel bad that I did that to you.' And then we held each other. I'm telling you, we haven't held each other for—I don't know how long. It felt good to do that."

Margie looks down and her hair falls across her face. She is lost in her thoughts. When she begins again she looks a little sad. "So, there's this problem I have with Peter. I have very little patience. But I think we're going to come out of it. I want to come out of it. I think he does too. It's painful for both of us."

****

The kids are all on Peter's bed. Peter is leaning against the headboard, Lynn is in the middle, and Annie is at the foot of the bed. The girls are in a silly mood. They keep giggling.

"None of us liked each other in the beginning," Lynn says. "Except I liked my mother and Peter. I didn't like Annie and I didn't like Margie." Lynn laughs. "And Annie didn't like us."

Annie says, "When I first saw them I go, 'I hope I'm not friends with them for long.' " She giggles. Annie wedges her body down between the wall and the bed so that she's standing on the floor and leaning with her stomach and arms on the edge of the bed. "Then when they said we were gonna live with each other, I go, 'OH NO!' " Lynn and Annie look at each other and burst out laughing.

Peter watches the girls. He patiently waits for them to stop laughing. "Well, I don't like Margie and Annie too much," Peter says in a serious, even voice. "I don't really think they're the greatest." Annie giggles. "I think we'd get along better if we were just a family—just mother and Annie and Lynn and I" Peter shakes his head, and makes a face. "I mean Lynn and I and Mother."

"And Daddy," Lynn says.

"No," Peter snaps at her quickly. He shakes his head, disgusted.

The school the kids attend is largely made up of children from the army base. At the main door of the school there is a framed picture of a general. The kids' school is in the middle of a large open field. From the asphalt playground there are mountains far to the west, and a few homes far to the east.

In Peter's classes many kids wear jackets with 'Japan' or 'Korea' embroidered on the back which their fathers brought back from overseas. The school is reminiscent of those fifteen years ago where the emphasis is on well-behaved, clean children. The boys are likely to have short hair, and the girls are likely to wear dresses. The kids in general are very polite, at least when speaking to adults.

It's Saturday. After cartoons each of the kids cleaned their rooms. Margie and Lois vacuumed and straightened the rest of the house. Peter's room is very orderly. His models and his rocks and his radio are all neatly placed on his table and shelf. He vacuumed his room, made his bed carefully, and hung up his clothes.

"I have to go to the bathroom," Lynn says.

"Again?" Peter asks.

"One or two?" Annie laughingly wants to know.

"One."

"Lynn!" Peter tells her, "Don't say that. Say I have to whisper." Peter is starting to giggle now, too.

Lynn is laughing so hard she can hardly talk. "I have to whisper," Lynn manages to squeak out.

"Then whisper in Annie's ear," Peter tells her. They all crack up. Annie presses her face in the mattress. Lynn has tears in her eyes. She gets up and runs out of the room. Peter laughs and shakes his head.

By the time Lynn comes back the laughing has stopped. She climbs onto the bed. But then she takes one look at Annie and they both start laughing all over again. Lynn starts humming a song in a high voice. The song has no words, just a rambling la-la-la. Lynn has sad eyes with long eyelashes. As she sings, a laugh builds inside her like a bubble. Each laugh seems to have to press its way out past those sad eyes. Lynn is enjoying the funny mood everyone's in. She has a look on her face like she can't wait for the next joke to be made.

"I have secrets for making and keeping friends," Annie says.

"What are your secrets?" Peter asks her.

Annie thinks a moment. "I don't want to tell," she decides.

"Oh, come on," Lynn squeals.

"Yeah, we won't listen," Peter kids her.

Annie makes a face, struggling to decide whether to tell or not. She holds one finger up to her lips. "My secrets for keeping friends are," Annie speaks slowly, "... being nice to them... going up and talking to them..."

"I've heard that one," Peter tells her, disappointed.

"... Giving them candy," Annie continues, talking louder in case Peter interrupts again. Lynn starts laughing. "And not being like Darth Vader."

"Wow," Peter says. "I do all that and I still won't keep friends. And how do you get them?"

Annie begins squeezing herself down further in-between the bed and the wall. As she squeezes, the bed inches out from the wall, and she moves further and further down. Lynn watches her and laughs.

"Usually, when someone asks," Peter says, "I just say my mom and Margie are roommates. I think they don't want the word scattered around because people would tease us a lot."

"They ask, 'Is that your sister, is that your brother?'" Annie mimics a nagging voice. "I say, 'Sort of.'" Annie has sandwiched her little body between the bed and the wall so only her arms and head are sticking out. "It's like when I cut my face. Everyone used to ask me, 'What happened to you? When did it happen? How did you do it?'" Annie has two scars on her face from an accident when she fell carrying a glass as a baby. "One time I went, 'Oh, just forget it!' And that's the best thing. Because I don't like to talk about it until—until it gets to the point where I have to lie."

Peter is hugging his pillow against his chest. "You can just say, 'Why are you so nosey, why do you need to know all this stuff?'" Peter tells Annie. "Because you should be able to trust your friends. You know? You should be able to trust them not to get so much into your personal life." Annie is watching Peter. She's got her head and arms resting on the mattress. "If I were the one asking, I really wouldn't want to know. 'Cause it would be their life," Peter says. It wouldn't bug me if they didn't want to tell. I wouldn't go around teasing them and all that. I wouldn't spread stuff around the world".

Lynn starts to talk. "There's these two twins named James and John." Lynn is speaking very solemnly in her high voice. "If they knew, they'd be teasing us a lot more." Lynn is taking time to think between each little statement she makes. Peter and Annie are patiently letting her talk.

"We all wait at the bus stop together, and sometimes James and

John call me and Annie dog faces." Lynn stops for a moment. "On Valentine's Day, Annie and me both wore dresses, and we had to wear boots with them because of the snow. They teased us about that, about wearing boots with our dresses."

Lynn looks at Annie. Annie nods her head in agreement. Lynn has an indifferent expression on her face. It's as if she is being teased and she's not going to let herself care.

"Our mother tells us to ignore them, so we don't say anything."

"It doesn't work though," Annie tells Lynn.

"I know," Lynn answers thoughtfully. "But we still ignore them, because it may work."

****

"We have a lot of 'my mom said' around here. We both knew that had to stop." Margie looks out the window and the sun reflects off her glasses. "Actually, it seems we rarely have a fight that isn't somehow concerned with the kids. It's been that way ever since the beginning. It's been very difficult for us to put the two families together."

Lois is out, doing errands. When she gets back the whole family plans to have a meeting. The idea is to talk about things, about feelings, out in the open. This is the first time something like this has been done in an organized way. Although it's become apparent that it's needed, Margie is nervous about the prospect.

"What's amazing, though, is how quickly the kids have accepted each other," Margie says. "In the beginning there were problems of jealousy, not wanting to share. 'Annie gets two, why don't I?' But now that's so minimal. At this point, it seems typical of any three children living in the same house.

"The kids just started relating right away as brother and sister. I went to an open house at their school not long after we'd all moved in together. This was when Lynn was in kindergarten and Annie was in first grade. I walked into Lynn's room and there was a book she'd made entitled, 'Our Family', and it had a picture on the cover of all five of us. Then I walked into Annie's room and there was a picture that said 'This is me'. The next picture said, 'This is my family', and again it was a picture of the five of us.

"The three of them are very close. I think Peter has more devotion to Lynn, but I think if it involved anyone else outside his home he'd be right there to take care of Annie too. And vice- versa. It's really something how quickly they've developed that." Margie looks out the window again. A few clouds have appeared. They are moving to the east in a slow, lazy motion. "Sometimes I think it's too bad the adults can't follow in their footsteps."

****

"What does your father do?" Annie asks Lynn. She's asking Lynn questions that kids on the playground ask. Annie is still squished down between the bed and the wall. Lynn is kneeling on the end of the bed, looking excited and nervous.

"He works out in California," Lynn says.

"Oh, yeah," Annie asks. "Who do you live with?"

"My mother."

"Is that your sister?" Annie points to herself. She's trying her best to be very serious.

"Welllll," Lynn and Annie both start giggling. "Sort of."

"How is someone 'sort of your sister?'" Peter asks.

"She's like my stepsister."

"So your mother remarried," Peter says.

"No, she has a roommate, and that's her daughter."

"A man roommate?" Peter keeps pushing.

"A roommate who's a woman," Lynn says. She keeps giggling. This is all a huge secret that the kids never talk about. The subject is rarely brought up, even inside the family. Just kidding about it makes the kids nervous.

"Here, I can answer those. Ask me the questions," Peter says, as the girls are both laughing. Peter sits up and crosses his legs. He is holding a pillow in his lap. The bed is a mess from all the jumping around. The other pillow and the bedspread have fallen onto the floor.

"Who's she?" Annie points to herself.

"Umm, my room—I mean my mother's roommate's daughter." Peter is already starting to laugh.

"Oh, your mother has a roommate?"

"Yeah."

"A man?"

"No."

"A woman?"

"Yeah," Peter says.

"Do they sleep in the same room?"

Peter stops to think. Lynn is crouched on her knees with her arms tucked in between her legs and her chest. The expression on her face is as if she can't bear to watch.

"Do they sleep in the same room?", Annie asks again.

"Wait a second," Peter giggles. "Let me think a second." The girls start laughing.

"No thinking!" Annie yells. This breaks everyone up.

"I have to go to the bathroom," Peter says.

"Say whisper!" Lynn yells.

"I don't have to whisper," Peter answers, "I have to shout." They all go crazy laughing. Lynn falls over on her side. Peter covers his face with the pillow. Lynn tries to grab the pillow from him. She pulls it and Peter falls over on his side. Annie pushes on Peter's back from where she's sandwiched in between the bed and the wall. It's a mad, laughing, free-for-all.

The laughing subsides after a while. Peter goes and comes back from the bathroom. He gets on the bed. By this time the room has become quiet again. The sound of a car honking outside can be heard, and a radio is playing upstairs. Annie climbs out from in between the bed and the wall. She sits down under the window and crosses her legs. Lynn moves over and squeezes in between her and Peter. The kids are all on the bed, leaning against each other. Everyone is silent, lost in their own thoughts.

"If I were to tell my dad," Annie says finally, "he might take the matter into court. I might have to go where my mom doesn't want me to go, and I probably would never be able to see my mom again." She pauses. Everyone is looking straight ahead, Annie too. "So, I try my best. But I just think, 'What if I accidentally told my dad? Then what would happen?' " Annie has her hands folded in her lap. She looks worried. "One day I almost did. I said, 'That's where my mom goes for her meetings.' Dad said, 'What kind of meeting does she go there for?' I started to open my big mouth. So I go, 'Oh, Nothing!' "

A enormous responsibility is placed on a child by telling her, 'Here's a secret, but you can't tell it or you might get taken away from your mother.' That's a tremendously big secret. And to a child, it is an almost inconceivable consequence of telling it.

Annie shrugs her shoulders. "So far I keep on forgetting and I start telling something," she says. "Probably someday I'll have to spit it out and tell somebody. But I don't want to take the matter to court. If my dad wins that would be a problem. If my mom wins that would be a problem. Either way, it would be a problem."

Lynn is fooling with the hem of her sweater. "They'll never say for the kids to go with their dads," she says. "All the court does is pick the ones who are treating you the worst." Peter and Annie both look at Lynn surprised at what she's said. Lynn even looks surprised by her comment. She tries to explain. "Our dads were nice, and our mothers—they're OK. I think Margie's OK." Lynn's voice trails off.

The room grows quiet again. Annie crosses her arms and bites on her lip. Lynn is twisting the bottom of her sweater in her fingers as Peter begins to talk.

"I used to think that I wanted to live with my dad. He used to take us to all kinds of neat places, especially after he left he did." Peter picks the pillow back up and hugs it. "But we stayed with him during last summer and it wasn't how I expected it would be. I didn't like the way I was treated. We weren't treated like we were loved or anything. I mean, I know I was loved, but they sort of didn't really care for me— or Lynn."

Peter is blinking like he does when he's nervous. Lynn looks at him for a moment and then turns back to her lap. Peter pushes his glasses up on his nose. "We were always being yelled at, for every little mistake," Peter says. "Even the ones that are hardly noticeable we'd get in trouble for.

"Like one time we were supposed to take naps there and didn't fall asleep. We just rested. We got in trouble for that." Peter sniffles. He wipes his nose on the back of his hand. He looks over at Lynn. She doesn't look up. "It's awful strange for a teenager to have to take a nap, you know?"

Peter is thinking. He seems tired. It's been a long week. "See, we went to visit him for a summer just after the divorce—and one day he kept us. So they went to court. They went to court and all that..."

The wind is blowing outside. You can hear it against the side of the house. Peter is talking very quietly. He reaches for a Kleenex from the table, and wipes his nose. He tosses it at the wastepaper can. It misses.

"The decision came and it said that we had to stay with our mom, and we could only see our dad for one month. I didn't know how I felt, you know." Peter looks up. His eyes are blinking back tears. "I felt sad and I felt happy. Because I loved them both."

****

Everyone is in the living room for their first ever family meeting. Margie starts first. "One of the reasons I get involved if you're arguing with one of the girls," Margie tells Peter, "is that their arguments are different. I wonder if you see it that way." Peter is lying on his stomach on the rug. He's fooling with a couple rocks he has in front of him. He's not looking at Margie. Margie, Annie, and Lynn are on the couch. Lois is in the big chair next to where Peter is lying on the floor.

"See, when I hear the girls arguing they sound equal," Margie says, "like they're on the same level. One isn't overpowering the other. But when I hear you arguing with the girls, there's a big, big power play going on. I think it gets off-balance real fast and I step in to balance it somehow." Margie is leaning forward as she talks to Peter. Peter still isn't looking at her.

"When Peter and I fight it's over, like, who's boss around here," Annie says, interrupting. "If I didn't go to sleep he would say, 'You should go to sleep.' I'd say, 'No, my mother didn't tell me to go to bed.' It was like I was telling Peter that my mother is boss and not him, and he was saying he was the babysitter and he was boss."

The sun is going down. It's giving an orangish glow to the hills, which can be seen through the sliding glass doors to the right of the couch. Lynn is absorbed in picking at the nail polish she put on a week ago. It's a light red color, but most of it is gone already. She's working on her baby finger at the moment.

Lois has been watching Peter. "Most of the time when we go out the door," she says, "we do instruct Peter what to cook. Or we'll be sure he's aware of the phone numbers where we're at. In that sense he's in charge."

"I don't see it as him being in charge at all," Margie says. "In fact, I'm very uncomfortable with that. I don't think the girls need anyone in charge of them. I think they could handle themselves no matter what the situation was." Margie's voice is very definite. Since Peter won't look at her, she is talking to Lois.

"The girls are at an age where they're responsible, they can be responsible. They can exist in the house by themselves, without us, without Peter, and they'll be fine. I think if Peter didn't fill in for Lynn as if she wasn't capable, then we'd see a real growth, a real strength come through in her." Lynn looks up from her nails and smiles. "So now we're asking Peter to let go, and that's not easy." Margie watches Peter on the floor. He's not acknowledging her in any way. She turns back to Lois. "I've been the one that started pushing for that. For asking Peter, telling Peter, ordering Peter to let go."

Lois looks upset. She's not good at simply grabbing her children and hugging them. She was raised in a big family where little physical affection was shown. But as she watches Peter at her feet, flipping the rocks over and over in his hands and refusing to even look at anyone else in the room, she is leaning towards him and it seems that that's exactly what she'd like to do.

The girls are daydreaming on the couch when the doorbell rings. Margie goes to answers it. It's Barbara, the girls' friend from down the street. "Are Annie and Lynn home?" Barbara asks.

"They're busy," Margie tells her. The girls are looking over the back of the couch. Barbara can see them. She's standing at the door staring at them. "They're busy right now," Margie repeats.

"Okay," Barbara says. She reluctantly starts to back up from the door. Lynn waves to her as Margie closes the door. Margie comes back and sits down on the couch.

"There were times when we lived in Michigan, and Lynn was a toddler," Lois begins, "when I'd say to Peter, 'Keep an eye on her, don't let her go in the street.' And even here, when he first started to be the babysitter, there were times when we asked him to stay awake. We used to ask him to stay awake until we got home. That might have given him the impression that he was in charge."

Margie rubs her eyes underneath her glasses. The room is quiet as Margie and Lois lock eyes for a long moment. "It isn't that I don't appreciate the responsible way Peter behaves," Margie says after a while, "because I do. I know all three of you—well, you behave a lot differently than my brother and I did. I'm really impressed with it. I'm proud of it. I don't want you to feel unimportant."

Margie has been leaning further and further forward as she talks. She's trying to will Peter to look at her. "Peter, I do feel more secure knowing you're here. I don't know what to say." She is speaking very gently now, there is a pleading tone in her voice. Peter is lying on his side, his head is at his mother's feet and his back is towards Margie and his sister.

"Remember when I first moved in, Peter? Before the court thing, before all that. It seemed like we got along great. It really did. You and I went fishing, we went hiking out at the farm. But now nothing I do seems to be enough. If I do more, you still find some reason to say I don't like you."

Margie pauses. Everyone is quiet. "I don't know," Margie says, "maybe it has to do with the trial in Milwaukee. I read what you said in the Judge's chambers about me. From what you said, it didn't seem that you liked me, not at all. I was surprised and hurt by that," Margie says, her voice subdued. "Because up until then it just didn't seem that way to me. I thought we'd gotten along really well."

Lynn is playing with the arm of the couch, tracing designs on it. Annie is watching her. Sunlight is coming in through the window and shining on the wall. The street outside is still.

"Peter, what do you feel about what we're saying?" Lois is getting exasperated. It seems like Margie has softened and is making a conciliatory effort. She wants Peter to respond. But Peter is lying with his head on his arm, holding a rock in each hand.

"I don't know," Peter says barely above a whisper.

Lois waits a moment, and then continues, the impatience growing in her voice. "I want to know if you understand, so I'd like you to tell me what we've said."

"That you want me to back off," Peter's voice is soft and wavering

"How come," Lois coaxes.

"Cause they can take care of themselves."

There is silence again. The girls are watching Peter. "Do you like that?" Margie asks him.

"If it's okay with you, it's okay with me!" Peter's voice cracks. He sounds like he's starting to cry.

There is the noise of a helicopter overhead. Slowly it dies away. Lois watches Peter with a look of anguish in her eyes. "As far as saying that the girls will be able to handle everything that comes up, I don't know that everything that comes up in my life I'll be able to handle," Lois offers, trying to ease things.

Margie jumps in. "I still don't understand Peter," she says. "You sound angry, like you're getting the raw end of the deal."

Lynn tries to say something. "I think I know what he feels."

"Well, I'm asking him right now," Margie snaps at Lynn. "Do you feel picked on, Peter?"

113

"Yes," Peter answers quickly.

"Well, you're going to have to tell us what it is we said that made you feel picked on." Peter doesn't answer. "Would you turn around here and join us, please," Margie asks. Peter doesn't move. "This is so typical of our conversations, for them to end up like this," Margie says, her voice suddenly showing her irritation, "him pissed off—being totally uncooperative."

"The way I feel," Lynn says in her soft, high voice, "is that I guess Peter thinks that he's probably not loved right now."

Margie is shocked by the frankness of Lynn's statement. She looks at Lynn, not knowing quite what to say. From the expression on Margie's face, you can see she's very hurt.

"Was it something I said?". Margie asks Lynn.

"I guess," Lynn says.

"Or was it the tears that made you think that?"

"I guess it was about what you said."

Margie sits back against the couch. The room is still. The sun is streaming into the room through the sliding glass doors. It reflects against the wall and shines on the mantle.

Lois speaks to Peter. Her voice is serious, no-nonsense. "OK, I'm finding this really difficult," she says. "The position that you're lying in on the floor—I can't see your face, we can't make eye contact. There's no way we could hug one another or show any affection."

Lois is looking down at Peter. Her voice is stern and it's hard to tell if she is angry at Peter, or if she is, in fact, asking him to hug her. "Right now all the attention is focused on you, Peter," she says. "I think that's basically what you want, some attention. But I don't like the way you're getting it. I don't feel any cooperation, any response. I want something besides shrugged shoulders."

Peter suddenly turns around. He's crying and shouting at the same time. "All I ever get is criticism, nothing else! You don't really care for me! You never—why won't you do things with me? No more you don't!" Peter has raised his body up on his arms and he's facing everyone.

"I don't see you do stuff with me, go fishing, sledding. Only once you've done it. And you said you'd play games with me. You haven't!" Peter jumps up and runs out of the room crying. He runs downstairs and slams his door.

Margie looks confused and upset. Lois seems close to tears. There's a long silence. Peter can be heard crying downstairs in his room.

"He's probably going to be embarrassed in the book that he cried," Lynn says.

Lois starts talking very softly and slowly. It's as if she's afraid that any loud noise might send her running out of the room, crying, too. "I think," she says, her lower lip trembling, "that Peter never really got angry at me for the divorce and the custody battle. He never really let me have it for that, he never did. The blaming is part of it, I guess. But it's not what's going on inside."

Lynn looks over the back of the couch towards Peter's room. She looks down at Annie who makes a face and shrugs her shoulders. "The kids used to tell me over and over that if I changed my religion their dad and I could get back together again. I would stand there saying, 'No Peter, no Lynn, that's not true.' Didn't he say that, Lynn?"

"What?"

"Didn't your father say that?"

"I guess so—well, no, I'm not sure," Lynn is speaking in a very tiny voice.

"He didn't?" Lois says. Margie gives a surprised laugh. "What did he say then about he and I getting back together?"

"Nothing." Lynn's voice is more certain this time.

Lois shakes her head. "Both of them, they've never really got mad at me, at us, for the divorce. They've never screamed, ranted, fussed— broke down in tears. It was hard for all of us, incredibly hard," Lois looks at Lynn, and Lynn smiles the way she does when she's nervous. A big smile appears suddenly, stays for a moment, and then disappears. Lois looks over at Margie. They exchange a sad look. "I'm still waiting...I'm still waiting," she says.

Update:

Margie Weston and
Lois Roberts

Spring, 1983

Margie:
Joe, you called this morning and asked us to put this tape together. It's about 11:30 at night. We wanted to be sure to get it together for you tonight and get it mailed, otherwise we might never get around to it.

First of all, I no longer work at the power plant. Lois and I now share ownership in a roller rink and a food drive-in. We both work 10-16 hours a day, which has been a physical drain, but there are a lot of rewards in it too. Lately, I find myself suffering from some guilt in not being around the kids more. I'm sure I'm going to have to find a level where I'm not working quite so many hours, so I can spend more time at home.

Annie is 13 years old, a seventh grader. She's active in band. She plays the flute. She's also very active in speed skating at the rink. Just recently she's developed an infatuation with a young man over at the rink and wants to spend a great deal of time skating all of a sudden.

Basically, she seems to be a normal 13-year old. She misses her dad a great deal, and she's going to visit him this summer. I feel my relationship with her is very open and rewarding. So I'm really happy with that.

Peter is also very active in speed skating, and is doing very well at it. And he too has fallen in love with a girl. He's less involved in school because his whole social life is centered around the roller rink.

Lois:
In some ways people might say that Peter is slow for his age. He hasn't started dating. This girl he has a crush on, he just sees her at the skating rink. Also, he's seventeen and he doesn't have a driver's license yet. In South Dakota you can get a license at fourteen. But I just think he'll get around to things in his own time. He's quiet but he's very responsible. He works for us over at the rink after school and on weekends, and he's a big help.

Lynn is more involved in school activities. That's because she's not as interested in speed skating. She and Peter are going to be spending the summer with their grandma this year, and there's a chance their father will come visit them. They haven't seen their father in three years. But neither of them is aware that he might come down there because the grandma didn't want to get their hopes up in case he doesn't.

Margie:

The three of them spend a good deal of time alone here at the house. That's not always a good thing, but Lois and I both appreciate how well-behaved our children are, and how well they take care of themselves. I hope we never take that for granted.

Also, we've noticed that the older the three kids get the more concerned they are that their friends might realize the relationship between Lois and I. For example, Annie was going to have a slumber party for her birthday, and she was very worried that the girls would wonder where Lois and I slept. I told Annie, "Gosh, they'll all be in bed before Lois even comes home." But she was still worried.

Annie went ahead and had the slumber party and no one asked. But the next weekend Lynn had her slumber party. Lynn wasn't even concerned that her friends would wonder where her Mom and I slept, but then, low and behold, someone asked. I'm not sure how she handled it, but it was just kind of ironic.

The bond between the three kids is stronger now than ever. Lois wanted me to be sure and mention this. It's something we're very thankful for. The three of them rely on each other, they trust each other, they talk, they support each other totally. And that's really helped—being in the situation that they're being raised in.

(Pause). God, I'm tired.

Lois:

I'm tired, too. I'm trying to think of things to say but I'm so tired...hopefully this will do.

We wish you the best of luck with this book, Joe. We're sorry it took so long to get this update to you. Talk about guilt complexes. Every time someone would say, "Did you read this or that book?" I would think, geez we have to get this sent out. So here it is, finally. Keep us posted and good luck.

2022 update to the Weston/Roberts family

Joe – Hello Annie, how are things in South Dakota?

Annie - All right.

Joe - How old are your kids?

Annie - I have two boys and a girl, ages 17, 15 and 13. The girl's my oldest. She's a senior.

Joe - Wow. They are growing up.

Annie - It went by too fast.

Joe - You were eight at the time I interviewed your family. You were young but very precocious, and you had an interesting way of describing things. This is how you described your situation. "Okay, I don't like calling people gay. I don't think it's fair. People who don't know what gay feels like, get mad about it, and they don't like it. Some people think it's wrong. And the people who think it's right probably are and some people don't even have a choice. Because when you're it, you don't know what it feels like when you're not it. And if you're not it and you get to be it, you're probably like it." From a child's perspective, that sounds pretty accurate. When did you first realize that your mom was lesbian?

Annie - I don't know that there was ever really a moment when I went, oh, now I know. My mother and father got divorced when I was five. And it was shortly thereafter when she started living with a woman. So, I guess I just always went, okay, this is what it is.

Joe – So that was pretty much how you always saw your mom.

Annie – Yeah. I think the feeling I had most as a kid was that I had to try to make sure that my father didn't know. Not that the world didn't find out, but that my father didn't know that she was. I think that was the earliest that I was focused on her being gay,

Joe - Why couldn't your father know?

Annie - Lois, who we were living with, her ex-husband was trying to take her kids away. They went through a whole court thing. And part of what was brought up, the reason why they felt that kids shouldn't stay with Lois, was because she was gay. My mom was afraid that my dad might do the same thing. But later I realized that he knew all along. I don't know how he knew, but he knew. So, we didn't really have to keep it from him. Which was kind of funny because of how worried I was.

Joe - Well, at that time, in 1979 or 1980, it was difficult to live openly as a gay parent. And I would think that in South Dakota it was probably harder than in most states to be openly gay. You said you tried to keep it from your father, did you also keep it from your friends for fear that they wouldn't understand?

Annie - I never talked about it, I guess. Most of my friends had been to my house at one point or another, so they kind of understood. But they never really asked me too much about it. I don't know what they thought. They never, I don't ever remember friends mentioning it really.

Joe - Do you remember when you first told a boyfriend about it?

Annie - There was one man that I dated much later, I was in college, who came from a very religious background. I remember telling him about it and I was concerned about what he would think. But he just kind of went, well, she lives far away. And then we ended up breaking up three weeks later anyway, so it didn't matter.

Joe - What was the attitude towards your family situation in South Dakota, when you think back on it.

Annie - It seems to me that the attitude here in South Dakota is, you can do whatever you want just don't bring it up to me constantly, no matter what it is. Whether it's, you know, who you love or what diet you're on, just don't keep hitting me with it all the time. My friends' parents might have said to my friends, you can't go over there to spend the night. I don't know. I didn't really ever want to have people spend the night. But they didn't say anything to me about it. I don't remember hearing anybody saying to me, your mom is a sinner or a bad person or any of that. I really don't.

Joe - Well, that's good. But still, it's a difficult secret for a seven or eight year old to have to keep.

Annie - Yeah, it was hard. I didn't want to mess it up. Especially I didn't want to accidentally say something to my dad. So, if my dad asked me about my mom, I would keep my answers very general. I said, "I don't know," a lot when I was younger.

Joe - So how was your relationship with your dad?

Annie - My parents got along well. I mean, as far as divorced parents went. There was troubles of course, just typical troubles, like with child support and all that stuff. But after I grew up, my dad and my mom got along really well, until he passed away about six years ago.

Joe - Oh, I'm sorry to hear that. How about your kids? Do you remember telling them about your mom?

Annie - I talked to my oldest, my daughter about it. And she was just like, oh. She never really asked a whole lot of questions. My youngest son, he just says, "I don't care, you can be straight, gay, whatever, it doesn't matter to me." You know, that's just their attitude.

Joe – Have your kids spent a lot of time with your mom.

Annie – My mom's always been a big part of their life, from the time they were very little. Even if they didn't know until later exactly what her lifestyle was. But they were always around her, so it wasn't a huge shock. I think when they were old enough to understand what gay was, is when we kind of talked about it. But it wasn't ever a big deal. Also, my daughter has quite a few friends who are gay, and they're out in high school. And she has a couple friends, like three friends, who are transgender. So, she's just kind of like, well, there's all kinds of different things going on in the world.

Joe – That shows that the world has shifted in 40 years. 40 years ago, you couldn't tell your friends, you couldn't tell your community. And now, high school kids are able to come out as gay and come out as transgender, in South Dakota. I mean, isn't that a just a paradigm shift?

Annie - Completely. Yeah.

Joe - That's very encouraging to hear that you can be open about being gay while in high school in South Dakota. And I guess if you can tell your friends in South Dakota, maybe you can do it anywhere.

Annie - Yeah. That could be true.

Joe - You talked about feeling guilty in the book. You said you felt guilty about your parents' divorce. You also were jealous that Peter and Lynn still had a dad. And then they went through a divorce, you said in the book that you felt like maybe it was your fault. Did you struggle with guilt when you were young?

Annie - Yeah, I did I guess? There was quite a bit of turmoil that surrounded me. And I think I felt like, you know, it was all my fault that things in the house and in life were just kind of crazy and up in the air. And I blamed myself. I didn't know why. I worried that it was my fault that my parents got divorced. And I think that I still do feel guilty about things pretty easily, even things that aren't my fault necessarily.

Joe - Maybe that happens to kids who go through a divorce young, because they don't understand why their parents really broke up.

Annie - But I will say that when I found out that my mother is lesbian, that relieved the guilt a little bit. Because I'm like, it's not my fault that my dad wasn't a woman. So that kind of relieved any kind of guilt from them divorcing that I may have put on myself.

Joe - At the end of the book, your mom writes a little update and talks about having bought the roller rink. As the owners of a roller rink your mom and Lois were very much a part of the community. And I would think that people would know, whether or not it was spoken out loud, the community had to suspect that your mom and Lois were gay? Or could they still hide it?

Annie - I don't remember anybody ever really talking about it. But looking back, I think people knew or suspected. There were a lot of people, kids, who hung out at the rink all the time. And although they never really said it to me, I think everybody knew. That's just the feeling I had at the time, it was just kind of an unspoken thing.

Joe - If they knew, did you feel hostility from the community? Did they treat you any differently?

Annie - No. I look back on that time when my mom had the roller skating rink as one of the best times in my life. I had friends and a hobby, you know, a sport that I loved. And nobody gave me grief about any of that. So yeah, I think they just accepted me and accepted whatever they knew about my life. And they probably knew.

Joe – I think it's wonderful that in South Dakota, in a small town in South Dakota, you didn't experience any hostility, and that the community wasn't rejecting your family.

Annie - I can't say that they didn't talk behind our backs. I remember explaining to one friend that, both my mom and Aunt Lois got divorced. And so, we just kind of moved in together to share expenses. And they just went, oh okay, you guys all live together. So, I don't, I can't speak to what my mom experienced. But I didn't really ever see any of that judgmental attitude, you know, the judgments from other people.

Joe - And how old were you when your mom and Lois broke up?

Annie - I was 14

Joe - You must have been a freshman in high school. Was that a difficult breakup?

Annie - Yeah, it was, it was difficult. There were a lot of fights. I ended up getting involved in one. It wasn't physical, but I ended up-- I think Lois had moved out and she came back and they were arguing. And I remember going out and telling her to just leave.

Joe - In the book they talked about how your mom had issues with Peter and how your mom felt that Lois didn't treat you the way she should. But in the update on your family, both parents said, we're so happy that the kids get along so well. Did you get along with each other?

Annie - Yes and no. I mean, we got along pretty well. We'd have our normal, step family issue fights and all that stuff. But after my mom and Lois broke up, then the relationships fell apart. We just lost touch.

Joe - Did you ever feel, growing up in a home where your mother and her lover were lesbian, did you ever worry that you might become lesbian? Did that stress you out at all?

Annie - Yes, I did. I was concerned about that for a while, when I was younger? I never really was-- I don't think I ever was attracted to women. But I think I was kind of afraid that I might end up being that way. It's funny, because I was worried about what society would think a lot, even though my lived experience was different. At the time, I didn't think that people knew my mom was gay. I thought we were keeping it a secret pretty well, since we didn't talk about it openly. I thought it was hidden from people. And so, I thought, especially trying to keep the secret from my dad, that that was a lot of pressure. And I felt like, this is too hard. I hope I'm not gay because I don't want to have to keep this from people. I think that's what I was worried about the most. It was that if that happened, if my attraction was to women, what I was worried about the most was that I didn't want to have to try to keep it a secret.

Joe - The burden of that?

Annie - Yeah, yeah.

Joe – Originally, when I put out this book, I called it *Whose Child Cries*. The title comes from a proverb, a saying, "He cares not whose child cries, so his laughs." I chose that title because it meant that people only worry about their own kids, they don't worry about what other kids are going through. But when I republish this, I'm going back to the original title I had, A Secret I Can't Tell. And I think that really does sum up what almost all the kids in this book had to deal with.

Annie – I like that title.

Joe - I think looking back on it now, with your daughter having openly gay friends and openly transgender friends in high school, in South Dakota, it really shows that we've come a long way. It seems like, finally, the LGBT community can live their lives openly and hopefully not be fearful. It's amazing the progress that's been made. So, thanks again. And say hi to your mom for me.

Annie - I will I will.

Joe - Nice talking with you. Take care.

Annie - You too, Joe.

§

CHAPTER 3

The Granger Family

Jamie, age 16
Tom (Jamie's father)
Justin (Tom's partner)

I thought marriage was a bed of roses," Jamie says, sitting on her bed with her legs crossed. She's the only one home. "You know? You have a house, a car, two point two kids. You have a back yard with a picnic table and you eat outside. You have a cat and a dog, and the wife sits at home and darns socks while the husband goes out and earns a living. He comes home and calls out, 'honey, I'm home!'"

Jamie laughs to herself, she shakes her head. "Well...that's not what I see most marriages to be like, but that's how I want my marriage to be." She laughs again. "Except I don't want to darn socks."

Jamie is a thin, fragile-looking girl, with short, light brown hair and almond-shaped green eyes. Her eyes are very compelling. They're beautiful and expressive. People tend to stare at her eyes when they meet her.

Jamie is sixteen. She grew up the oldest of four children, on a farm in Montana. Her family at that time lived in a big, white farmhouse with dogs and cats and horses. Now Jamie lives with her father and his lover in an apartment in Seattle, Washington. Her parents were divorced when she was twelve. Her two sisters and her brother still live with her mother in Montana.

"I couldn't live in a situation where nobody talked, where people weren't physical towards each other," Jamie says softly. "But, you know, when things are really bad in your life, sometimes you don't— you don't think about the bad things. All you think about are the good things.

"My parents fought a lot. They weren't very happy. They never hit each other or anything like that," she says, picking at the red polish on her fingernails. "But they were always yelling in front of the kids. Like at the dinner table, my mom would get really upset. She'd go bananas, she'd just go crazy. She'd start screaming and yelling and throwing things."

Jamie draws her lips across her teeth the way she does when she's nervous. She is sitting very still on her bed. "They fought about money. My dad would bring my mom dresses that were really expensive when we didn't have any money for groceries. My mom would get irate and they'd argue. Dad was trying to make my mom happy by doing things for her, by trying to make the house look better, or buying things for her. I don't think he made her happy, you know, personally, so he tried to make her happy material wise. They didn't show that much affection. They didn't spend much time together."

Jamie has been living with her father, Tom, and his lover, Justin, for three years, on and off. After the divorce Jamie first lived with her mother. A year later she ran away from home to come live with her dad. Jamie then lived with her father, her aunt, her father again, in two foster homes, and now once again she's back with her dad. She has had difficulty finding a living situation that is comfortable for her. Jamie is very sensitive to the problems that go on in families. Wherever she is living, she seems to tune into the problems. Then, having found them, she becomes very disappointed.

"You know, it was funny," Jamie continues. "My parents would fight for a long, long time and then they'd ignore each other. My mom would say things and my dad wouldn't even acknowledge her. He would just tune her out.

"See, Dad was losing money left and right. He lost money on the pigs, and on the horses, and he wasn't making any money at the shop. We got into debt, thousands of dollars in debt. So Mom had to go back to work after she had Mickey."

"When I was a little kid and my parents would fight, I'd get so upset I'd have rashes on my arms and legs. I used to scratch them like crazy. The rashes didn't bother me until they'd fight and then I would just itch," Jamie says. She runs her hand along her leg and smiles a nervous smile. "My mom would put baking soda on them. It was nerves, I was worried about my family breaking up. This was when I was about seven. See, my mom and dad always used to scream at each other, 'I want a divorce, I want a divorce.'"

****

"When Jamie was three years old," Tom says, "Rita took her to see a psychiatrist. Her mother would tell her to do something and Jamie would just disregard it. This had gone on from the time she was a tiny little kid. Rita would say, 'no, no', and slap Jamie's hand. Jamie got to the point where she'd say, 'no, no', slap her own hand and do it anyway. She thought slapping her hand was a prerequisite and after that she could do what she wanted."

Tom is short and thin, with dark hair parted on the side, and a moustache. He has deep lines around his eyes, more deeply etched than most people who have lived only forty-two years. Tom dresses casually. He prefers Levi's and a nice t-shirt to a suit. Tom speaks slowly, and when he laughs, his face often shows a certain sadness.

"Jamie didn't care if she pleased her mother. She would harass her mother during the day, she wouldn't mind. And as soon as I walked in the house at night it was, 'Hi, Daddy' and a big kiss. She'd bring me a beer, bring me a newspaper. She'd do everything that a wife would many times do for her husband.

"Jamie kind of upstaged her mother, kind of slipped into that role to get into my good graces. And I could never see that she had done anything wrong. She was just a perfect little kid. However, I hadn't seen all the trouble she'd caused all day long."

Tom is sitting at the kitchen table. He looks tired. Jamie's still at work, and Justin's not home yet. Tom closes his eyes for a moment. A whistle can be heard coming from the train yard in the valley below the house.

"The next younger child, Kim, wanted to please her mother but never knew how. When Rita was nailing her, Kim would get so frustrated she would begin to stutter. Rita would get impatient and slap Kim. Or she'd say, 'I don't know why I waste my time with you. You're not worth it. You pee in your pants, you don't do anything right'— she'd go on and on and Kim would dissolve into tears.

"Amy was the youngest of the girls and she would never question her mother. Rita would tell her to do something, and she always did it with a smile on her face. But Jamie wasn't like that. She didn't care if she pleased her mother or not."

Tom works as a hairdresser in a shop that he owns in Seattle. Back in Montana, he graduated from college in biochemistry and worked in a lab for several years. He wasn't happy with that, and it was Rita who first suggested he try hairdressing. He eventually had his own shop there as well. But in Montana, in addition to hairdressing, Tom was raising hogs and quarter horses in an effort to make extra money. He was working almost all the time. Life in Seattle is very different from life on the farm.

"When Jamie was about a year old, Rita first went back to work," Tom says, leaning on the table. "Rita's a nurse—she worked three to eleven. I'd pick Jamie up from the babysitter, fix dinner and spend the evening with her. We'd go to my mother's and visit, we'd go to the park and play, or get an ice cream cone. I'd take Jamie around in the convertible. She and I spent every evening together and got really, really close.

"Kim was born two years later and Rita quit working. She was there at night and we were relating as man and wife. So Jamie was no longer the center of my attention. Also, I had opened a new business and was working late hours.

"Kim was born with this thing where her throat muscles would just totally give out and collapse. She'd be drinking from her bottle, her muscles would close, and she'd turn blue. Whenever Rita would feed her she would have a 15-gauge needle standing by to do a tracheotomy in the event Kim couldn't breathe. Then Amy was born, and she was born without her right hand. That was another traumatic thing for Rita. All this took attention away from Jamie. And Jamie was being a little stinker and resenting Amy just as she had Kim."

Tom rubs his face with the palms of his hands. He takes a deep breath and lets it out with a sigh. "When Rita got pregnant for the fourth time she wanted to have the baby aborted. She was afraid something would be wrong with that baby as well. I have an aunt who is only four foot two, and my sister has a daughter who is four foot four. Rita was convinced that there was some sort of chromosome imbalance on my side of the family even though the doctors said there wasn't any connection.

"As it turned out Mickey was born perfectly healthy, everything was okay. But Rita insisted I have a vasectomy anyway. We weren't going to have any more children." Tom shrugs his shoulders. "So I did."

****

"My dad didn't know half the times when we got beat up," Jamie says. "I didn't tell him because I was scared that—that there'd be another argument, and my mom would probably get madder at us." Jamie is still in her nightgown. It's a white nightgown with lace at the neck and the sleeves. The material billows around her, making her seem even tinier than she is. Jamie's bedroom smells of patchouli oil, a perfume that she wears. Behind her, on the wall over her bed, are posters of Peter Frampton and Blondie. There is also a poster of a forest scene, with green moss and sunlight shining between the trees.

Jamie's closet door is open and the line of hangers is full of all sorts of colorful clothes. Clothes are perhaps her greatest interest. She likes to have the latest fashions. Jamie has a part-time job, and most of the money from that goes to expanding her wardrobe.

"Mom used to tie us up in chairs," Jamie continues. "My little sister, Kim, had a problem with her bladder. She used to wet her pants. Mom would tie wet pants around Kim's neck. She used to call her skunk and elephant, call her pig. She was always really mean to Kim.

"Mom used to pick us up by our hair or pick us up by our ears and swing us around the room. She used to kick us. She would get us in a corner and slap us until we'd get on the floor and cower from her, and then she'd kick us."

"What could Dad do?" Jamie asks. She is speaking softly, with a dull, tuned-out look in her eyes. "Mom would fight with him and he'd just... he just got to the point where he wouldn't say anything because it would get her mad and cause a fight. They had such big arguments. They would last for a long time. I guess Dad came to the conclusion that she was more important than us kids," Jamie shrugs. "If I were to get married and have kids, my kids would be important to me, but not like my husband. I think to save the peace between them he just wouldn't get on her case about it."

Jamie tilts her head onto her shoulder. It's already 9:30, and her first class starts in fifteen minutes. Jamie isn't in any hurry to leave, though. She often goes to school late or skips school entirely. Jamie missed so many classes at the public school that she had to transfer out and go to an alternative school. This new school has much less pressure; it's less rigid in its approach to the students. But Jamie's not very concerned about missing classes there either.

"My parents finally went to a counselor and he said they should sell the farm and get another house, start over. I remember I was really unhappy when we moved and I would take it out on my sisters. I used to hit them with horsewhips. I saw my mom doing it so I thought, you know, I'd get some reaction out of them that way." Jamie laughs uncomfortably. "One day I went out to the playhouse and I told Kim she had to choose between me and Amy, who she liked the best. I told her if she didn't choose me I'd hit her with the horsewhip. I told Amy she had to choose between me and Kim. Amy and Kim had always been so close. They were always together and I was alone.

"I was chasing them around the parking lot with the horsewhip when my mom came out. She grabbed the horsewhip from me and she beat me to a pulp." Jamie starts to giggle uncontrollably. "Then she tied me in a chair and stuck me in the corner until my dad came home—and that was a good two hours."

Jamie crosses her arms. A smile is frozen on her face. "I always wanted to be the big shit and tell my sisters what to do," she says. "I was always mean to them. They were always together, and I thought maybe if I beat them up they'd be scared of me and they'd stay with me." Jamie laughs, a nervous laugh. "I always wanted to be like a mother."

****

Three months ago Tom, Justin, and Jamie moved into this apartment. It's not as nice as the one they had been living in, but it's quite a bit cheaper. Tom decided that it was time to start saving towards buying a house. This apartment is nothing fancy but it serves their needs. It has two bedrooms, a living room, and a small kitchen. In a city of hills and views of the bay, their apartment looks out on other apartments and a railroad yard.

The house is a split-level, square, green building. Tom, Jamie, and Justin live in half of the top floor. As you walk in the door, you enter a hallway. The first room off the hallway is Tom and Justin's bedroom. It has a large double bed, and two simple, inexpensive dressers. On the wall is a painting of a nude man. The next room off the hallway is Jamie's, with her posters, the smell of incense and the stereo going most of the time. Then there is the bathroom, followed by the living room and kitchen. The kitchen is small. It is a narrow walkway with the stove and refrigerator on one side, and the sink and counter on the other. The living room has a cabinet T.V., a soft couch, and a big easy chair. The apartment is simple, functional and comfortable, and it will do for the time being.

Tom is sitting at the dining room table. The light from the big window looking over the valley shines on the side of his face. "I'd come home from work sometimes and one of the girls would be tied to a chair because they wouldn't mind their mother," he says. "Rita might have told them they weren't supposed to do something and they'd done it anyway. This was like when Kim was three or four and Jamie was maybe six years old.

"When Rita got mad she'd lose total control, totally lose control. She would grab the kids and shake them so hard her fingernails dug in. She wouldn't even realize it. That's the way her mother had dealt with her, and that's the way she dealt with her kids."

Tom leans forward in his chair. "There was a time when Rita thought Kim had said profanity. Rita made her take a handful of detergent and put it in her mouth, to wash her mouth out. Well, of course it made Kim sick," Tom says. "She began to gag and she ran to the bathroom and started vomiting. While she was vomiting and spitting up all these suds, Kim was taking toilet tissue, wiping her mouth and spitting, and then throwing it in the wastebasket. Rita came in and saw this. She got upset with Kim because she had wasted all that toilet tissue. So Rita took all this filthy, sudsy, vomitous toilet tissue, put it in a plastic sack and tied it around Kim's neck. And Kim was made to wear it."

Tom is speaking in an even voice, staring intently in front of him as if he is seeing the scene unfold. Tom shakes his head and sighs. "I came home that evening and Rita said, 'Kim's in her room. She's being punished.' I went to see.

"Kim was in a room where the sun came in from the west, through this big window. The window couldn't be opened, and it was really hot in the room. Kim was lying there, beet red from perspiration, and she was asleep. She was still sort of sobbing, because she'd cried and vomited so much. She was sobbing in her sleep.

"I walked in there and woke her up and she started crying all over again. I saw all this junk around her neck. I didn't know what it was. 'What is this?' I asked Rita, and I took it off Kim's neck.

" 'There you've done it again,' Rita starts shouting. 'No matter what I do to discipline the kids you don't agree with me, you don't support me.'

"But how could I support something like that?" Tom asks with his hands out in front of him, looking confused. He pushes his hair back from his face. "'I can't support something like this,' I told her."

****

"I can remember when I was six years old," Jamie says. "Mom had a huge garden, she had all these vegetables. But she'd never go out there and weed it." Jamie laughs. "My dad called my mother, Blanch, and dad used to say, 'Blanch, Blanch, out on a ranch, how does your garden grow? With beans and tomatoes and peas and potatoes and a whole damn bunch of weeds.' " Jamie's eyes shine as she giggles, remembering.

"A quarter of the garden was flowers, a quarter was vegetables, and the rest were carrots. At least that's how I remember it. I hate carrots. But I remember helping my mom pull those carrots out and we had the best time. We just laughed and giggled. It was fun. That's the only time I remember my mom and I alone together having a really good time."

Jamie gets up and goes to her closet. She looks through her clothes for something to wear. Her closet is stuffed with clothes. It's difficult to even move the hangers to the side to get a look at things. Jamie picks a blue dress, and she takes a pair of blue tights out of her drawer. She goes into the bathroom to change.

She comes out looking very striking, wearing dark make-up around her eyes, and red lipstick. The dress is sleeveless and cut above her knees. Jamie looks very pretty. She takes a pair of simple, white, low-heeled shoes out of the closet and slips them on.

"My mom was beautiful," Jamie says. "She was gorgeous, she was like a model. She looked perfect." Jamie checks her make-up in the mirror. Satisfied, she sits down on the edge of her bed. "My mom was the type of lady that would walk into a party and everybody's head would turn. It's like on TV when the star of the show walks in and everybody looks at them. That's how it was with my mom.

"My mom's got the nicest eyes of anybody I know. She's got a real strong face and she's very proper looking. She has manners, really nice manners. My mom always holds her head up high and it looks like she respects herself." Jamie smiles self-consciously. "I think appearance wise I'm like my mom, in some ways. I turn people's heads. But not like my mom did."

Jamie's boyfriend's name is Todd. He's two years older than she is and a senior at her high school. He's a bass player in a band and very serious about his music. Todd is nice looking, with curly brown hair. He's also quiet and polite. Jamie is in a hurry to move out on her own. She often talks about her and Todd getting an apartment together.

Todd doesn't contradict her but he admits he's not sure they are ready. He will explain to Jamie that they don't have good enough jobs and that neither of their parents like the idea. Jamie says that she knows all that, but she wants to try it anyway.

Jamie lowers her voice, even though no one else is home. "My mom used to scare me about sex," she says. "My mom used to scare the hell out of me. She and I used to talk about sex all the time. In fact, that was our main topic of conversation."

Jamie pulls her skirt down to her knees. She rests her hands in her lap. "See, my dad used to breed horses. I think the most violent act of sex of any animal is with horses. They kick and bite. It used to scare me to death. I used to scream and cry when my dad would breed the mares to Keeper. My mom used to say, 'That's what it's like. That's what it's like when you have sex.'

"My dad would talk to me and he'd say, you know, 'it's beautiful, it's between two people that love each other.' And he'd explain it a lot differently than my mom would. I'd think about what my dad said and I'd think about what my mom said. But you see, it seemed like the worst things—I mean, what my mom said was sounding in my head. I was afraid. I was frightened no matter what my dad said. Because my mom had said this."

Jamie clears her throat. She holds onto the edge of her skirt with both hands. "My mom used to make it sound like a nightmare. She'd say, 'When you have kids it hurts worse than anything in the world. When you have sex, it's painful. And in bed the man doesn't care about how it feels. It just—hurts.' She told me all this stuff," Jamie says, "and all I could see were the horses kicking and biting each other. I would see it, and it would make me sick to my stomach."

****

Tom looks up as Justin comes in the door. Justin is tall, with wavy brown hair and a thick moustache. He has long arms and long legs. He walks down the hallway to where Tom is sitting at the kitchen table and gives Tom a kiss.

"I'm taping," Tom says. "I'll be done in a minute."

"I'll just watch TV till you're finished."

"How was your day?" Tom asks.

"Over. My day is over, that's the main thing," Justin jokes. Justin works as an aide in a nursing home. He makes beds, changes bed pans, turns old people over so they don't get bed sores. Justin's been talking about changing jobs for quite a while, but so far he hasn't done anything about it.

Justin sits down in the big easy chair. He leans back and the footrest comes up and lifts up his feet. He takes the remote control off the table and switches the TV on. Tom has everything all ready for dinner. He gets up, puts the casserole in the oven and turns it on.

"I tried to talk to my wife but she wouldn't hear me," Tom says, sitting back down at the table. "She felt I was some sort of weirdo, too. If I put my arm around my daughter, or held her on my lap, she'd say I was encouraging her to have an incestuous feeling towards me. To allow my daughters to get in bed with me when I had shorts on and they had their little nighties, to lay next to them, or hold them—I was encouraging this."

The drone of the television can be heard in the background announcing the news. Tom takes a deep breath as he thinks. He looks down the hallway. "I felt that if I could sit down with the kids and rationally talk about sex, this was better than talking about it in front of my wife. Because she was right there in the driver's seat as the person who is experiencing sex with me. If she is telling them it is a dirty, rotten thing, they'd tend to listen to her. She was the one that was relating to it.

"Whereas, if she wasn't there contradicting everything I said, I thought I could probably make a better impression on them. I would say, 'This is the way animals act. Yes, Keeper has a huge penis, but at the same time the mare has a huge vagina to accept this. It's part of the courting program for him to bite her on the neck, or for her to tease him and kick at him. This is the way animals do it. But it's not done this way among people. They will court and kiss, and it is a beautiful thing. It's not a dirty thing.'"

Tom shakes his head as he tries to explain. "See, if I were to say something like that in front of my wife, she would undermine everything I had said. It came down to the fact that we had different views. When we did talk about it, it would be a big blow up and cause a fight between us. So I would try to talk about it without her," Tom says. "I would get the kids aside."

****

"I don't think if I had a child I would get mad at them for having sex," Jamie says. "I might get mad at them for doing what I did with Paul, and being blind to being hurt, and being used. But I wouldn't get mad at them for having sex. I've thought about this.

"I think you have to experience both good and bad sexually before you figure out what you want, you know. I'd never tell my kids, 'no, don't do that.' I wouldn't tell them to do it either. I think I'd just be honest and want them to be as honest as possible with me. I wouldn't want them to hide it from me and think, 'I'm going to get in trouble if I do this,' or 'I'm a bad person.'

"My mom told me that if I ever did go to bed with somebody before I was married, that she knew I couldn't handle it. I wasn't that type of person. She said she knew I'd freak out if I did." Jamie shakes her head. "Well, I think I did freak out at first. But now I'm okay, now I can deal with it." Jamie smoothes her dress out across her lap as she thinks. She stares out the window. The sunlight shines on her face and gives her skin a healthy pink glow. Jamie is already late for class, but it doesn't matter anymore. She's decided to skip school today. Or rather, she plans to go to school to find Todd so she can ask him to skip school with her. Jamie turns back from the window.

"When I think about two people making love, I think about the horses. That's what I think about," Jamie says. "When my girlfriends would talk about sex. I'd think about the horses, and it would make me sick."

"Paul couldn't figure it out. After we'd do something, I'd move away from him. I'd sit there and I'd be sick to my stomach. After I made love to Paul or Ricky, I couldn't stop all the things that were going on in my head. I couldn't put my mind on something else like I usually can. It's like—I'd get this pain in my stomach, and I'd feel like I was going to throw up."

There have been three boys Jamie has had relationships with. When she lived in Montana with her father, and through the foster homes, Jamie went with a boy named Ricky. They were very close. Ricky stuck with Jamie through a lot of confusing times. When Jamie moved to Seattle, she didn't know anyone and she quickly started going out with Paul. Tom didn't approve of Paul. Looking back on it Jamie doesn't approve of him either. She feels he was using her. But that relationship lasted only a short while. A few months after they broke up Jamie met Todd, and Jamie and Todd have been going together for over a year now.

"Every time I want to get my mind off something," Jamie is speaking so softly that it's difficult to hear her, "ever since I've been a little kid, I'd sing the song 'Winnie-the-Pooh'. My whole life, whenever I would get sad, or hurt, or feel bad or something, I'd just sing 'Winnie-the-Pooh'. It's weird. I'd sing that song to myself and I'd feel better." Jamie looks down, embarrassed. "But after being with Ricky or Paul, no matter what I thought of—I'd go 'Winnie-the-Pooh, Winnie-the-Pooh'. I'd sing the song, and I'd still feel sick.

"Sometimes Paul and I would be making love, and all of a sudden I'd move away from him. I'd tell him, 'Stop! Leave me alone!' It was really hard for him to understand. If he asked me why, I'd just tell him it hurt. But in my mind, I'd see that image. Not when Dad was breeding other horses, but when he was breeding my horse, Keeper. When he bred Sheba and Keeper, that's what I'd think about. That's what I'd see in my mind."

Jamie crosses her arms. She is staring out the window with an intense look on her face. "I remember it. I remember the brown barn, and the gate, and the haystack. I remember dad was holding Sheba.

"Mom had told me that when you are a virgin and it's the first time, it hurts the most. Sheba had never been bred. She had just come into heat. Dad was going to breed her to Keeper. I remember, I remember it perfectly. I sat there watching, and I screamed at the top of my lungs."

****

At dinner this evening Jamie didn't talk much. And she only picked at her food, leaving most of it on her plate. Tom and Justin spoke about plans to meet with a realtor to look at more houses tomorrow. They've already found one house they like, but they want to see others to compare it with. When her father asked her how school was today, Jamie replied, "the same as usual." Then she excused herself and went into her room.

Justin gives Tom a look to say, "she's doing it again." Jamie works late and misses dinner about half the time. Justin feels that for the times she does eat dinner at home she should take a turn and do the dishes.

She rarely does, though. Tom often says he'll have a talk with her about it, but he never seems to get around to it.

"Let's not go into that tonight, okay?" Tom says, and he waves to Justin to forget it. Justin rolls his eyes and starts clearing the table. He runs the water in the sink. Tom follows Jamie into her room.

"You know what I was thinking, Jamie?" he says.

Jamie is lying on her bed. "What?" she answers.

"Well—how about if I talk about some things between Rita and I, some reasons why we didn't get along." Jamie sits up and looks at her father. She's been depressed all day today, mopey and tired. She didn't feel like doing anything. "I was thinking," Tom says, "that if you want to listen, it might help you understand your mother. And it might help you understand why we didn't get along."

"Okay," Jamie says. She gets up slowly. Tom puts his arm around her as they walk back to the dining room table. Jamie sits at one end of the table and Tom sits at the other. Justin has gone back to their bedroom. Jamie rests her head on her hand. She already looks bored. Tom clears his throat. He turns the tape recorder on.

"When I married Rita, I had had very pleasant sexual experiences." Tom is looking at the tape recorder, making sure that it is turning. "I felt, 'Okay, I can help her.' But my hands were tied. Every time I tried I was causing blood, pain, crying, and rejection." Without raising her head off her hand, Jamie watches her dad.

"Rita was raised in a Catholic environment," Tom continues. "She was sent to Catholic grade school, high school. She went to Catholic school of nursing. She was brought up in a time when sexual promiscuity was absolutely taboo for young Catholic women. Rita and I dated for two years before we got married. We were engaged for five months. When it came to sex, we would always stop before we went all the way. Rita wanted to be a virgin when she married me.

"And then two weeks before we were married, we did go to bed together. We tried to have sexual intercourse, but Rita had a very tough hymen membrane that I could not penetrate. It was extremely painful for her. It started to tear and she bled, and bled, and bled. We thought the hymen had been ruptured, but it hadn't."

Tom is looking at Jamie as he talks. Jamie is still leaning with her head on her hand, but her face is taken on a confused grimace. "We tried it again and it was so excruciating she couldn't stand it. Finally, she went to her obstetrician, they took her to surgery and removed the hymen. And she healed. But her first sexual experience was an absolute total fiasco."

Tom pauses. He watches Jamie, waiting for some reaction. She doesn't give him any. Tom clears his throat. "We didn't try sexual intercourse again until we went on our honeymoon. By then she didn't feel the pain any more. It was comfortable, she could tend to relax. But that's where she became pregnant with you. And here again it was sort of a traumatic experience. It hurt like hell and when she could enjoy it, she found herself immediately pregnant and starting morning sickness."

Jamie sniffles and sits up very straight in her chair. She wipes her nose with her hand. Her indifferent look is gone.

"When you were born it was all a big mess," Tom says. "Rita was going to breastfeed you but she didn't have enough milk." Tom stops momentarily. He takes a breath and lets out a big sigh. "I remember she came home one night to feed you. She gave you all the milk she could muster, and you were still hungry.

"Rita started crying. She was looking for the formula card. She'd finally admitted defeat. I remember she was looking for the instructions on how to mix it. She went to pull a drawer out, and it came out all the way. It dumped all sorts of silverware and papers on the floor. Rita started screaming, she was angry at first. And then she sat down and began to sob 'Please don't send me to an institution', she said. 'I know I act crazy, I just can't help it.'"

Jamie is crying silently. She wipes the tears away with the palm of her hand. "Do you remember?" she asks. "Do you remember what I said to her?" Tears are rolling down Jamie's cheeks.

"I don't think your mom is rejecting you as a person," Tom says, speaking softly, trying to reassure Jamie. "Not at all. She really loves you, but you're a reminder of things that she has never been able to deal with—"

Jamie interrupts him. "Mom was having a lot of trouble with her periods. She said it was like going through labor every month. That's when she decided to have her hysterectomy." Jamie starts to cry. Her breathing sounds like panting. She shakes her head back and forth. "I couldn't understand. I told her that she wouldn't be a woman if she had a hysterectomy. That she wouldn't be my mom, that she'd change."

Tom looks so sad watching his daughter. "Your mother feels guilty. Each time you show up with your suitcase in your hand, you're forcing her to deal with an unpleasant time in her life—"

"I can't believe I said something like I did," Jamie says. Her arms are crossed over her chest and she is hugging herself. She keeps shaking her head. "I told her, 'I know why you got your hysterectomy'. I said, 'because you fooled around with Eddie Hall, that's why.' "

Jamie wipes at the tears on her cheeks. She rubs her hand across her forehead. "I can't believe I said that. I didn't realize how much I must have hurt her."

"It will be OK," Tom tries to reassure Jamie. "Give it time."

****

"We had financial problems," Tom says. "We were starting a business, we'd bought a new home, I was on the school board with meetings lasting until God knows when. Our time together was very short. Many times we would go to bed at midnight, just absolutely physically exhausted. I wanted to have sex. She didn't, but felt it was a duty. That made me feel like our whole sexual experience was very lacking. It made me feel like a glutton, like I was forcing her."

There is the sound of the trains clanking together in the valley, and a train whistle blows far away. Jamie's music can be heard faintly coming from her room.

After Jamie went back into her room, Tom fixed himself a cup of coffee. He takes it and walks back to the kitchen table. Tom sits back down and starts again.

"I loved Rita too much to go somewhere else for sexual gratification. I couldn't think of going to bed with a man at that time." Tom blinks several times. He rests his chin on his hand. "What I would do, is I would get totally involved in things that would drain my energy. That's why I was raising 100 hogs, I was on the school board, I was showing horses. I was trying to get myself so involved with everything else that I didn't have time to think about sex. As it turned out, that ended up making her feel even less of a woman. Before, at least I was trying once in a while. Now, I didn't even make an advance toward her.

"Little by little that's what separated us." Tom says, talking softly. He closes his eyes for a moment. "Then Rita became ill and she had a hysterectomy, I became sick and almost went on a kidney machine, one of the kids was scalded from the pressure cooker, Rita's sister died—and it just finally broke. It all blew."

Tom crosses his arms. "She was going to get out of the situation, and right now. File it, it had to be done. Within two weeks we were going to get a divorce, that was it. And we did. We got the divorce. I would think, 'I'm divorced and I don't really want to be. But maybe I do.' I wanted to see the kids. I wanted them with me. I felt totally frustrated and confused."

Justin sticks his head in the doorway of the living room and motions to Tom that he is going to sleep. Tom tells him to go ahead, he'll be there in a minute. Tom looks tired, he has dark lines under his eyes. But he's got himself thinking about all this and he doesn't want to stop until he figures it out. Tom runs his hand back through his hair as he tries to organize his thoughts.

"I was living in town and driving to this little community where my business was. I passed the house every day," he says, speaking slowly. "She had it written that I could feed the horses from quarter till nine until quarter after nine, or from quarter till four until quarter after four, but I was unable to see the children. She said that I was dangerous, and I might harm them. There was an injunction put out that stated I wasn't to visit them.

"I'd drive past the house in the morning to get things going there, and the kids would be waiting for the bus. They'd wave and want me to stop, but I couldn't because if I stopped I'd be in violation of the order. And Rita would be standing there watching out the window."

Jamie goes around the corner from her bedroom into the bathroom. She is wearing her nightgown, and she has a hair brush in her hand. Tom absently watches her. Behind Tom, through the big bay window, one can see the lights shining in all the apartments in the valley. The night is dark and it looks like a whole solar system spread out on the ground.

"Around the time of the custody hearing Rita was accusing me of being homosexual. I had had a couple experiences, but at the time I didn't think I was." Tom bites on his thumbnail. His eyebrows are pulled down over his eyes. "My attorney was talking to the three judges who might hear the case. One of the judges said that if I was homosexual, he would be very prejudiced. He said, 'as far as custody of the children, I might consider his daughters visiting him, but I would not allow his son to.'

"I remember I was very upset by that," Tom says. His jaw muscles move up and down as he grits his teeth together. "My wife is heterosexual, and the judge wasn't worried about my little boy being molested by her. If I were heterosexual he wouldn't have any qualms about letting my daughters visit me. But because there was the possibility that I was homosexual, 'Let's keep the little boy away from him. He might do something!' "

Tom shakes his head. He gets up slowly and pours his tea into the sink. One can hear the trains clanking together down in the valley. Tom walks over and stares out the window. The railroad yard is the only area not sprinkled with lights. It looks like a dark stripe in the middle of the valley. Again, there's the sound of trains clanging into each other. Tom cannot see the trains but he stares into the darkness, he stares and listens. The night is suddenly quiet again. Finally, Tom turns and walks down the hallway to his room.

****

Jamie is sitting on her bed in her nightgown. Her room is a mess. She's been "sorting out" clothes, deciding which ones she likes and which ones she's tired of. Her headphones from her stereo are on the table next to her bed. The stereo is still on, and a trickle of music can be heard coming from the tiny headphone speakers.

"When I'd live with my mom," Jamie says, "she'd be bad-mouthing my dad all the time. It was hard to sort out my true feelings about him. And the same with my dad. I'd be with him and he'd say things about my mom. He didn't do it as much as my mom did, but it was really hard for me. It was real easy to be on the wrong side."

Tom and Justin have gone to sleep. Jamie's not tired yet. She usually stays up the latest anyway. Jamie is sitting on her bed with her legs curled under her. Just her feet, with her red painted toenails, stick out from beneath her nightgown.

"There'd be one day when I'd hate my mother, and another day when I'd hate my dad. I'd be with my mom and she'd tear apart my dad, up one side and down the other. Then my dad would do the same thing to my mom. I was a twelve-year old kid saying, 'Wow, what's going on?' You know? And these two people whom I was supposed

146

to love and honor, they're ripping each other apart. What am I to believe? What am I to think about it?

"As it turned out, both of them kinda lost," Jamie says. "Because instead of making me closer to one and further from the other, it made me further from both of them. I'd think, 'they're both little kids for doing that.' Not only for doing it to me, but for doing it to my two sisters and my little brother. I really can't respect my family."

Jamie runs her hand back through her short hair as she thinks for a moment. "When they were getting the divorce my dad used to say, 'Boo' when he drove past my mom's lawyer's office. This was when it was just him and the kids in the car. But this one time, Mom was driving past her lawyer's office and my little brother Mickey said, 'Boo'. My mom about went through the ceiling." Jamie laughs remembering it.

"Mom called me up as soon as she got home. She yelled at me, she was so pissed. She said, 'I suppose you and your dad thought this one up, huh?'

"I said, 'I'm sorry, mom.' But when I got off the phone I rolled on the floor. I thought it was so funny. Just because it was so immaterial and stupid. It was really childish of both of them. Number one for my dad to say anything. And number two for my mom to call up and be pissed about it. You know? I mean, who really cares?"

Jamie stretches and yawns. She's tired and at the same time not sleepy at all. Jamie has trouble falling to sleep at night. She has different things she does to try to relax. One is to listen to music. The other is to get high. Each night she wonders whether getting to sleep is going to be difficult.

"When I lived with my mom," Jamie says, "every day she'd come home from work and she'd say, 'Oh, your father, he's such a bastard, he's a fourteen-year-old jackass, he's a faggot, he's this, he's that.' My dad took a trip to Alaska with Dave Hunt, and Dave was only eighteen at the time. So my mom kept saying he was a faggot. When Dad got back he was allowed to see us again, and I wanted to live with him so badly.

"My mom came home one day and she ripped my dad down so far. I told her I'd had enough of it and I wasn't going to put up with it any more. Right away my mom started saying what a SOB my dad was. So, I grabbed a couple things and I ran over to my dad's house. Mom chased me in the car. But instead of taking me back she brought over all my clothes and just dropped them off."

Jamie looks flustered, remembering that episode. In the state of Montana a child twelve years or older is able to decide which parent she prefers to live with. Jamie could have remained at her father's home even if her mother had tried to get her back. Her mother didn't try, though.

"About a week later Mom moved out of the house she was living in, and she moved to Watsonville," Jamie says. "She didn't even tell me she was going to Watsonville. She just moved and I lived with my dad."

Jamie stares across the room. She looks sad, but also distant. The house is quiet, everyone else is asleep. Jamie sighs and turns the tape over on her stereo. She climbs back in bed and gets under the covers. When things are going around in her head, listening to music is the best way to keep from thinking. Jamie takes the headphones off the nightstand and puts them over her ears. Resting her head back on her pillow, she closes her eyes.

****

It's a beautiful sunny morning in Seattle. The sky is blue, and there is only the barest trace of a breeze. Everyone's alarm clock goes off at practically the same moment. Justin gets out of bed and goes to the kitchen to start the coffee. By the time he gets to the bathroom, Jamie's already got it. He knocks on the door.

"I'm in here," Jamie says.

"I need to use the bathroom for one moment," Justin tells her through the door, figuring she's doing her make-up.

There's silence. Jamie doesn't answer. Finally the door opens and Jamie strides past Justin into her bedroom. "If you've got to use it, use it," she snaps.

Justin scowls at the closed door to Jamie's bedroom. He's an inch away from cursing her. A moment passes and he decides against it. He goes into the bathroom and closes the door.

During breakfast Tom tries unsuccessfully to make small talk. Jamie and Justin are both notorious for waking up slowly in the morning. They often are grumps at breakfast and Tom has found that it is better to leave well enough alone. Tom turns to the paper and reads as he eats. Justin borrows a part of the paper as well. Jamie eats quickly and excuses herself. She goes back into the bathroom to work on her make-up, and she stays there until she hears her dad say goodbye.

"I was having a lot of trouble dealing with things," Jamie says, sitting down at the kitchen table. She is wearing pink pants and a white blouse. Her make-up has been applied very carefully, and her light brown hair is brushed back from her face. "I couldn't hold friends. I was really mean. I was different. I guess I was behind them in a lot of ways. They were all doctors' children. They'd go out drinking and partying and stuff, and I didn't even know that kids did that. I was still into riding bikes with my sisters.

"My dad was partying a lot. He was still straight, from what I know. But he would sometimes bring guys home and have them live with us for a while. They'd sleep in different bedrooms, but they lived there. I was starting to hang around with a bunch of kids, and I was smoking cigarettes. I smoked weed one night with this guy who was staying at our house and he told on me. My dad blew up. He didn't care that this guy had done it, too. But I had been drinking and smoking cigarettes and getting into a lot of trouble anyway. So my dad sent me to stay with my aunt."

Jamie's eyes have dark eyeliner around them. Her cheeks have a touch of red, and she is wearing pink lipstick. The effect, all together, look striking. Jamie is sitting very still, staring intently across the room.

"I told myself, you know, I said, 'I'm not gonna smoke. I'm not gonna drink, I'm not gonna do anything. I'm just gonna get out of eighth grade and get into high school.' But my cousin was doing things ten times worse than I ever thought of doing, and she was a real influence on me. She was a year younger, but about two years in advance physically. She was Mormon. She'd go to church and the whole bit, and then as soon as church was over, she'd go out and party. I was the one who always got caught, though. When my aunt got fed up with me she sent me back to live with my dad.

"Dad had moved into a duplex in a very wealthy part of town. Dad and I started over, you know. The only problem was that Dad was working all the time, and I didn't know one single person. I met this guy named Mike, and he smoked too much dope. Mike smoked cigarettes, and he drank. We got in a lot of trouble together. I'd come home high and my dad would have a fit.

"One night I came home," Jamie says. "I'd been with Mike and I was really, really high. I walked in the door and my dad and this friend of his were smoking pot. Dad got mad at me, and then he called Mike and talked to him and stuff. I thought, how could you get mad at me for doing it, when you're sitting there doing the same thing? His excuse all the time was, 'well. I'm of age and you're not.' But I'd think, 'It's still illegal, you know.'"

Jamie stops talking. She looks to be sulking. The day outside is peaceful and still. The sky, seen through the big window behind Jamie, is a perfect blue with only an occasional streak of white. Jamie begins picking at the red polish on her fingernails.

"I knew my dad didn't approve," she says, "but there was nothing better to do. I started hanging around with my old friends and getting into trouble. We moved in with my grandma, so Dad didn't have to pay rent. Grandma would always catch me smoking and tell Dad. And I'd get into trouble." As if reminded, Jamie pulls a cigarette out of her purse and lights it. She takes a drag and puts it in the ashtray.

"One night I was supposed to come in at 11:30, but John and I were talking in his car in front of the house until 1:30. Dad grounded me. The next day I went over to see my boyfriend Ricky. See, the night before I'd gone out on him, and I hadn't told him.

"Dad called Ricky's house and said, 'Jamie, you get your butt home in ten minutes or I'm calling the cops.' We went home and my dad said to Ricky, 'Jamie's in a lot of trouble right now. She went out last night with John and she didn't get home until 1:30.' You should have seen Ricky's face drop," Jamie says.

"Well, I got mad. I got really mad at my dad. I got pretty mouthy, and he slapped me. I said, 'Don't you ever hit me again.' And he slapped me right in front of Ricky. Then my grandma said something and I called her a fucking bitch, and I ran out of the house. My dad ran after me and pulled me in by the hair. He said, 'Young lady, you are going to stay here and straighten up or you are going to come with me to a social worker.' I said, 'I'll go with you.' So I went with him, we talked to a social worker, and I ended up staying in a foster home."

Jamie's voice is without emotion as she tells the story. It's an old story, one she'd just as soon forget. Jamie brings it up for information, but she refuses to bring up all the feelings she went through.

Tom was about to move to Seattle at the time that Jamie went to the foster home. He said that he had been planning on taking Jamie with him. However, he felt if he couldn't trust Jamie to act right and be in on time in Montana, then he couldn't bring her to Seattle where he'd be working long hours and she'd be on her own a lot. He felt that Jamie could have chosen to stay with him, but she didn't. It was her decision.

"See, living in the foster home made me think," Jamie says. Her eyebrows are drawn together as she concentrates. "It put me in a neutral situation where I could think without having my mom saying, 'Oh, your dad is a son-of-a-bitch', or, you know, having my dad say something about my mom. I lived in a neutral situation where no one really cared who my mom or dad were."

Jamie takes a drag off her cigarette. She sets it back in the ashtray where the smoke lazily rises towards the ceiling. "In the first foster home there was another foster girl named Laurie. She was so perfect it made me sick. She was a little shit. She'd go behind the parents' backs and do something, but I couldn't say anything. I'd always get in trouble because I was really mean to Laurie. Sheri, the mother, was really jealous of me too. She accused me of fooling around with her husband. She got her hair cut like mine, she bought a bunch of clothes like mine. It seemed to me that she was really jealous because her husband paid attention to me. One day she slapped me around and they took me out of that foster home and put me in with the Desmonds.

"The Desmonds were very religious people. They were good people, but their daughter, Rene, was a junior in high school and she and I didn't get along at all. In fact, we had a fight one day and I got so mad at her I picked up the vacuum cleaner and hit her over the head with it." Jamie laughs. "She deserved it. She hit me in the face with one of my boots." Jamie sighs. "She was really jealous because I had a boyfriend and because she was about five foot two and two hundred pounds. She was huge." Jamie laughs again, a slow rolling laugh. "She was just the most bitter person I've ever met—besides my mother."

****

"She got in a terrible fight with Rene, the foster daughter," Tom says quietly, "and she'd had a big argument with her boyfriend Ricky about coming back to live with me." Tom clears his throat. "There were several things. She'd had another fight with her mother. Jamie became very depressed and I don't know why she did it, but she took a bunch of phenobarbital." Tom visibly winces as he says the words. "As soon as she did it, she was sorry. They took her to the emergency room and pumped her stomach, and she was okay. But she was really depressed and down at the time. She'd really had it."

Tom is sitting in a cafe. He has just finished his lunch. The cafe has big wooden tables, and Tom is sitting at the last one against the back wall. The waiter comes by and takes the dishes. He pours more coffee, and Tom thanks him. It's early for lunch, so the place is not crowded. This is a quiet, friendly restaurant with big windows and wood floors.

"When she was staying with the Desmonds, Jamie called and said that she would really like to come back and live with me. I felt, okay, but I've got to be honest about this. I have a lover, we're living together, and I want her to know. I called Jamie on the telephone," Tom says, "and I talked to her about it. That's when she wrote me a letter and told me, 'love is a rare thing. If you have someone you love, that's what's important.' " Tom smiles. He's saved the letter. It was a huge relief that his daughter would react positively to the news that he was gay. "It was a very nice letter," he says.

Tom watches out the window as people pass on the street. They are all wearing summer clothes; it's an unusually warm spring day.

"Anyway, she came to live with us," he says. "She started school. She introduced us to her friends"—Tom stumbles over the words— "as her parents. Jamie made no bones about the fact that we were gay. Most of her friends were very... accepting of the situation. She seemed to be very happy for several months.

"Then at Christmas she and her mother had a really bad time, another strong rejection. And that was the last time there's been any real communication between the two of them." Tom shakes his head slowly back and forth. He leans forward and rests his weight on the table. "When Jamie gets upset about one thing, nothing else goes right. She has to put the blame somewhere. I was the handiest, so was Justin.

"Jamie started coming down on us. She would be rude and ornery, and I can't say Justin was much better at times. She'd mouth off to him, and like I told him, 'she may not be right but she's sixteen years old. Don't come down to her age and start fighting.' She would say something nasty to him, and he would immediately come back with the same type of thing. It was like listening to two kids fighting, instead of an adult and a child."

The waiter comes by with fresh coffee. He has to wave to get Tom's attention. Tom looks at the man, confused for a moment. "Oh, no thanks. I'm fine," Tom says. The waiter leaves and Tom tries to find his train of thought. He presses his fingertips to his eyes.

"Justin felt kind of resentful toward me because I wouldn't backhand her or straighten her out. I guess maybe I was being lenient in a way." Tom's voice drops. He sounds tired all of a sudden. "But on the other hand, here's this kid—she's coming from a divorced family, a mother who has totally rejected her, moving in with her father who has a lover, into a gay situation, starting a new school, leaving old friends behind, making new friends, and trying to adjust to everything in a period of months." Tom rubs his forehead. The strain of dealing with all this for so long shows in his eyes. He looks slowly around the room as if he is noticing his surroundings for the first time. "It was all very difficult for her," he says, and he shrugs. "I guess I made allowances for that."

****

"In my book I don't see my dad with another man," Jamie says. "Sometimes when my dad's happy I feel like it's the best thing for him to be with Justin, regardless of my feelings. And sometimes I think it makes me sick."

Jamie sits back in her chair. She doodles on a piece of paper next to the phone. "It took me a long time to really believe myself, but I think it's great, you know, male-female, male-male, female-female, as long as a person's happy." Her pen moves quickly back and forth as Jamie fills in one area after another with dense blue lines. "And yet I can say that, but I don't feel my dad is really happy. He can say he's happy but I don't feel he's really happy. Maybe that's because I'm not happy." Jamie looks confused. "I mean, how can you love someone the way my dad loved my mother, and just all of a sudden totally turn off towards women? You can't."

Jamie picks up the phone and tries Todd's number. It's busy. She wants to see if he's left yet. When Todd called this morning, Jamie said she wasn't sure she was going to school again today. Todd said he'd pick her up, just to make sure she did.

"I feel like I take a back seat to Justin," Jamie says. "I feel like Justin is more important to my dad than I am. It used to be that my dad would do anything for me. He still gives attention to me, he just doesn't give it to me as much anymore. And besides, Justin used to be a prostitute in L.A. He was into taking drugs and everything. It makes me sick that my dad would lower himself to something like Justin. He wouldn't have liked my mom if she was like that.

"Justin makes me sick because of the way he smokes a cigarette. My dad isn't feminine like Justin is. My dad isn't, um, prissy like Justin is. It makes me sick to watch TV with Justin and watch him smoke a cigarette. Just because of the way he moves his hands. I have to get up and go in my room. I mean, Jesus—if you're going to be gay that's one thing. But if you're going to, you know, act the part I think that's another. I have friends who are gay. I accept people who are gay. It's just when you go to the extreme.

"My dad just ruined a relationship with a boy I really cared about, because dad didn't like him. And I'm not trying to ruin Dad and Justin's relationship. I just think it's very unfair for him to say, 'I dislike this person and don't think you should go out with him.' He'd tell me Paul was unimportant, that he was not good looking enough for me." Jamie looks up from where she's doodling. "Well, he was right about Paul. Paul did rotten things. He was using me. But still it was unfair for Dad to ruin our relationship."

****

"Jamie always made it a point to be really close to me whenever I was around," Tom says. "I think her mother might have felt that I was spending time and attention on Jamie that I wasn't spending on her. On the other hand, I think she was also relieved. The less we were together, the less she had to deal with us as man and wife, with the sexual aspects of the whole relationship. But Jamie's always been like this. She always had to be number one with me. It carries over here with Justin. She always has to have a lot of attention."

The restaurant is suddenly starting to fill up. It was practically empty a moment ago, and now almost every table is taken. The noise level has risen in the same proportion.

"Whether Jamie likes to admit it or not, I think she did feel threatened by Justin. I think she would really like to have me more to herself. And Justin felt the same way about Jamie. The two of them were kind of vying for first place with me.

"I think one reason that Jamie continued to have this relationship with Paul when I disapproved of it, was to act out the same role with me that I had with her. I was having a relationship that she disapproved of, and she had nothing to say about it. So why couldn't she have a relationship I disapproved of? Like, what's good for the goose is good for the gander."

The waiter comes over again. He stands next to the table and asks Tom if there's anything else he needs. The restaurant is full and the waiter is politely asking Tom to leave. "I'll just take the check," Tom says. The waiter puts the check down on the table and walks away.

"One time I was talking to Jamie about this boyfriend of hers, Paul I was telling her what I felt he wanted from her. She said to me, 'How can you condemn me for performing an act that is normal, when what you're doing is abnormal? It's perfectly normal for a man and woman to go to bed together. You and Justin do what you do, and you consider that all right. Then you condemn us for doing what we do.' She said 'You're the one who's abnormal.' "

Tom gives an ironic smile as he picks up the check. The restaurant is crowded and noisy now. Tom carefully weaves in-between the tables on his way to the front to pay the bill.

****

"I don't know," Jamie says. "I don't know what to think. It did make me sick when my dad told me he was gay. It made me sick to think he got in bed with a man. I walked in on them before. It made me sick to my stomach. I really mean it. I just went—'Oooh', and walked out of the room. My dad got really mad at me. But I didn't know what they were doing."

Jamie is impatient for Todd to pick her up. She's feeling nervous today. She wants some company, and she wants a rest from talking about all this for a while. These are stories she's tried to push out of her mind, and remembering them just gets her upset.

"Dad says that I didn't like anybody he went out with. Well, he's wrong, because I loved Jackie dearly. She's black, but I didn't care.

I loved Jackie and I wouldn't mind her disciplining me. She wouldn't do it just to push her weight around. It would depend on the person. If the person was a lady but she was like Justin, I wouldn't like her any more than I like him."

155

Jamie pours herself a glass of water, and leans up against the counter. "My dad can say he's gay, but I don't think he is. My dad can tell me up and down that he's happy, but I don't really think he's happy. I don't," Jamie says emphatically. "I think he's just kidding himself. I don't think my dad and Justin are going to last.

"This is just a phase my dad's going through, it's just lasting longer than most. I think Dad's just trying to see if this is what's good for him. But I think in the long run he'll find out that maybe it's not so good for him. I don't know. Maybe he'll find out that it's good for him, maybe."

Jamie is holding her glass in both hands. Her eyes are open wide as she talks about all of this. "I can't choose the person my dad is going to love. And, to tell you the truth, if I could choose, I'd choose my mother. Because in my eyes and in my head that's how I'll always see it, regardless of who my dad sleeps with or lives with or marries.

"I think one of these days my mom's going to get her act together. I really wish my parents would have worked on it because I think anything can be worked out. But I don't—I don't really think there's a chance of them getting back together. It just got too bitter, and too... too bad. You know? They fought too much. And there were things said that no one should ever say to anybody."

Jamie stares out the window with a worried expression on her face. "My dad despises my mother now, and my mom despises my dad. But I don't believe—they said they despise each other, but I don't really believe that deep down they despise each other, not totally." Jamie's voice is rising. She looks sad and confused. "They had to love each other at one time, to get married and have four children, and work hard enough to almost make it out of debt, and almost make it. You know?"

The doorbell rings. Jamie almost jumps. She runs to the door to let Todd in, and as soon as he walks in Jamie throws her arms around his neck. She gives him a big hug.

"Hey, what's this?" Todd asks smiling sheepishly.

"I missed you," Jamie tells him, as she presses her face against his chest.

****

The workmen across the street are pounding away, building what the sign describes as "deluxe condominiums." The tall, square structure hugs its side of the street and blocks the afternoon sun, as Justin's little Triumph pulls up. Justin and Tom stopped on their way home to look at another house. This one was okay, but they were really impressed by one they looked at last week. That one was an old Victorian in a neighborhood near downtown. The neighborhood is a little rough, but the houses there are more reasonably priced.

Justin goes to the refrigerator and pours two glasses of iced tea. He sets them on the table. Tom comes out of the bathroom and sits down. He is dressed in white corduroys, a blue t-shirt, and a dark blue windbreaker.

"Let's see. It came to a head here a while ago," he says. "Jamie decided that it wasn't working. She didn't want to stay here anymore, she wanted to go back to Montana. She said she loved me, she wanted to stay with me, but not with Justin. I was more or less forced to make a choice."

Justin sits down at the table. He leans back in his chair and sips his tea. "I let Jamie know that in a few years she was going to be gone anyway. She wouldn't think twice about leaving me alone. I was planning my future for the rest of my life," Tom says. "I told her, 'this isn't just my home, this is Justin's and my home. We came into this together.' Justin had welcomed her into his home—from that point on it was her home as well. And it could be a family situation. But it wasn't up to me to make the choice." Tom looks over at Justin. Justin offers no comment. Tom begins to smile. "So Jamie said she was going to a foster home. That was it. If this was his home, my home, we could have our goddamn home. We could stick it. She wasn't going to stay here."

Tom adjusts himself in his chair. His smile gets bigger. This is one story that turned out well. He can afford to smile about this one. Tom begins speaking in a gentle, soothing voice.

"I had a long talk with her. I told her, 'Jamie, I could allow you to run away and go to a foster home,' I said, 'but you would be going through the same thing in a period of time that you're going through here. The difference is that you'd be going through it with people who don't have a gut level love and feeling for you.' "I told her, 'I would rather go through all the bad times and all the baloney that you think is coming down here, with you. As demanding and ornery as I can be, nobody is going to stand by you and see you go through this thing like I will. Because I really care. I don't think you can find a foster parent who will care as much as I do.' "

Tom brushes his hair back from his face. He sighs and continues. "I said, 'I know this may seem like a bummer situation, but I would rather be here to work it out with you than let all the counselors and foster parents do it. Because in time it will work out. And I think it will work out faster and better if we're together. Besides,' I said, 'I'm kind of selfish, I want you here.' "

Tom's face spreads into a big grin. He looks over at Justin. For the first time in days he looks wonderfully happy. "Anyway," he says, "Jamie ended up staying."

****

"I have my dad on a golden pedestal. It's really unfair for me to do that to him, but it's hard for me not to feel that way. I decided to stay with my dad," Jamie says, "because there has always been something very special between us that nobody could ever replace and nobody could ever take away. No matter what my dad did, or what I did, I think it will always still be there.

"I might be angry at him for a while, but I could never lose it totally for him, lose my feelings totally. We had a talk and Dad told me he was very happy living with Justin. I thought, if that makes him happy, it has to make me happy. Because I love my dad."

Todd and Jamie are sitting in a diner a block from school. It's where the kids hang out if they're not in class. Jamie has talked Todd into skipping first bell. They're having coffee and donuts. This school she goes to now is very unstructured. Attendance is encouraged but not required, teachers rarely lecture, the kids work mainly on their own.

The school is in an old two-story building. It has wood floors and beautiful trim around the doors and windows. There's an informal lounge on each floor where students are always gathered, talking and smoking. The school even has a day care room for students with young children.

"I don't associate with a lot of people now," Jamie says. "I don't hang around with a crowd any more. I have a few close friends I've known since I first moved here." She looks over at Todd, who's eating a donut. He smiles at her. "I used to not be able to keep friends. Like when I lived in Montana. Someone would be my friend for a month or two, and then they wouldn't like me anymore. But now it's not that way. I have friends I'll probably know for the rest of my life."

It's overcast outside. The sky is filled with big clouds. In Seattle two sunny days don't often follow each other. Jamie has her back to the window. Todd is watching the kids pass by on the street.

"Even though some of my friends can handle my dad, not all of them can," Jamie says. "Sometimes I would go out with guys, before I met Todd, and it would be real important for me to make a good impression. They'd find out that my dad was queer and they wouldn't go out with me again.

"I'd tell them, 'You know what's going on in my house?' And they'd say, 'what?' 'Well, my dad and Justin live together as a couple, and they're lovers.' They'd freak out. They'd walk right by me in the halls and wouldn't talk to me. But that didn't happen with Todd," Jamie says. She smiles at him across the table. "Todd's really a special person. I don't know what it is about Todd, but I can be perfectly honest with him, about anything." Todd breaks into a big smile. "He didn't freak out. He really doesn't care what my dad is. He only cares what I am."

Jamie sweeps her hair back from her face. "Like I was talking to a friend on the phone yesterday. I asked her if she'd like to eat dinner and spend the night at our house. She said, 'I don't know if my mom will go for that, because I think she knows about your dad.' My dad went over there the other day to pick me up, and after he left her brother said, 'Oh, boy, isn't he cute? He seems like a bloody faggot.'

"I told my friend, 'I feel bad about that. I feel bad that your family feels that way. You're my friend and I want to be able to get along with your mom and dad just as well as I get along with you.'

" 'It doesn't matter what they think,' she said. 'It doesn't matter to me. They're not here to judge you.' " Jamie shrugs. "This girl hates her parents. She told me. She can't stand them. But I felt bad that her mom couldn't be open enough, and broad-minded enough, to handle something like this. She's such a religious, godly woman. She's so clean. Their family is very, very religious."

Jamie looks over at Todd. She sighs. Todd reaches across the table and takes her hand. He is very affectionate with Jamie. When they are together he usually keeps his arm around her, or as they sit somewhere, Todd will lean over and kiss her on the cheek for no special reason. Jamie likes that, she likes that kind of attention.

"I used to always want to take my friends home to my house," Jamie says. "And then I'd think, um, my dad's pretty weird sometimes, maybe I shouldn't." Jamie laughs. Todd laughs too. "Like he might say in front of my friends, 'This is Jamie's mother', about Justin. It's a big joke, ha-ha-ha. Or my dad might be sitting on the couch playing with Justin's foot." Jamie's smile fades. "To me. I'm pretty used to that. But to someone else it looks pretty weird. It looks pretty weird to me, but to someone else from a straight home, to come over to my house and see something like that—" Jamie rubs her forehead. She shakes her head as she thinks about it. "—I'd just rather not be embarrassed."

****

"Well, if Justin is in the living room," Tom says, "and I'm going out, I'll give him a quick kiss or something like that. But we don't sit around holding hands, or fondling, or embracing. I wouldn't do that with Jamie's mother and I wouldn't do that with Justin.

"When I was married I might tell Jamie's mother that I love her and put my arms around her and give her a kiss, to show affection. But unless we were alone I wouldn't show passionate affection." Tom laughs. "I wouldn't embrace her and bend her over backwards and lose my tongue halfway down her throat. No, I wouldn't do that with a woman and I wouldn't do it with a man either."

Justin laughingly shakes his finger at Tom. "You watch yourself, young man," he says. Tom smiles.

"One time I remember, we were all in the kitchen and Justin came over and gave me a big hug. Jamie saw us and said, 'hey, I need a hug too.' So, she started squirming up in between us. She wiggled in so that Justin and I had our arms around each other, and Jamie was in the middle with her arms around both of us.

"I could sense Justin's feeling of tenseness. He felt she was intruding—"

Justin interrupts. "I didn't want to let go. It was just that I wanted to be next to Tom at that particular moment. Jamie came squirming up in-between us, and I didn't want to be bothered with her at that moment," Justin says in an apologetic voice. "That was my moment. Any other time of the day or night would have been fine. But I got really upset about that."

"See, I felt much differently than Justin," Tom says. He gives Justin a sympathetic smile. "Instead of being angry I felt, 'you poor little cuss.' Jamie wanted to be a part of it, she wanted to share it. She didn't want to be threatened that Justin was taking away something that she couldn't share, that she couldn't experience, that she couldn't have."

Justin agrees. "I couldn't tell her to beat it," he says. "I wanted to, but I couldn't."

"I felt good about it," Tom continues. He nods to Justin, so that Justin won't feel put down. "But I felt like it was kind of a breaking point, really climactic. Jamie finally came and crowded in between us. She was saying, 'hey, you two have something special, but remember me. I'm in the middle. I want to share it with you.' "

Tom is smiling. He leans back in his chair. "I knew Justin was upset, but I didn't look at it like 'this is our moment, get away.' I was really excited about it."

****

"I'm interested in Todd, I'm interested in moving out on my own and I'm interested in making money," Jamie says. Todd has gone to class. He wanted to take Jamie with him but she wasn't ready to go. She said she'd be along in a minute.

"I'm interested in art, all kinds of art. I like to make things with my hands. I can go to art class and the time goes by so fast. Or I can go to another class and it seems like I'm there for a hundred years." Jamie puts her hand on her forehead as she thinks. "My dad says I just like punk rock music, but I have some classical albums and when he's not there I listen to them. I would never let him catch me, though. He'd probably give me such a hassle." Jamie giggles. "I like to shop, I like to buy clothes," she says. "I'm interested in me. I'm interested in people I want to be interested in. And I'm interested in being better than my mom and dad."

Jamie only has classes half a day. Then she takes the bus downtown to her job. Her job is telephone soliciting people to buy condominiums in Hawaii. Jamie likes working. She especially likes making her own money. Jamie doesn't have that same enthusiasm for school. She rarely misses work, but she often doesn't go to classes. And even when she does go, for the most part she's just going through the motions.

"I get really bored with schoolwork," Jamie says. "I feel like I've gone through school and haven't participated. I haven't taken what I should have, I haven't learned anything. You know? I've learned, but I haven't really learned. Not how I'm capable of learning. Because I'm smart. I'm a smart person. I should know how to snap those math answers off just like that." Jamie snaps her fingers. "But I don't. It's because I'm lazy, and because I don't feel like it." Some kids come into the diner and sit at the counter. Jamie takes that to mean that first bell is over. She should get going if she's going to make her next class. The kids are talking and laughing, making a lot of noise. Jamie stacks her books up in front of her.

"My dad expects too much of me, and I can't live it out. I think that's why we have our problems. He has me on a pedestal," Jamie says, looking concerned. "I don't think he should expect me to be the way he wants me to be. I should just be. You know? I should do what makes me happy, as long as I don't hurt anybody, or as long as I don't hurt myself.

"When Dad has expectations, sometimes I can live up to them and sometimes I can't. When I don't live up to them he's upset and hurt. But like I tell him, 'if you'd just keep your nose in your own business and not expect things from me, then we'd get along a lot better.' " Jamie suddenly seems angry. This is an argument she's had with her father more than once. "But Dad doesn't see it that way. He doesn't understand. I've tried to explain it a hundred times and he just doesn't grasp it. It goes in one ear and out the other."

It appears that Jamie is going to say something else, but she stops herself. She glances up at the clock. Second bell has already started. Jamie gathers up her books and rushes out the door to class. Her lips are moving as she talks to herself, walking down the sidewalk.

****

"When she would get home, she'd be on the phone until five o'clock," Justin says. "I would say, 'Jamie, is your homework done?' I might tell her that it was her night to do the dishes. Or I might calmly try to tell her to put the ironing board away, or take her clothes out of the dryer—just little things like that."

Tom is watching, letting Justin talk. "Jamie would get really resentful, like I have no business saying those things to her. And, in a way, I guess I don't. I don't want to be her parent. The last thing in the world I would want to try to do is replace her mother, or to try to establish myself as another parent.

"I would rather clean the house myself, you know? That way it gets done to my satisfaction. Her room is her problem, her laundry is her problem. That way it saves a lot of arguments. She won't get mad at me. And she won't start yelling, 'You don't have any right to say I should do this, or do that!' "

Justin is tall and lanky. At twenty-seven he is fifteen years younger than Tom. Tom and Justin are very different. Whereas Tom, for years, worked two and three jobs at the same time, Justin has had very little regular employment. Before he met Tom, Justin lived in L.A. where he was something in-between a prostitute and a personal companion for certain wealthy men in that city.

However, whatever Justin was in L.A., he doesn't seem to be anything like that in Seattle. He works as a nurse's aide in an old folks home here. It's not a job he likes but he plans to do it until he finds something better. He dreams of someday opening a flower shop. Justin and Tom have a quiet life. They go out once or twice a week. Other than the fights concerning Jamie, they rarely argue. They've been together for almost three years already. And each year seems to get better.

"I'm still impulsive, but I'm much more stable than I was," Justin says. "I think I was trying to use Jamie to help hold me down and not noticing it. I would do that by acting like a parent, by treating her like a kid. And that would really aggravate her."

Justin is smoking a cigarette. His cigarette is held lightly between his fingers as his hand droops down. Tom is leaning back in his chair, just listening. "I think if I were a next door neighbor Jamie and I would get along fine. That is until I would come over for dinner a few times, and her father and I became friends. Then I would be stepping on her territory. Not because I was someone going to bed with her father, just because I was someone taking his time away from her. That's our basic problem, right there."

****

The night is dark and the street lights are on as Jamie gets on the bus to go home. She worked at her job six hours today, in addition to going to school this morning, and she's exhausted. The bus has only two other passengers as it winds up and down the hilly streets of Seattle. Jamie absently watches out the window.

"I look like my mom. I look almost identical to my mom," Jamie says. "My dad sat down one day and told me right straight out, 'Jamie, you look like your mother, you act like your mother, you're a carbon copy of your mother. You remind me—especially when you get mad—you remind me of your mother. Sometimes the resemblance is so strong I can't stand to be around you.' "

Jamie shakes her head. "That's not fair to me at all. I don't see any reason in the world why—why someone could tell me that I'm wrong for wanting to get out of this situation. We don't fight as much as we used to. I just decided I wasn't going to any more. If I don't make Dad mad at me, and if I don't scream and yell at him, then he's not going to scream and yell at me. And if he does scream and yell at me, I just tune him out. I tune my ears out. That way I'm not reminding him of my mother."

When the bus stops at Woodland Street Jamie gets off and climbs the steep hill home. There's a note on the kitchen table from Tom. It says, "Justin and I are out for a couple hours. Your dinner is in the oven." Jamie opens the door to the oven and takes out a plate with rice and fish. She sets it on the table.

Jamie picks at her food. She takes a tiny bite of fish and a fork full of rice. She doesn't have much of an appetite. Todd is supposed to stop over later, around nine. Todd also works an afternoon job. After he goes home from work, he often takes the bus to Jamie's. He can only stay at her house an hour before it's time to go home, and that's a lot of traveling for an hour together. But Todd doesn't seem to mind.

"Sometimes my dad wants me to be a little kid, and sometimes he wants me to be an adult," Jamie says. "He'll have me do a little kid thing one moment and I turn around and he'll expect me to do an adult thing and handle an adult thing the next. He does this to me. I end up running around in circles all the time, until I'm exhausted and I can't handle it.

"Like the exact time when I talked to him on the phone and he told me he was gay he said, 'There's something that I didn't tell you before. I want to open up and tell you—I'm gay.' I said, 'Okay, there's something I want to tell you about.' This was in the same conversation.

'You accused me of not being a virgin when I lived with you, and I was, but I'm not anymore.' And he freaked out."

Jamie leans on the table. She rests her head on her hand. The apartment is quiet and still, and almost every light in the place is turned on.

"My dad gets hurt, but he gets himself hurt. It's his problem if he's disappointed when I don't go to school. It's not really that bad. It's not that bad if I skip school. And if it is that bad, then it's for me to deal with. I'm the one that should be disappointed.

"Everybody disappoints everybody," Jamie says emphatically. "I mean, nobody can—you can't expect anybody to always be good and always do good. That's impossible. I'm always disappointing my dad. And he's been disappointed a lot."

Jamie takes another bite of her fish and then she pushes her plate away. Jamie hasn't had much of an appetite lately. And sometimes when she does eat, afterwards she feels sick. Jamie stares out the window. The lights in all the homes in the valley are shining brightly.

"I can remember when we lived on the farm and my mom was going to leave my dad. This was way before the divorce. I walked out in the barn to go feed my horse and I saw my dad. I had never seen my dad like that before. I mean, I had seen my dad cry, but I had never seen my dad sob. He was holding onto the neck of his horse, sobbing.

"I don't think he knows that I saw him. But it made me feel so bad. It made me feel really disgusted toward my mother." Jamie's voice is shaky. It sounds on the verge of cracking. "If that was Todd, I'd be out there talking to him. I wouldn't be in the house calling him every name in the book.

"I think they're both little kids," Jamie says. "I want to be better than they are. I mean, he wasn't a little kid in that instance, because I don't think you're a little kid if you cry. But I think my mom was a little kid by not understanding, by not taking the adult route and going out there and saying, 'hey, okay, let's work this out. I do love you, Tom. You're my husband. We have four children, we've got a beautiful home. We can make something if we work together.' But she didn't do that. Instead, she's in there calling him every name in the book."

****

"I don't consider myself a gay person," Tom says. "I really don't feel gay. Gay, to me, has been painted as very deviant, and I don't feel that way at all. I'm just a human being who prefers to go to bed with a man I can relate to in a way I haven't been able to relate to women. If I were living with a woman, I'd be doing exactly the same things, fulfilling the same responsibilities, that I am living with him."

Tom and Justin are in a gay bar downtown. Justin is playing pool while Tom talks. The bar is made up of an area with tables, a long bar with stools in front, and there is the one pool table with the light hanging from a cord above it. Tom is sitting where he can watch Justin as he plays pool.

"I can accept things now. I can say, 'Oh, yes, I messed this up but next time I won't do it as badly.' When I was married I couldn't do that. When I was married and I screwed up it was, 'Oh, boy, I've really done a good one this time. I'll never be able to rectify this mistake.' I'd feel really badly, and I'd beat myself to death over it.

"I wasn't making enough money. I wasn't getting the house remodeled when my wife thought we should do it. I didn't put in a garden when she thought we should have a truck farm, I had horses when she didn't like horses. I got involved in raising hogs when the market was up, and then the price of grain went sky high and the hog market dropped so low that I lost $3,000 in one year. And that was money I was going to use to remodel the house. I felt guilty about my judgments, my goals. I began to feel that my profession was a feminine profession, that I shouldn't be in it in the first place."

Justin makes a good shot and motions to Tom, "did you see it?" Tom shakes his head. The bar is practically empty. People will start coming in a little later, around nine or ten.

Whenever Tom gets to talking about those years of his life, and about his family, he can't stop all the thoughts that come racing back. Thoughts of his kids who he hasn't seen for two years now, thoughts about those years in Montana. Justin leans over the table, he shoots.

"I think I lost a lot of trust when I was married," Tom continues. "I spent a lot of time feeling badly about what I had done wrong. The main thing I did wrong in my marriage was trying to fulfill someone else's expectations of me, when I just couldn't do it.

"I know Justin cares about me, and I care about him very much. But when something gets to feeling too good, I almost feel like—wait a minute, I should sit down and analyze this. Am I letting myself get into a situation where it's all going to blow up? Am I going to wind up back where I was again?

"This is very difficult for me," Tom says, squinting his eyes. "Because right now we're looking into buying this house. There are so many things—the papers, the appointments, the credit reports, everything. It's bringing back all the memories about when Rita and I bought our house. And then after we did, and we were all excited about getting it, everything blew up. It wasn't right at all.

"I keep thinking it isn't going to happen this time. I'm being cautious to make sure it won't, but I have no way of controlling it. I mean, I have really been nervous and anxious lately. I want this house more than anything. But on the other hand, it would almost be a relief if the woman called today and said, 'you don't qualify. You can't have the house.' " Tom looks over at Justin. Justin smiles at him from across the room where he's sitting next to the pool table. "Then I wouldn't have to worry about it. I wouldn't have to go through everything I've been going through."

****

"I don't think my mom had any more head trips on her than she's laid on me," Jamie says. "And I overcame them." The clock over the sink says 9:00. That's when Todd said he'd be by. Jamie has been anxiously listening for him. "It's obvious that my dad loved my mom that he loved her as much as Todd loves me. At least I think he did.

"My mom can tell me sex is dirty until doomsday now and I'd laugh in her face. I don't really care what they say about sex. They don't experience it like I do, with Todd. I'm the one with Todd, not them. In fact, I don't think sex is dirty, even a one-night stand. You learn, I learned from it. It might not be what I would choose to do now, but I'm glad I did some of the dumb things I did. Now I know that a one night stand isn't half as important to me as being with Todd."

Jamie gets up and walks down the hallway to the door. She turns on the porch light. There's a breeze outside. The wind makes an eerie whistle as it blows around the corner of the building. Jamie stands there in her pink pants, her white blouse, and her white shoes. She looks very pretty. But one moment Jamie seems very attractive, and the next moment, looking at her, she seems worried, and an unhealthy kind of skinny.

"I've found love, and give and take," Jamie says. "If I couldn't find it at home I was going to find it elsewhere. Now I'm happy because I can come home and instead of thinking, 'God, my dad doesn't tell me he loves me enough, or he doesn't do this or he doesn't do that', and thinking negative, I'll come home and I'll think about Todd. Then it's easier for me to handle things. It's easier for me to think, 'Well, Todd does love me. He does satisfy me and make me happy and make me feel good.'"

Jamie sits down on the windowsill. She rests with her back against the window. "I'm just giving myself a break right now, for my own sanity, you know?" Jamie's voice is low. "I haven't thought about my mom, and I really haven't thought about my dad and Justin for a couple months now. I'm not dealing with some things that I should have dealt with when I was younger. But the reason I'm not dealing with them is because I can't, and because I don't feel like putting myself through the wash any more.

"I just got to the point where I was tying myself in knots trying to figure it all out," Jamie says. "The problems with my mom and dad... I still don't have those figured out in my head. I still don't have everything set and exactly worked out with myself. But I'm not going to go through it any more. It's done and over with. So why go over it and over it and over it. That's how I see it at this point."

The doorbell rings. Jamie jumps up to let Todd in. "You're late," she tells him.

Todd smiles. "I know," he says. Jamie is looking at him like she's angry. "This is the quickest I could get here." Jamie suddenly takes his hand.

"Come on," she says, "keep me company while I finish this?" Jamie pulls on Todd's arm as she practically runs back into the kitchen. Todd follows her smiling.

****

The bar is just filling up when Tom and Justin decide to leave. They aren't ones for staying out late. Tom is not in any hurry as he drives his blue Toyota through the quiet downtown streets. Justin relaxes with his head against the headrest. "Jamie has never really accepted the divorce," Tom says. "She loves me, but in a way she's sort of angry because I put her in this position. Her mother did too, but Jamie can't get to her mother. So she gets to me."

Justin smiles. "That's the truth," he says.

"I worry about the other kids," Tom continues. "I worry that Rita will put her attitudes on them. If my daughters engage in sexual activity, I wonder if they're going to be made to feel like Jamie did, that it's dirty, and nasty, and wrong. Or if Mickey is more artistic, if he doesn't like to play ball and all those things, is he going to be made to feel inadequate? I got this bitter letter from my daughter Kim a while back. She wrote about suspecting me of being gay. She said I might fool the psychologists and the social workers, but I couldn't fool her, she knew what I was. It was a Kim I'd never heard before. It sounded just like her mother."

Tom's disappointment can be seen in his eyes. He hasn't been with his three kids in almost two years. After he moved to Seattle he visited them twice. But each time his ex-wife made it so difficult that Tom decided there was no chance of his kids accepting him until they were away from their mother.

Justin looks over and sees how upset Tom is. He puts his hand on the back of Tom's neck and rubs it gently. "I just hope that someday my children will see that this has made a better person out of me," Tom says. He sighs. "I didn't go off into a corner someplace, turn green and get two heads. I love my kids just as much as I ever did. I'm still concerned about them. I want to see them, I'd love to have a relationship like before. I just don't think that's possible right now.

"But I think it's sort of interesting," Tom says, his voice becoming angry, "that Jamie is doing better here. She's doing better living with Justin and me in a homosexual environment, than she was living in a straight environment with her mother and me. I'm not saying that everything is honky dory, that we don't have problems. I just think that that situation was much more damaging to the kids than the one that we have now. You know? She's doing okay here."

Justin slides over next to Tom and puts his arm around him. As they drive down the empty roadway the streetlights sweep slowly across their faces, first one light, then the next, then the next. Tom's jaw is locked tight. He stares in front of him with an brooding intensity that is lost on the quiet, empty street.

****

"See, when two people are married," Jamie says, "first off, they don't have any children. You know? Then they have kids and the family's molded. They're stuck together. They've got to be a family. But with Justin and Dad and me, we don't have to be a family. I don't have to be here. It's just like they're going out together, you know?"

Jamie is sitting against her headboard, propped up by two pillows, with her knees are drawn up to her chest. Todd is lying across the bed sideways.

"I always wanted to marry someone who is like my dad—but is straight." Jamie laughs. "I want to marry someone who has high morals and is honest and sincere." Suddenly Jamie shakes her head. "I shouldn't even say that because I don't want to get married. I think marriage is for the birds.

"I want to live with someone. Then after living with him first for a long time, if it works out, then I'll think about getting married. Because I've seen marriages where people think that everything is going to work out so beautifully, and everything is going to be a bed of roses, and then it turns out to be a hell of a mess. You don't end up just hurting each other. Usually in the outcome there's a couple of kids who get screwed up too."

"Any family you're talking about in particular?" Todd asks Jamie, jokingly.

She kicks at him with her bare foot. Todd jerks to cover his stomach, but her toes only brush his shirt. "Maybe," she taunts.

Todd grabs Jamie's foot. He pulls it towards him. Jamie strains to hold it back. "Damn you," Jamie calls out, giggling. She is straining to pull her leg back, but it's no use, because her whole body is sliding down the bed towards Todd.

"Todd! Don't!"

Todd puts her foot in his mouth. He gives it a bite, right on the big toe. Jamie screams. Todd releases her foot. "That didn't hurt," he says.

Jamie scoots back up to the headboard. She hugs her legs to her chest again. "It did too," Jamie says. She pouts and scowls at Todd. He just shakes his head. Suddenly, she starts laughing. She extends her foot to Todd. "It didn't hurt. Here, you can do it again." Todd takes her foot and pretends like he is going to bite it, but he doesn't. He sniffs at it, makes a face, and puts it down.

"Todd!" They both break out laughing.

"There's no guarantee that Todd and I will be together forever," Jamie says when she gets control of herself again. "Just like there wasn't any guarantee for my parents. I just hope if we don't stay together we don't put each other through what my parents put each other through and do the things that they did to each other." The room is quiet again. Jamie's smile has faded. "I know they still could have been friends if they wouldn't have ripped each other up one side and down the next. Both of them did. Neither of them is innocent in that respect.

"And Todd and I, both of us have gone through a divorce, both of us have gone through hassles with our parents. We've just had to deal with a lot. Todd's brother committed suicide and that really hurt him," Jamie says, looking at Todd. He doesn't show any emotion. "We have the same outlook on a lot of things. We feel we're close enough, and we care enough about each other, to stick together through anything."

Todd sits up on the bed. He looks as if he's not sure he wants to say what he's going to say. "I'm not disagreeing with what you said. But you know how you always told me, and it's true, that you can sit there and hate me."

"Not anymore."

"Not anymore?" Todd asks. "It wasn't that long ago that you would just sit there and tune me out and everything."

"It's true," Jamie confesses. "I can get mad at him and say I hate him, and it's just because I'm angry or because I'm hurt. Just like my mom did. You know? When Todd would make me mad. I'd tell him that I hated him. I'd feel that way until I could get calmed down to the point where I could get my senses about me again."

Neither of them speaks for a moment. Todd is sulking. He is wearing a distant expression. Jamie grabs his hand and pulls him towards her. At first Todd doesn't come, and then he moves up close to her. Jamie puts her arms around him. Todd starts to relax. He looks at Jamie and half smiles. She gives him a big smile back, and he kisses her on the top of the head.

"I wonder," Jamie asks, "I really wonder heavily if my parents cared about each other when they got married like Todd and I care about each other." Jamie picks the jewelry box off the table next to her bed and puts it in her lap. It's a heart shaped, metal box with red and white glittery stones on the top. "I wonder if something like what happened to them could happen to us. But I think I'm strong-willed enough to not let it happen, and I think Todd is too.

"I have a feeling that if my parents had stuck it out, they'd be happier now. If two people care enough about each other to get married, you can't just lose that. It doesn't just go away. It's just that the bad things overtake the good things sometimes."

Jamie puts her hand on top of the jewelry box. Her face is sad, but it also has a strange calm to it. She opens the jewelry box, looks inside, and then closes it again.

"I think we're good together," she says. "I think Todd and I are really good together. I've always, my whole life, wanted to be with somebody who loved me and cared about me. Not just a parent, somebody who would love me and care about me as an individual, and not a child. You know?" Jamie smiles, embarrassed. Todd reaches over and squeezes her hand. The jewelry box gets knocked over and the contents, earrings and necklaces, spill out onto the bed. Jamie giggles. "That's always been really important to me, always," she says. "And I think I've found that."

Update:

Jamie Granger

Spring, 1983

Joe,

In the few years since you wrote the chapter on our family I've gone through a lot. We all moved from where you visited us, and then Dad and Justin broke up. Justin moved out and I lived with my dad and finished high school. Then I went to beauty school and got my license.

Also, Todd and I broke up. He was busy in his career and I was in beauty school, and things just weren't working out. We went through a real hairy situation in the end. It got a little physical, physically violent. But we're still friends.

Right now I'm really happy. I met Randy, and we've been together for eight months. He's a really neat guy. We lived with my dad for a while, but now we've moved into a nice little house that we're working hard to fix up. We're at the point where most of the painting is done.

It's nice having a house with just the two of us living here. My friends all have roommates, and wild parties, but I'm not into that at all. I don't party, and I don't smoke pot anymore. I've gotten out of drugs completely. When I drink my limit is one. And I'm working really hard too.

I have a job at a nice salon. I'm also taking classes, learning how to cut hair better. I'm trying to get my life together. I have a lot of goals, things I want to do in the future. I want to do something really creative, something like art with hair.

It's working out better for all of us now that Randy and I moved into our own place. Dad and I are getting along a lot better. I think in the long run Dad and I will be better friends because we're not living together. The last year before we moved out, Dad and I fought the least we ever did.

Living with your parents after a while gets to be a real pain. When you're living with someone else they put a fix on your life. A long time ago I decided that I couldn't judge my dad, because he was him and I was me. But since I've moved out it's easier to be friends. I look at him through different eyes, since what he does is not in front of me all the time.

I haven't really seen my mom, hardly. I saw my mom, not this Christmas but last Christmas, for one hour. It was really weird. A lot came down on me. My mom's a really weird lady. I mean, Randy and I get along really good, usually. But it depends on where I'm at, where my frame of mind is. Because if I'm thinking about what my mother said to me and what my dad put me through, of course I'm going to be nauseated and freaked out about certain things, like sex. But if I let myself go, and I just think about what's going on between Randy and I, then it doesn't disgust me, you know?

It's a struggle for me to deal with things in everyday life—my anger, dealing with my anger is a struggle. Sometimes I deal with it the way my mother and father taught me to.

I fight, I let my aggressions out on other people whom I care about. I have real heavy mood changes up and down. These are things that I used to not really understand, but I've taken a look inside and gone, "why do I do this?"

If Randy and I get in an argument it might not be because he did anything wrong, or because I did anything wrong. It might be because I used to get angry at my dad when he did the same thing a long time ago. That's really hard to break away from.

But like I said, I'm really happy right now. I'm working towards a lot of things. Randy and I have a good relationship, a good friendship. We're working on it all the time. We're committed to one another. And Randy's a really special person.

The only thing I'm having trouble with is dealing with what I've been taught. But I think the more I work on it the easier it's going to be for me. My parents didn't set examples for me in a lot of situations. Because my morals and beliefs, my feelings and goals, the way my sexuality is—I don't know. It's really hard for me to explain because I get lost and start thinking about all those other things that get going in my head.

It's just that for me, I feel I have to break away from what both of them taught me. I need to go my own way. I feel that the way that I'm searching and the way that I'm seeking—that it's going to be right for me. It might not be right for my dad, or for someone else. But I think it's going to be right for me. And that's what I'm going on. That's what I'm hoping.

2022 update to the Granger family

Joe – Hello Jamie.

Jamie - I am just juggling balls right now, Joe, and spinning plates. I want to talk to you, and there is so much to express. But I really don't know what kind of take I could have that would make my dad and his partner look good.

Joe - Well, I'll ask you a few questions...

Jamie - But I love them. Even though my dad's gone.

Joe - If you don't want to talk to me now that's okay too. If you want to wait, we can wait a few days or a week if you'd like.

Jamie – No, that's fine. So my take as a child of gay parents, it's that straight or gay it's called humanity. How do we treat each other? How do we honor each other's differences? The deal is for me, I didn't come here for diversity, I came here for unity. I'm here for the greater light in the world. I'm an artist first, you know, and then I'm a woman, or I'm straight, or I'm this or that, you know. So, I don't know why we can't identify with people as people first, instead of labeling.

Joe - How did things go with you and your father since the book.

Jamie - Yeah, what happened with my dad was horrible. And it's very sad. And my mother's still alive. She's really rigid and angry, and vindictive and hateful toward me, because I loved my dad. I sat in her living room and said, I'm going to break the chain mom. All this negativity toward family members and exiling people and holding them hostage is no longer serving anybody. So, I'm going to love you, regardless of what you do, or where you go, or what you say. I'm going to love you in spite of yourself.

I was about 20 when I started doing counseling because I got in a relationship and I knew I needed to figure out why things were not working. And it was clear that both my parents were like children, they behaved that way.

Joe - What was it like living with your father after the book came out,

178

you were about 16 at the time.

Jamie - We were very, very close. And then I got my hairdressing license, and that's what he wanted me to do. I wanted to go to school for marine biology and he wanted me to follow in his footsteps. So, I got a scholarship to a beauty school and I ended up working alongside my dad.

Jamie - And then I went to Europe and I studied with some of the best hairdressers of that time. I was in Scotland and I modeled and I had photographs in high fashion European magazines because people thought I was beautiful. I didn't know that when I was young, because my mother always said I was ugly and stupid and my life was in the toilet. She was super abusive to me and anything that I did good wasn't good enough for her. And it's interesting at 58 years old to look back and say, I sure have taken a lot and it's a wonder I'm not crazy or vindictive or spiteful, but I'm not.

Joe - Were you open with your friends about your dad being gay?

Jamie - Always. And that's another layer of it, Joe. All my friends in high school were gay kids that didn't understand what they were or who they were. But they knew that I was an accepting person and so I ended up with really close, good friends all my life, many of whom were gay. And it's kind of interesting, because I'm not gay. But my best girlfriend in high school was. And she came from a very staunch, Free Methodist family that founded a church. And they were so hard on her.

Joe - You had so many things to deal with back then, even before you moved in with your dad. I think you'd lived with different family members, then you lived in a foster home, then you came back to live with your dad again.

Jamie - It's true, I went through living hell. And the thing is, nobody else in the family really knew what I dealt with, or what was really in the mix for me. They think that I just moved to the city and ended up having a really good time. I was in my late 20s and I had been doing a lot of counseling, Joe, trying to figure out where I was at. I truly did some strong work. And I realized that there's a lot more going on than just gay, in my family of origin. There's selfishness to the point where I feel like, honestly, I never should have been given to my dad to help him grow up.

Joe - What do you mean by that?

Jamie - The hard part was that I was his firstborn daughter. And in his eyes, I was his precious daughter and that's how he treated me when mom and dad were together. But his boyfriends hated me. They were jealous of me. They wanted to be the number one. Dad would choose guys that were like children and not emotionally developed. And then I was in the way.

Joe - So, there were step parent kinds of problems?

Jamie - It got worse when I was working with my father. We opened a salon together in the U district and I caught my dad messing around on his boyfriend. And it wasn't just with one person. I sat there for a year and watched him. And then after that he would come up to me and say, "God, Mark and I are so monogamous, and I'm so happy in this relationship, and just treat Mark like he's your mother", you know? He'd say these things to me.

Jamie - And God, my father manipulated. I was the kid, Joe, that was on his team, supporting him. I love my dad, with all my heart. But I sat down at one point and asked him, "what possessed you to get married and have four kids if you're gay? What would be in your head not to be true to yourself and know that what you're doing would affect your children, and my mom, and the ripple effect of that in our lives? What were you thinking? I just need to know."

Jamie - And he said, "I didn't know I was gay. I had no idea." Well, when we had his funeral, there were black and white pictures set out from when he was in the Navy. And there were things written on the back of those pictures that made it very obvious that this man was my dad's lover in the Navy, okay?

Joe - You had such a confusing education about sex. Your mom told you sex was terrible, was painful, and that men were selfish. Your father tried to be more positive, but it sounds like his example wasn't great either.

Jamie - Oh my God, Joe, after you did the book Justin and my dad broke up. And my dad had a revolving door of young men in and out of that place, and it was just horrible. At one point I knocked on the door and said, "look I have important stuff to do tomorrow. I have tests and you guys are keeping me awake." That's usually what the parent does.

Jamie - So looking back on my life, and my dad admitted it, he said, "I was the kid, you were the little adult". I said, "I know, I didn't get much of a childhood". I grew up having to be very serious and understand big people things when I was little. But the perspective of a child is a very different thing than the perspective of the woman pushing 60. My father got involved with men that were really problematic via alcohol or drugs. It's not my world. I had plenty of that growing up. So now I'm satisfied with my career, making pottery, throwing beautiful tea pots. That's what I like to do for fun.

Joe - When you were younger, you said that if you had sex with your boyfriend, usually you would get this bad feeling in your stomach and have to pull away. Did that continue?

Jamie - I actually met someone. I did not like this music at all when it came into Seattle. But I had a group of friends that ended up getting really, really rich and really, really famous. And this young man came after me like white on rice, and he ended up being in one of the world famous bands. So, I had a life at that point where I flew around in a five star Lear jet, and traveled all over the world. And we were going to get married and live happily ever after. But my family came after that energy so crazily. I realized there is no way that I will ever have peace and marriage. We will have to take on my entire family for the rest of my life. It's too big.

Joe - That's a shame.

Jamie - It was a nightmare. Now I live a peaceful, calm, meditative, quiet, beautiful life. Dad's life was chaos all the time. There was always something going on. Whereas now I'm very celibate single. And if I meet the right man, he's gonna have to be the right man. So yeah.

Joe - You said that your mom was scary when you think of--

Jamie - I opened up my own business at 24. Not a lot of people do that. But I'm a go getter. And I started doing hair on my own. And I did really well for myself because people liked me. I've been through a lot, and in the process I've learned a lot. I know that I'm here to help. And that's why I believe I've been through these things, to come to a place of understanding and maybe be there to help others.

Joe - That's wonderful. When you look back on it, what do you think about living with your dad and him being a gay parent?

Jamie - I don't think my father truly was gay. I have a theory. And I may be wrong, but I may be right. Some men consider themselves gay, and they call themselves gay, so that they can get away with the quirkiest shit as they possibly can. And it's a behavior that doesn't have to do with gay, it has to do with lying and manipulating and getting your way no matter who it hurts. And I watched that with my dad. And it was a disappointment to me when I found out truly where he was coming from.

Joe - But when you say you don't think your dad was gay, if he wanted to manipulate people, he could have been with women and manipulated them, but he chose to be with men that--

Jamie - He did that too. Yeah, he manipulated women. I have a deep spiritual life. And I think it's what saved me. I don't have a belief system like, oh, if you're gay you're going to hell. But what I would like to say is this. Women or men, what I feel is that you need to have a lot of love and care and dignity to take on that beautiful opportunity to help a person grow in the world. And I think people have manipulated, because they want to have a little mini me, and a protege of themselves, instead of the individual that they've been given.

Joe – It sounds like you're saying that you weren't taken care of, you weren't encouraged to be yourself.

Jamie - Exactly. I was supposed to be who somebody wanted me to be instead of me. And when I figured that out, the only thing I could do is be me and live well in my own heart. And step in a way of light and soul and develop that in me. But the more I did that the further away I got from my family.

Jamie - It's like I don't even think about whether people are gay or straight. What you're doing in your bedroom with a partner is not my business. And if you're happy with that person, then by all means, because love is love. But I saw a gay relationship that worked to manipulate, and I didn't see real love. And I guess it's my opinion that we don't knowingly hurt people that we love, just to get whatever we need. That's not loving.

Joe - But that doesn't necessarily have to do with your father being gay. Are you saying that your father wasn't very developed as a human being, and neither was your mother?

Jamie - Exactly. I'm trying to say that gay or straight, the bottom line is, you have to have a foundation for the child to grow. And if you're so busy in your sexual life, and your escapades, you don't have time to raise a child. Most of the time in a straight relationship when you have kids, sex kind of goes out the window while you're raising them. You know? And then you can find your way back to each other or not. Or maybe it stays that way. I don't know.

Jamie - But what I saw is that dad got his way. He wanted to have me live with him. But once he had me there, he just left me to my own devices, left me alone most of the time. And I kind of felt like I was kept like this little doll or something. But I'm not plastic, I have a human heart, and it's beating. My dad got what he needed. He played out his life on his terms. And his last words were, "I was here to have a good time." Those were his last words. That's what my sister told me.

Joe - I was here to have a good time?

Jamie - Yeah. That's what he said to my sister when he was crossing.

Joe - That's a pretty unusual thing to say…

Jamie - I love my dad very much, and I thought we'd work things out. I went and helped him take care of himself when he was sick. So honestly, the way that I look at it is-- it's not just gay. It's hyper sexual behavior. With my father, yes, he was gay and he liked men more than women. But there's a lot more going on that I've had to figure out that doesn't necessarily flow in a gay relationship, that can flow in any relationship. And it's unhealthy.

Joe - You call it hyper sexual?

Jamie - Yeah, I do. And I'm the opposite. It's like, Don't Touch Me!

Like, Don't get close to me. I don't want to play those games.

Joe - That reminds me of something you said in the book. You said, "my parents didn't set examples for me in a lot of situations, because my morals and beliefs, my feelings and goals, the way my sexuality is, I don't know, I need to go my own way." How would you describe the way you are?

Jamie - It's a way of loving. Because what they showed me was not love at all. And I have to go in a way of love, self-love first. You have to love yourself to love others. Otherwise, you're just displaying, peacocking. You have to have self-love and enough integrity to hold your own moral code. And I do. I'm looked at as the uptight one, but I'd rather be seen that way and laughed at than to go in the direction that my dad did. Because a relationship is a great arena for growth in life. And if you can grow with someone, and grow old with someone, there's substance in that relationship. But if you don't really have self-love, and you're always looking for someone else to validate how fabulous you are, then you're not really loving yourself. So how could you love someone else?

Jamie - And I know that sounds really stupid and contrived, but it's real. Because if you have a relationship without love, then what you have isn't a relationship. It's shipwrecked. It doesn't grow. It has no life force and it isn't moving. And eventually it will implode. And that's why I don't play games with people. I would never want to hurt anybody. But what my dad would do is, the minute he had a boyfriend he'd just throw me out.

Mom and dad were fighting over me to have custody. But once dad got custody of me, he just left me to my own devices. And that made it so that I didn't want to create my own family. I didn't trust.

Joe - So, when you say you're different than your parents, would you say that your parents were both selfish people?

Jamie - Absolutely. In my life, I have been stripping down to find the truth. And I find that their reality had nothing to do with mine.

Joe - You have been through a lot. You've had quite a journey. It sounds like you've experienced so much, some of it pleasant some of it unpleasant.

Jamie - I learned a lot through really working on myself and realizing that I was the mistaken zygote. I didn't fit anywhere. And that's okay. It's best that way. You know, what else do you do?

Joe - A zygote is a cell? Is it an embryo or something?

Jamie - I'm making a joke. Like the stork dropped me off in the wrong place. Like if I look at my life I'd say, I wish I was born to parents that actually supported me in anything. Instead of having me support them in their thing. Because parents that are children do that. Parents that are adults don't do that to their children. Right? And dad admitted it, he was like, "you were the little adult and I was the kid, and I wouldn't have made it without you. Thanks for being there for me coming out."

Joe - When I wrote this book, there was so much anti-gay pressure from society, that everybody in this book went through a heterosexual marriage before coming out as gay. They either hadn't realized they were gay yet, or couldn't admit it to themselves, or they were trying to prove to themselves that they could be straight. And then they admitted their sexuality to themselves and came out to the family. At that point the family went through a separation or a divorce. But sometimes when the gay parent came out, they had repressed their sexuality for so long that now they were going through something like a second adolescence in terms of their sexuality.

Jamie - That is exactly what I witnessed with my dad. He just went out, like, how can I say it... like a six point buck. And he'd bring people home, different ones every night, I'd have to hear it. I grew up around some pretty weird stuff. And that's not about being gay or straight. It's just that when he came out of the closet, he came out like a six point buck. I'm not kidding you. It was not easy to be around. He brought people home that were my age. And I'd be like, "Dad, come on, goodness, stop this."

Jamie - But eventually, once he found Mark and they were together, he just stayed with Mark. So, they basically got married. And later, my dad said to me, when he was really sick he would say, I could never love anybody like I love Mark. And then reality check-- dad, you were messing around on Mark. When Mark found that out he was really hurt, and then they worked things out and they got married. I think having my dad be the way that he was made me more likely to say, "no, this isn't healthy."

Joe - What you're saying is that any parent, gay or straight, who is so interested in their sex life, to the exclusion of being a parent first, is going to be bad for the child?

Jamie - Exactly. It isn't about gay or straight. It's about respect and love.

Joe - And looking after your child, should be the most--

Jamie - Exactly. When I turned 24, Joe, I rented a four-bedroom house and I opened my own business, at 24. And I paid my own taxes, and it worked really well. My clients loved it. I did three generations of women. And I learned a lot about myself and my abilities. But once I got things going, my mom came in and moved right by me and literally just picked my world apart. So, with the parents that I had, it's a wonder I survived and had any success.

Joe - When you're a child you are stuck with your parents. That's whose responsible for bringing you up and you can't do much about that.

Jamie - Truly, I brought myself up. My dad was interested in men and attention. There was little room for me. And at this juncture in my life, I'm trying to figure things out. People may want to come up to me and touch me and get all in my stuff. And I'm just like, No, Thank You! Six feet of distance with this COVID thing? I think I started that 16 years ago.

Jamie - So, yeah, I am warm but I'm well protected. And at this point in my life, I'm just in a state of shock about how I've been manipulated. So, I'm trying to take my life back after what I've dealt with. And I've taken a lot of guff from people. There's something about me that people don't listen to my boundaries, and they don't hear what I'm saying. Because I'm soft spoken. I'm small. Unlike a lot of people, I remained in good physical shape. Although I have fibromyalgia and a blood infection. And I think it's from a dog bite, not a tick bite.

Joe - Well, you've been through a lot. You've learned a lot.

Jamie - Yeah, well, I've been through a lot but I'm not gonna let it make me feel like I'm damaged goods. That's just the way it is. I will get through it. And I feel like now is the time in my life to really look at what I've worked for all my life, instead of feeling like I'm imprisoned by someone.

Since I have no kids, no pets, I pretty much could do whatever I need to do. So I will.

Joe – That sounds like an excellent plan.

Jamie - I'm so glad you called me, Joe. I'm sorry about all the rigmarole to get to talk with me.

Joe - Well I hope you find the right place, and the right environment. I think it'll all work out for you.

Jamie - Hey, the very best to you, Joe. And if you ever need any more info, give me a call.

Joe - I will. Well, it was great talking to you.

Jamie - Thank you, Joe. Take care.

Joe - You too, Jamie.

§

CHAPTER 4

The Leonard Family

Eric, age 8
Beth (Eric's mother)
Jeffrey (Eric's father)

Eric sits us up very straight on the couch. "My name is Eric Leonard," he says. "I come from Montreal, Canada—" he pauses for a moment—"Quebec, Canada, I should say. I live in a gay house. My father's gay. He lives with a gay friend whose name is Tim Brannan. And that's about all."

It's Saturday afternoon and Eric is sitting stiffly in the basement of his father's house. He is eight years old. He has blondish brown hair which is cut straight across the front at his eyebrows and hangs over his ears. Eric is tall for his age, and a tad on the heavy side. And he usually wears a pair of large square glasses, as he does now.

"Gay is a word that means men are loving men, or sometimes it means women loving women," Eric says. "It's very different from what some people are. And some people just DONT, AB-SO-LUTE-LY DON'T approve of gay people."

Eric's eyes are open wide behind his glasses. He is very intent on what he's saying. Eric has been interviewed many times, but always with his father, Jeffrey, never alone. Jeffrey is very involved with gay rights issues. Because of that, he and Eric have had a certain amount of media attention over the past few years. Jeffrey feels that he and his son are a positive example of a gay man raising a child, and he has brought Eric along with him to be interviewed by newspapers, magazines, and even on a talk show. So, Eric knows what he wants to get across. It's just a question of putting it into the right words.

"I think that gay people are fairly new. I think people are used to having plain husbands and wives doing their own thing without any gay people around them. And they don't even know what gay is. They don't even know the word.

"When someone says faggot, homosexual, and all that stuff it's sort of...well, faggot means gay to all those people who don't like it. The word is different. It's sort of different because it means that gay people CANNOT be allowed to live." Eric thinks for a moment. He squints his eyes. "It's not that they should die. They should just not be. Like, they should not EXIST."

Eric is speaking slowly. His whole face moves as he talks, and he uses his voice to emphasize his point. Eric seems nervous. His knees

are rocking back and forth as his hands are tucked under his thighs
However, the more he talks, the more he loosens up.

The basement is half Eric's father's study and half furnace and
storage area. The couch Eric is sitting on separates the two halves. The
study side of the room has two lights on, but the furnace area is dark
The light doesn't seem to penetrate into that part of the room. The
darkness is tucked in between all the metal parts of the furnace and
stuffed around all the cardboard boxes. Eric has his back to all that.

"Gay people bother straight people because straight people DON'T
KNOW. They just DON'T realize what gay people are, and what life
they are living. They just DON'T realize that gay people are part of our
society, and actually they're sort of twice as good as regular people."

Eric pushes his hair back from his face. "Gay people are, um, people
who in some ways are... more understanding, more knowing... and
more willing to stay put for a long time without complaining. Straight
people are just not like that. Unless they understand gays, and
somewhere along the line they want to be gay." Eric crosses his arms
tightly across his chest. He nods his head. "Straight people just don't
understand each other," he says.

****

"I'm a dream separatist," Jeffrey says. "I'm not moving to an
isolated place where I can only be in touch with gay people. I live in a
city and Eric goes to a heterosexual school. He watches heterosexual
TV. I think he has access to a far wider range of experience than any
child in a heterosexual family does."

Jeffrey is sitting at the dining room table. It's an antique oak table
with claw feet. There's a cup of coffee in front of him and the steam
still rising off it. Jeffrey is in a hurry. He has to leave for work soon
He teaches literature at a college in Montreal. Besides his teaching job
he is also involved in many projects within the gay community
Consequently, he is very busy. His schedule is such that he often has
to slot things into a few minutes here, and a few minutes there.

"The kind of thing that bothers me," Jeffrey says, "is the mythology
of heterosexual marriage that Eric is constantly subjected to. It's there
throughout the whole culture. We do have to live in a culture, but there
are things I won't subject myself to."

Jeffrey takes a sip of his coffee. He blows across the top to cool it down. "I cannot stand a neighborhood situation, whether suburban or intercity, because it's so predominantly heterosexual. And I will not move into one even for Eric's sake. If I could find one where I would feel at home, I would consider moving. But I haven't seen any sign of one.

"Eric goes to an alternative elementary school. Even though it's kind of a counter-culture school, the ruling ethos is still very straight and very nuclear family. I tried intentionally to become involved with his school, but I simply could not go with that for very long. I didn't like being around the other adults. Despite the fact that we had kids the same age, in the same school, we had almost nothing else in common. There was nothing I was passionately interested in that they could understand, or wanted to understand, or wanted me to talk about."

Jeffrey often wears a concerned expression. The lines around his eyes give him a thoughtful appearance which people trust. On the other hand, he sometimes seems humorless, which he isn't. It's just that his sense of humor, like his private life, is something he shares primarily with his friends.

Jeffrey is thirty-five years old. He has short brown hair combed to the side, a mustache, and he wears gold wire-rim glasses. His triweekly trips to the YMCA are another commitment he rushes to. His exercise program of running and lifting weights keeps his medium build in good shape for a man his age.

"It's not that I'm giving Eric more access to gay than to straight," Jeffrey says." What I think I'm doing, or what I'm trying to do, is give Eric a language and a permission to be in touch with his emotions. Fathers relating to their sons transmit male qualities, with male in quotes—qualities such as stiff upper lip, non-emotional, non-tender, controlling, intellectual, distant and so forth. I feel the real experience, for me, is one of developing alternatives to that way of father-son relating. And this is very much the same as what gay men have to unlearn about how men are supposed to relate to each other. We develop qualities that are supposedly unmasculine or non-masculine, non-competitive, non-aggressive and so forth."

Jeffrey's voice is very even when he talks, unflappable. If he wants to emphasize something he will put a space after a word rather than raise his voice. As Jeffrey talks, Eric comes downstairs. He fixes himself a piece of toast, pours himself a glass of orange juice, and goes back upstairs. Eric is watching TV in his room. He's waiting for Jeffrey to tell him when it's time to leave for school.

Jeffrey closes his eyes for a moment while he thinks. He takes in a big breath and opens his eyes. "I would be happier if Eric grew up to be gay," he says. "I could relate to him better. I've told him that at least once. Well, this past week I remember saying it to him. We were talking about a questionnaire that I was filling out that asked if I was gay or straight."

Jeffrey's hands are clasped in front of him. He leans forward. "I said to Eric, 'if you're gay I'll probably have a lot more in common with you, and it will be easier.' I don't think I said happier, I think I said easier. I mean, I would have to think very hard to think of close friends of mine who are straight." Jeffrey pauses. The sound of the T.V. can be heard faintly from upstairs. The cat is lying on the chair next to Jeffrey, purring. "But I also tried to make it clear to Eric that I'm really very fond of him and that I hope the relationship will be a nourishing one no matter what."

****

"Something I should say, which I don't know if I want to go in the book or not, but I just want to be clear about where I am..." Beth is talking fast. She smiles as she tucks her hair back behind her ears. "Since I separated from Jeffrey I've been dealing a lot with my own sexuality—as we all do—and what I realized a month ago, was that I really needed nurturing from women. I was ready for another sexual relationship with a woman if that happened, if that worked out." Beth breaks into a wide smile. "And it has happened."

Beth has straight brown hair parted in the middle which falls below her shoulders. She has an aquiline nose, and one can't help but notice the dark lines under her eyes. Even when she's smiling her deep set eyes look tired. Beth dresses conservatively. She wears warm clothes and dark colors. And her fingernails are bitten down to the quick.

"I think it's important to say my history. I had sexual relationships with women when I was twenty-one. I didn't know about lesbianism or anything like that. I just did this thing and it was lovely. It was always, 'well. I'm gonna do this and that's fine, and then we'll all grow up and get married'." Beth laughs, a nervous laugh.

"With Jeffrey it was more, 'I want to be normal'. He had told me that he felt he was gay. But I assumed Jeffrey was in the same place I was. And I didn't think about it much, except that it was interesting that he had this thing in his background that I had in my background."

The arrangement that's been worked out is that Eric stays two weeks with Beth and then two weeks with Jeffrey. It's like a co-custody agreement without a divorce. The apartment where Beth and Eric are living is made up of a first floor and a basement. The first floor is three small rooms; a dining room, a living room, and a kitchen. The basement is one big room that's been remodeled. The floor has a thick blue carpet and the walls are paneled with rough cut pine boards. When the sun comes in the small windows, it reflects off the boards and gives the room a warm orange glow.

The basement is where Beth and Eric both sleep. Beth's bed is on one side of the large room and Eric's is on the other. At the back of the room is a little carpeted stairway with three steps leading up to a bathroom and a closet. Beth is sitting on the steps.

"In my heart of hearts, of hearts, of hearts—", Beth says, giving a sudden big smile, "—I would probably prefer that Eric not be gay. It's for very, sort of, selfish reasons too. Like grandchildren and needs that I have around a nuclear family. There's still that yearning in me that revolves around those kinds of family relationships. Because I never really had them. As soon as Eric was born Jeffrey immediately started backing off. He started pulling away.

"But I don't have any qualms about Eric being gay. I suppose that comes from who I am. I haven't ever felt bad that I have had feelings for women. I haven't ever felt uncomfortable with my sexuality. I've always felt that who I love is who I love. There are times when I love women and there are times when I love men." Beth gives a loud laugh. It lasts only a moment and then Beth's face slowly becomes serious again.

"I mean, I've always felt that if my son chooses to be gay, then he chooses to be gay. I would deal with it the same way I deal with anything in him. 'How do you feel about it, kid? I feel good about it if that's what you want.'" Beth picks at the rug with one finger. "I feel comfortable knowing he has options. I don't feel comfortable with the idea of him not exercising those options because he might feel his parents want him to be a certain way. That would really upset me."

Beth's home is not elaborate, but it's cozy. Eric seems to feel more relaxed here. He and Beth play together; indoor games, outdoor games. They act out silly little plays. And Beth doesn't care if he messes up the apartment. She's not neat the way Jeffrey is.

There are two small windows in the basement and those are both in the corner behind the stairs. They look out on the driveway. The night-light is on outside. Inside, there is a row of track lighting in the center of the ceiling, with three lamps that point in different directions.

"Eric went through a period where he was kissing everybody at school, the boys and the girls," Beth says. "It got him in a lot of trouble, but he did it anyway. I remember at one point he told me that the kids at school didn't like him. And when I asked him why he said, 'Because I like to kiss. I don't see why people don't like to kiss. That's what I was taught to do.' "

Beth shrugs and holds out her hands as if to say, what can you do? Her eyes are open wide. "This kid's been taught that to be open, nurturing, and loving is a positive thing. He goes around in school kissing all the kids, even though he gets flack for it. He doesn't understand what's wrong. And he doesn't feel bad that he does it," Beth says with a wide smile on her face, "even though he knows it makes him different."

****

The basement is chilly. Eric doesn't seem to notice, though. He is sitting in the corner of the couch, holding onto the bottom of his t-shirt with both hands. His knees are shaking back and forth. He seems full of energy.

"The kids at school know that Jeffrey is gay. They know very much. Almost every day... well, when I don't like people I run after them kissing. See, they don't like kissing." Eric pushes his hair away from his face. "But even before that, they would call me faggot. They knew my dad was gay so they did it. They're just saying it to me instead of my dad, because they're afraid. They're afraid of my dad.

"Faggot is NOT a nice word," Eric says. His forehead is wrinkled up and his eyebrows are lowered over his eyes. "Not at all. It hurts my feelings when they say that."

Eric's worn-out gym shoes dangle above the floor. He's leaning on the arm of the couch. In front of him is a low coffee table, and across from that is Jeffrey's desk. One light hangs from a cord above the coffee table, and a big table lamp is at his elbow. Neither seems to give out a very bright light.

Eric pushes his glasses up on his nose. "When I'm grown up I would probably like to be gay." Eric laughs, a quick, nervous laugh. "I would like to be very much. Because it seems to me to be a very nice life—to be gay. Sometimes it isn't, sometimes it is." Eric's voice starts to crack. He swallows.

"Straight people DONT understand each other. And I'm like every straight person," Eric says. "I like gay people but..." Eric searches for the words. "I'm one of those people who likes gay people but who has all the habits and all the features of a straight person. I'm all straight. I'm just straight." Eric shakes his head, looking confused. "Like, I'm not gay, I'm not homosexual. I'm not a faggot. I'm not heterosexual— I'm none of that stuff!"

Eric's eyes shift around the room as if he is looking for what it is he is trying to say. He looks worried, and sad. "I am very different from the people I'm talking about. I'm not good. I'm NOT a GOOD person." Eric's voice starts to waver. "I have lots of things that I just don't like to do—but I do them, and I don't know why." Eric stops speaking. He takes several deep breaths. He starts again.

"I fight a lot. About nothing. I don't get angry. I just, oh, say there's this kid at school, okay? And he's just doing something and ignoring me, right? He doesn't even notice me. I just come up to him, for fun, and kick him. I don't know why I do it.

"Like with my friend Justin. He's very nice to me, and only sometimes fights with me. And all the time he fights with me we know we want to fight, just sort of practice." Eric's voice is low. He seems on the verge of tears. "It's just a habit that I do. I know that I shouldn't, and I try to stop. But I can't."

****

"I have trouble with a child's messiness," Jeffrey says. "Eric's room is a mess, completely. But his room is the one place I don't tamper with. I won't define the living room as a place that he can leave crayons and shoes and everything all over.

"I feel like the only honest thing I can say, whether I like it in me or not, is 'this is my house—this is not your house. I live in it all the time, you live in it half the time. I take ultimate care of it. You don't have the responsibility yet.' "

Jeffrey looks at his watch. He calls up to Eric to start getting ready to go. He continues, "Eric probably has the notion that there are only certain times, certain ways, that he can fit into the household as I run it. If I have people in, then he is either with us on our terms or he is asked to leave. If I am working or reading or whatever, then he has to fit into that or go to his room and entertain himself."

Behind Jeffrey in the living room is a black, baby-grand piano. The piano has a carved flower design on the front. It's very beautiful. When Jeffrey was younger he was quite accomplished on the piano, and he hoped to be a concert pianist. Every day he would practice for several hours. In the end he wasn't good enough, and he had to give that dream up. Now he plays his piano just to relax, or he plays a harpsichord he keeps upstairs in the guest room.

"One of my goals in parenting," Jeffrey says, "was to minimize at least the most obvious distinctions between grownup and child. So, I decided early on that Eric would call Beth and I by our first names, that his bedtime would be close to our bedtime, that his basic pattern of living would be close to ours. What I wanted to do was eliminate the authoritarian versus subordinate roles."

Jeffrey looks out the window. The light from outside reflects off his glasses. "But there's a lot of other stuff that's still there. I think I'm pretty much a tyrannical controller in many ways that I don't see too well. Indeed, this other emphasis has even blinded me to ways that I do control. For instance, with our reading. I don't tell him not to read certain books, but I do act as a censor. I'm ill at ease with the kind of sexism that runs through all the children's literature. Even the Bible, I think it's culturally valuable, he should know it. Yet it's tied up with so many values that I would just as soon not transmit."

The street Jeffrey and Eric live on is very quiet. It's made up of older, brick, two-family houses. Jeffrey's home has oak floors and intricate woodwork around the doors and windows. The windows facing the street have a design made of stained glass in the top panel. The house is in the Queen Anne style of architecture. It's very charming, with built-in cupboards and nice little details all around.

For the past year and a half, Jeffrey's lover, Tim, has shared the house with Eric and him. Tim's a graduate student working on his Ph.D. in chemistry. He works nights in order to have the lab to himself.

So, most evenings he doesn't get home until Eric is already in bed and asleep. Jeffrey and Tim are a couple, but they don't have a standard view of what that means.

"Tim and I don't go out much together," Jeffrey says. "I think the whole nature of our relationship is that we are private. We have a very deep relationship within these walls. I imagine that people who don't know that we are living together wouldn't even suspect, and people who do know might well think that we are simply sharing a house. Very few people know anything at all about the degree of emotional involvement and mutual nourishment that we mean to each other.

"Ours is a relationship that is growing and changing. When Tim has sex in the park or sex in the baths, or has a visitor here who spends the night with him, I'm only threatened if I think there's something wrong between us. If things are right, then I can really quite genuinely delight in that. I know how much fun it is to have sex with all that means— an intimate relationship with another person, being able to talk or not talk, whatever. I know how exhilarating it can be to be involved with someone that way even on a fairly casual basis. Right now I feel so meshed with Tim, we meet so many of each other's needs, that no one else is likely to be able to threaten that.

"I have no reason not to think that Eric sees friends coming over here, or me or Tim staying elsewhere overnight, as more or less the equivalent of his spending the night with his friends. When his friends come to stay they play together, they sleep in his bed, they wake up and watch TV, or whatever. And I don't sense that he sees anything unusual about my friend Keith coming over. He may have dinner with us and then stay the night with me. In fact, I wonder if Eric is even aware that there is such a thing as dull monogamous relationships among parents."

Jeffrey looks at his watch again. "I really have to go," he says. He doesn't get up though. He taps his fingers on the table as he looks out the window. It's a gray day outside. From where Jeffrey is sitting, he looks out on the backyard and the garage. The garage is empty; Jeffrey doesn't own a car. And the principal use of the backyard is for cutting through to get to the busy street where the buses come.

"Tim made it clear when we talked about living together that he did not want to take on regular childcare responsibilities. So, I think Eric is likely to see Tim as primarily involved with me emotionally and not with him." Jeffrey picks up his coffee cup and saucer. "But I do get the feeling that Eric is really very fond of Tim. He's quite physical with Tim in terms of playing, or in terms of hugging. Indeed, Tim has detected, and probably rightly, that when I have another visitor Eric is a bit protective of Tim and that relationship."

Jeffrey turns towards the stairs and calls out, "Eric! We should get going." Jeffrey puts his coffee cup in the sink. He stands just inside the doorway to the dining room, wearing a solemn expression.

"I don't think I've ever used the word love about my relationship with Tim," he says. "And I don't really want to." The TV goes off upstairs. There are jumping around noises. "I've made so many verbal commitments in the past. When I think in terms of the word love, it has for me so many deceptive meanings... controlling, dominating, fitting someone else into my pattern. It's a word I wish we could scratch from the English language."

The sounds of Eric running down the steps are followed by Eric charging into the dining room. He's wearing a t-shirt which isn't tucked in, and his big, hooded winter coat. "You ready?" Jeffrey asks.

"I've been ready," Eric informs him loudly.

Jeffrey puts his hand on Eric's shoulder. "We're going to have to hurry if I'm going to make my class on time." Jeffrey takes his coat off the hook and his scarf. He's wearing blue jeans, a button down shirt and his boots are still unlaced. Jeffrey bends down, and without lacing them up, he ties a bow in each one.

"You have everything?" he asks Eric, speaking softly.

"Yeah," Eric answers. Eric is carrying his lunch, which Jeffrey made for him. Jeffrey opens the sliding glass door. The two of them walk out onto the porch, into the snow.

"Zip up your coat," Jeffrey tells Eric. Eric does it. They walk across the yard and go through the hole in the fence. Neither of them has a hat on. A trail of white breaths of mist follows them as they walk to the bus.

****

Beth works for a department store in a new high-rise building downtown. She got tired of making pottery for a living and decided to try something different. Working in a department store is very different.

At 4:30 Beth files out of work with everyone else. She walks two blocks to a huge shopping mall that resembles a space city. It has an all-glass exterior and it covers an entire block. Beth passes by all the shops as she comes to an area filled with green tables and green chairs. The tables are surrounded by fast food restaurants of every description. There are bagels, tacos, burgers, pizza, egg rolls, and a juice bar. Beth buys a cup of coffee and sits down at the corner table. She takes off her coat as she begins to talk.

"Jeffrey had told me long before we were married that he was interested in men, but at that point he didn't want to be homosexual. It wasn't until Eric was born that he changed. That's when Jeffrey started going to gay political meetings. He came out in a reverse way almost, by joining groups first. It wasn't until Eric was nine months old that Jeffrey first slept with a man."

Beth picks up her cup and holds it in her hands. "Jeffrey's very different now," she says. "We both are, but with him it shows a lot more because he's chosen a totally alternative lifestyle." Beth takes a sip of coffee. She gives an uncertain smile.

"For a long time, every Wednesday, he would go to a meeting after work and then stay downtown with a lover overnight. That was as far as it went. I would be home alone, but I dealt with that and it was okay. Then as the years went by he started being out more and more. That's the point where things started getting hard for me to handle.

"I'm not a political person, not in the sense that Jeffrey is. I'm not involved in organizations, I don't go to meetings." Beth pushes her hair behind her ears. "When Jeffrey was always gone at his gay meetings I'd say to myself, 'of course Jeffrey has to do this. Jeffrey is so brilliant, so this, so that—so together.' That was one of my hang-ups, thinking that everything he did was more important than anything that I would ever want to do.

"Every time Jeffrey took a step back from me, in order to be more active politically—more active in his love affairs, I would just close off more. For the last few years I was with Jeffrey, I was just totally shut down. I developed a very simple life where I didn't have to feel or think about a whole lot." Beth rests her chin on her hand. She has a far-away look in her eyes. "It's like being dead all the time," she says.

A few of the restaurants are closing. Workers are cleaning off the counters and squeegeeing off the glass that separates each restaurant from the eating area. An older man starts wiping the tables off. He moves from one table to the next and tosses the trash into a metal garbage can on rollers. The man is heavyset and has a weathered face. He works slowly and automatically, with little interest in what he's doing.

Beth is staring into her cup. She looks up and sighs. "I had such trouble with the demands of a baby," she says. "It got off on the wrong foot because Eric never slept, and I was exhausted, and Jeffrey wasn't there. I was soooo tired. I had been sick almost the entire pregnancy. For two years after Eric was born it was like every day for me was survival.

"I would think, 'What can I do to get through this day?' That's how I felt. I didn't have any friends because we were in a new city. Jeffrey was off teaching, or at his meetings. And I didn't have the energy to do anything about it. Every day, my priority was just to get a little bit of rest. That was it."

Beth bites on the edge of her styrofoam cup. "I just retreated more and more and more. I don't really remember what I did with Eric. I had to feed him, I had to get him to bed. I had to love him and make sure he was happy. I don't mean happy-happy—but remaining open, you know."

Beth shuts her eyes. She seems flooded with all those memories. When she opens her eyes again, they're teary. She blinks several times. Her voice is lower now, softer. "I managed somehow to do all the right things, quote, unquote. In some of those cases my heart was in it. But in a lot of them my heart wasn't. Because I was so unhappy."

Most people have already left the eating area. All the restaurants are in the process of closing. The older man comes by and asks Beth if she's through with her cup. She nods and puts it in his barrel. The man wipes off her table and goes on to the next. Beth crosses her arms. She tries to remember where she was.

"When Eric was two, I put him in day care," she says.

"From that point things began to get better. I was able to rest some. I was able to get a job and help support us. At that point I started enjoying being with Eric more."

Beth smiles. "Eric and I have a lot of fun now. We clown around a lot. We do whole scenarios. If we're at the park, we're both climbing on the equipment. I don't get hung up on things like dirty clothes. I'm usually right in there getting just as dirty as he is.

"Of course, there are times when I have to be his mother. Like, 'No you can't do that right now', or 'I'm sorry but you really have to try to eat this.' That kind of stuff." Beth laughs, a slow, easy laugh. "But I really enjoy doing all those things with him. And now that he's older I enjoy his company very much. I value the time I spend with him."

Beth closes her eyes and rubs them slowly with her fingertips. "It's time to go, ma'am." Beth looks up, startled. The older man is talking to her. He has deep lines in his face. "We're ready to close," he says.

"Okay," Beth answers. She looks around. The place is empty. Beth picks up her purse and puts it over her shoulder. "I'm sorry if I stayed too long," she says.

"Nothing to be sorry about," the man tells her. She smiles at him, and he half smiles back. He walks away.

Beth looks around surprised that everyone has already left. It seems like she only arrived here minutes ago. She starts down the long hallway. The stores are all closed. Dresses and shoes hang in every window. Beth hurries her pace. There's something spooky about a mall this big when it's empty. She puts her hands in the pockets of her coat. Her heels echo as she walks on the tile floor. Click-click, click-click.

****

"Not all straights are bad," Eric says. "Just plain old straight people are okay, if they have one exception, which is..." Eric is thinking, searching for the words he wants. He finds them. "...that they believe in gay people. Like they don't hate gay people. If they improved of it, sort of. And they went out for dates with gay people."

Eric relaxes his shoulders and leans back against the back of the couch. He takes one of the big pillows and puts it in his lap. He hugs it to his chest. The light is on over the coffee table and the table lamp is on as well. Eric is sitting in between the two lights, where they overlap. Eric raises his eyebrows as he begins again.

"Almost all Jeffrey's and my grownup friends are gay. Except for my mother, she's not. But she likes gay people. She believes in gay people." Eric pushes the pillow back onto his legs. "Beth likes Jeffrey," he says, "but in a very kind way. She sort of loves him. But in a very... kind way." Eric shakes his head, unsure if that's what he means to say.

Beth and Jeffrey have been separated for over two years now. They both live in Montreal proper, but quite a distance from each other, certainly too far to walk. Eric goes to the same school he always went to, and that offers some continuity to his life. When they first separated Eric would spend one week with Beth and then one week with Jeffrey. Everyone found that too confusing, though, so they decided on two weeks with each parent. That's the way their arrangement stands now.

"Like sometimes, after a year or twenty years—" Eric says, still trying to explain this "—oh, let's say a year, a couple who is straight who have been separated and haven't been seeing each other, finally gets to see each other. Say the man is named Joe, and the woman is named Carrie." Eric is looking up towards the ceiling thinking out loud. "And say that Joe is going to be at Carrie's house. Joe is just sitting down on the sofa reading the newspaper when Carrie opens the door. 'Joe!' she yells and runs over to him. Joe puts down his newspaper. 'Carrie!'"

Eric waves his arms in the air. His voice is filled with the excitement of his story. It echoes through the basement. Eric lets his arms drop. He shakes his head again. "Beth believes in gay people," he says. "Like she thinks we're not awful and horrible, and she doesn't call them faggot. But Beth and Jeffrey can't do what Joe and Carrie did."

Eric makes a face. That also didn't exactly come out the way he meant it. He punches the pillow and squinches up his face. "They can do it. They can do it," he says, "but they hate it. They always kiss each other, all the time. But they don't go—" Eric picks up the pillow. He hugs it and makes mushy kissing noises. "Mumm, Muuumm, Mumm."

****

"Beth and I talked before we were married," Jeffrey says, "and told her that I was homosexual. I thought it was not a problem, though, that I had conquered it or something to that effect." Jeffrey is sitting on the piano bench, his back to the piano. "I'm pretty sure that I didn't think it was something that would be vanished in terms of my personality. However, I did feel that I would be able to live happily heterosexually." Jeffrey smiles. He leans back against the piano. "That was a long time ago," he says. "People change quite a bit."

At six o'clock, it's already been dark out for an hour. The street light in front of the house shines in through the window. Occasionally a car or a bundled up person, will pass on their way home. Eric is upstairs in his room, watching TV. Tim is at the lab and probably won't be home before midnight.

"I don't think I ever considered not having children," Jeffrey says. "We decided to delay a couple of years, and not have a child immediately. But there never seemed to me to be any question, of course one has children.

"The year of the pregnancy was a loaded year. Beth was having a very hard time psychologically and physically. I was in my first job situation, and it required all kinds of things that I'd never had required of me before. It was a very emotionally straining time."

Jeffrey seems more comfortable talking politics than personal life. He doesn't talk easily about his marriage. His voice keeps the same even tone. He just talks faster, and his face tightens around the eyes.

"When Eric was born," Jeffrey says, "my immediate reaction was one of immense depression. I remember standing in the subway and it descended on me like a big cage. The heterosexual family trap. I thought, 'I've got responsibilities now with a capital R. One takes out insurance policies. One watches the way one crosses the street because there's a baby back home.' There was just this big cage of the heterosexual life that was going to trap me," Jeffrey says. "And nothing seemed to me to be more desexualized than the heterosexual husband."

Suddenly realizing what time it is, Jeffrey gets up and hurries into the kitchen. He grabs two pot holders, opens the oven, and pulls out the stew that's been cooking. He takes off the top. The steam rises, bringing with it a rich, thick smell. Jeffrey pokes the carrots and the potatoes with a fork. Satisfied, he turns the temperature down and puts the ceramic dish back in the oven.

Jeffrey walks over to the windows at the front of the house. He looks up and down the street. Cars are parked along the curb, or in the driveways. Everyone is home from work already. Lights are on all down the street. Just having his face close to the glass, Jeffrey can feel the cold outside. He sits down in the chair beneath the window and lays his head back against the cushion.

"After I admitted to myself that I was gay, I thought that it would take a tremendous effort to preserve the marriage, but I wanted to. I had no sense of how we could end the marriage other than destructively. Beth was in a very bad psychic state. One of the things I have realized is that I married her, in part, because I thought I could save her. And I felt that to end the marriage would only make her situation worse.

"But I depended on it as well. For me the marriage was a kind of validation of anything and everything. I couldn't imagine myself without marriage. I used it. I think in ways I still do use it, or use being a parent, as a kind of validation to a straight society."

Jeffrey is speaking softly, with no hint of anger or confusion in his voice. His eyes look worried, though, he is squinting as if looking into a light.

"We've never had any disagreements about the question of custody. We both will remain jointly responsible for Eric. We will share time with him as nearly equally as possible." Jeffrey smiles. "Eric is able to talk about things in his life and help with the decisions that need to be made. He makes it clear that he likes both of us and he doesn't like both of us. He enjoys being with Beth more of late than with me. Because at this point I haven't sorted out my life enough to make room for him.

"I forget what the sentence was that he said—" Jeffrey closes his eyes and tries to remember. "We were in the process of working out the separation, and we were both very worried about Eric. We were trying to talk with him about it all and trying to make sure he had a chance to say whatever he wanted to say to get any feelings out. He finally looked at Beth, or me, or whoever, and he said, 'I wish you both would stop worrying about me worrying.'" Jeffrey laughs. "Eric can think for himself," he says.

****

As people walk by on the sidewalk Eric can see their legs through the basement window, their legs and the bottoms of their heavy coats. The neighborhood is quiet for a Saturday afternoon. The sun seemed to be about to peek through for a minute, but then the clouds came back.

Eric adjusts himself on the couch. He yawns. He's been talking for three-quarters of an hour already, and he's getting anxious. "Well, my day-to-day schedule at Jeffrey's is—I'll just tell it, I won't tell it in detail." Eric is sitting on his hands. "...I get up about 7 and read or watch T.V. until about 7:30. Then I get dressed. I just goof off until about 8:00 when I go downstairs, eat breakfast, and get ready to go to school.

"When it's time, I walk through my backyard and get to the bus stop. I wait for a bus and take the bus to a subway. I get on the subway, I go eleven stops, and I get off at a stop called St. Peters. I go up the stairs from the subway and get on a streetcar. By then I feel like falling asleep in class." Eric rolls his eyes and makes a face like he's drunk or something. He wobbles his head back and forth.

"I get off the streetcar at the fourth stop, which is called Oak Street. I turn right and then I tuuuurn, let's see... left. Then I turn right, then I turn, let's see..." Eric has his hands over his eyes. His lips are moving as he thinks to himself. "Forget it!" he says finally. "I get to school. I stay there till three o'clock. Then I come home and goof off. And I just stay here till about 7:30 when my dad comes home." Eric shrugs. He kicks at the front of the couch with the heel of his shoes.

Eric is wearing his brown corduroy pants and a yellow t-shirt with a blue star sewn in the middle. Eric doesn't play any sports in the neighborhood, and there are very few sports played at his school. One thing Eric is good at, though, and very much enjoys, are computer games. His specialty are the space games. They take a lot of skill and practice, and Eric plays them whenever he can.

It so happens that Eric can practice the computer games even at school. Eric goes to an alternative school with a very unique setup. Children can arrive or leave school at any time. They can study or play, according to their own inclination. And all punishments are given out by a rotating committee of kids formed from the group. The only real rule is that during the morning the children must do quiet activities so that those who wish to study will be able to. The school has a small computer which has programs for the space games. Many of the kids spend a good part of each day playing, and watching others play, the space games on the computer.

"When I'm home alone in the afternoon I do lots of things," Eric says. "I watch TV. I make haunted houses in my room. I set booby traps all over the place." Eric laughs excitedly. "I might put something like a foam toy on top of the door, or sometimes I lean a baseball bat against it. Then when Jeffrey opens the door, the thing falls down." Eric laughs loudly. "It scares the hell right out of him!" he says.

Eric kicks his feet against the front of the couch again. He's fidgety. He picks the pillow up and puts it in his lap. Then he rolls it down his legs onto the floor. Eric continues talking in a bored-sounding voice.

"In the evening Jeffrey makes dinner. He doesn't like eating early, so when I'm eating he just sort of hangs out in the basement and does all his essays from school. After dinner I go upstairs and watch TV. Later he comes up and has his dinner." Eric picks up the pillow and rolls it down his legs again. As it passes his feet he kicks at it, but misses. He leaves it on the floor. "About 9:30 I get ready for bed. I read comics till about 11:30," Eric smiles, to show he's exaggerating. "When I get real tired, then I fall asleep."

Eric puts his head back against the back of the couch. He rests there staring up at the ceiling. "See, there's one week where I'm alone, and then there's another week when I'm not alone, Jeffrey gets home early and we eat dinner at the same time. I sort of like it both ways. Because when I'm alone, on about Friday I get tired of it. Then when I'm with Jeffrey, I sort of get tired of him and want to be alone."

Suddenly Eric sits up. He makes a face, puts his arms out and lets his hands flap back and forth weakly. "Ohhh, I don't want to do anything," Eric mimics Jeffrey. "I just want to lie down and rest." Eric lets his head drop onto his shoulder like he's asleep. He falls over onto his side and makes snoring sounds.

"Mission boringness!" Eric says in a loud voice which is muffled against the couch cushions. "Your mission, if you should choose to accept it..." His voice trails off as he laughs gleefully to himself.

****

"We continued to have sexual relations until, I would say, four years after Jeffrey came out." Beth is cleaning up the kitchen. "That's right, for about four years. We didn't have sex that often, but we had it. It was the same kind of sex we'd always had." Beth puts the dishes in the sink. Eric should be getting home from school anytime now. "There came a point where I decided that I didn't want to sleep with Jeffrey anymore. I didn't know why. I just knew I didn't like what was happening in my life. It was that simple.

"What's interesting about the whole thing is that Jeffrey decided at that point that we should go to therapy because I was not having sex with him. Here he'd been going out with his men friends for four years..." Beth gives a soft laugh. "He was very upset," she says.

Beth puts the last of the dishes in the sink and squirts in the detergent. She turns on the water. It splashes off the plates. Suds start bubbling. Beth wipes off the table with a sponge. She wipes off the counter. A mound of white suds is rising in the sink. Beth takes a swipe of the suds in her hand and watches them disappear. She turns off the water.

"A lot of other things were happening that I was having trouble dealing with. Like all these parties were taking place at our house and there would be a lot of gay men necking in my kitchen and stuff. I really resented it. Also, Jeffrey was working in his spare time for the gay newspaper and he was literally always gone.

"Jeffrey and I had talked about eventually not being together anymore. We had been talking about that for a long time before the separation. We had even said to Eric many times, 'Well, you know we're not always going to be together.' " Beth wipes her hand on a towel hanging next to the sink. "Eric actually adjusted to it very well, I think. He'd really only been used to having one or the other of us around anyway."

There's the sound of someone walking up the porch steps. Beth runs around to the door and opens it just as Eric rings the bell. "Hellooo," she says in a singing voice. Eric is carrying his book bag. He walks in the house dragging his feet. His boots are untied and his heavy coat is unzipped. He looks tired. "What took you so long?" Beth asks. "I expected you a half hour ago."

Eric smiles. He likes the attention. He sets his book bag on the table like a little man home from work. "I was playing kickball at school," he says in a matter-of-fact voice. He picks up a paddleball toy off the table and starts trying to hit the ball attached by the rubber band. Suddenly he doesn't seem tired anymore.

"Give me a kiss," Beth says. She bends down and kisses Eric on the lips. Eric smiles and goes back to the paddleball. "Watch TV or play in here for just a little while," Beth says, running her hand through his hair. "I have to finish things in the kitchen. It will only be a few minutes."

Eric goes paddleballing into the living room, his shoelaces trailing behind him. He drops his coat on the couch and turns on the TV. Beth goes back into the kitchen and starts on the dishes. She takes a glass out of one side of the sink, wipes it with the sponge, and puts it into the other sink.

"Jeffrey and I agree almost down the line when it comes to raising our kid," Beth says. "We agree on what's the best way to handle Eric in a situation where he is angry, in a situation where he is being selfish in a situation where we're balancing our needs with his. There's constant consultation. We both babysit and we borrow money from one another.

"But what's nice about it now is that Jeffrey and I don't rely on each other. In many ways we're more together than we ever were. Because we deal with each other as real people now. I don't call Jeffrey up and say, 'What do I do now?' And he doesn't call me up to ask what to do It's like, we discuss things but there's not a dependency at all. We each have equal input and then a decision is made." Beth smiles her wide smile. "It's working," she says. "That's all I can say about it. My sense is that it's working."

Beth finishes washing the dishes. She unplugs the drain and lets the soapy water out. Turning on the faucet she begins rinsing the plates and setting them in the rack to dry. Beth picks up the silverware in one handful and rinses it under the faucet.

"There was a period of time when Eric was hitting kids at school a lot," Beth says, her face suddenly serious. She turns off the water and leans against the counter. "They called us in and we both went." Beth tucks her hair behind her ears.

"At the time I was living in a building where there were other kids for Eric to play with, and also Eric and I would play tennis and do all kinds of physical stuff. Then Eric would go to Jeffrey's and be expected to be a lot quieter. At my house Eric would be going 'rummn rummm.'" Beth makes a motor sound. "But at Jeffrey's he had to go more inside.

"I told Jeffrey, 'You're going to have to do other things with him. And Jeffrey recognized that and dealt with it. I'm assuming that's what happened because the hitting stopped."

Beth looks out the window above the sink into the front yard. The yard is outlined by the faint light that shines through the window from the house. Beth takes a deep breath and lets it out with a sigh. She turns on the water and hurriedly rinses out the sink."

****

"Beth takes me places where I would like to go. Jeffrey doesn't," Eric says. 'Oh oh, it's time to go to a meeting,' and I have to go too because I'm with him. And then the meeting lasts, say, from 7:30 to 11:30.

"When I go to those meetings I get so BOOORRED! I never listen. If I do I get even boreder. If I listen to one word I go, 'UUUGGH!' " Eric slaps his forehead and acts like he's about to faint.

Eric is sitting on the edge of the couch. He suddenly sounds excited. "Tomorrow I'm going to my mom's house," he says. "It's going to be spring soon and we can play all sorts of games we can't do in winter." Eric gets up and goes over to Jeffrey's desk. He picks up the stapler and fools with it. Then he picks up a pink quartz rock that Jeffrey uses as a paper weight.

"Sometimes I get really lonely without one person," Eric says. "But then sometimes I don't like Jeffrey as much as Beth. Well—," Eric thinks for a moment, "—let's just say that I have a lot more fun with her than I do with him. That's for sure."

Eric puts the rock down and goes back to the couch. The room is quiet. Eric flicks at a piece of fuzz on the arm of the couch. It doesn't move and he keeps flicking. Finally, he picks it off and tosses it on the floor.

"My parents were never divorced. All they are is separate. They separated because they were arguing too much," he says in a matter-of-fact voice. "They're happy living apart, but they're not happy—umm, living together. They told me that. They said they had too many arguments—but I didn't care.

"I thought it was only bad if they had an argument every day. Like, first day," Eric breaks into a high-pitched whining sound, "'yahyah yah yahyah'. Second day, 'yahyahyah yah yahyah.' Third day..." Eric goes through each day, one at a time, and each day the screaming gets louder and longer. By the time he finishes the seventh day he's totally out of breath.

"And that's the whole week," he says between gasps for air. Eric sticks his tongue out, exhausted. He laughs. "That's not them. That's a family who argues every day. They didn't argue every day. I thought they had to argue every day not to like each other."

Overhead there's the sound of footsteps, and then water running. Jeffrey's and Tim's voices can be heard faintly coming from the kitchen. Eric looks back over his shoulder toward the sounds. The water stops and there's clanking of dishes. Then the footsteps go across the floor and up the steps. The room is quiet again.

Eric leans back against the back of the couch. The furnace kicks on with a "thunk." Startled, Eric turns around. He looks into the dark part of the room behind him. There's only the soft "whurring" sound of the flame burning the gas. Eric turns back. He crosses his arms over his chest.

"I always wanted to be as far away as I could when they argued," he says. "But I'm very curious." Eric gives an embarrassed smile, "I would peek." His legs are rocking back and forth again. "But I would never listen to their arguments. I would just turn off my ears."

Eric sits up straight. He adopts an English accent to his voice, the accent of an English gentleman. "RAUTS!" he says, "A SECRET TO MAUNKIND!"

****

The sounds coming from the piano are not musical. They are alternately a handful of notes banged at once, or single notes played at random. Eric is "improvising" for his father.

Looking at Eric's face you would think he was in pain. His jaw is set, his eyes are wide, and his lips are drawn tightly across his teeth. With his right hand, Eric uses one stiff finger. He pushes a series of arbitrary notes, or the same note over and over. With his whole other hand, he pounds all the notes in a general area. Jeffrey sits behind Eric. He shows little emotion as Eric plays.

Jeffrey would like Eric to practice the piano regularly. To encourage him, Jeffrey tells Eric that it doesn't have to sound like music. It should sound like whatever he wants, whatever he's feeling. Still, Eric doesn't rush to the piano. It would appear that he plays mainly to please his father.

The last notes die out as Eric finishes. Eric's hands are shaking. The wide-eyed, wild look on his face as he was playing is slow to vanish.

"That was very interesting," Jeffrey says calmly. Eric looks at Jeffrey and nods his head. "I liked the part where you were alternating a single high note with a group of low notes. The piece had a lot of momentum at that point." Eric nods again. He looks exhausted.

"You should do this more often," Jeffrey says. "You could even practice in the afternoon before I get home. In time you'd find that

211

you would achieve more control over what you wanted to communicate."

"Maybe I will," Eric says. He gets up and starts toward the steps, dragging his feet.

"Take your books and things," Jeffrey reminds him. Eric picks up his books and a picture he made at school. He goes slowly up the stairs, holding onto the bannister. A moment later the TV can be heard coming from his room.

Moving to the dining room table, Jeffrey takes his coat off and puts it on the back of his chair. He sits down. The cat jumps up on the chair next to him and Jeffrey absently pets it. He scratches it behind its ear and the cat pushes against his hand and purrs.

"In the past I've done a lot of reading to Eric. It's one time that we are doing something together that he enjoys and I enjoy, so I don't want to put it down," Jeffrey says, and he smiles. "But now that Eric has started to use the transit system on his own, I think that I'm going to have to start designing another time for us to read together. Because up until now most of our reading time has been on the subway.

"In fact, since he was little the pattern has been that I entertain him when he's here with me, and I'm trying to change that pattern now. As yet, I don't think Eric has a strong sense that he can do what he wants in this house, within the limits that I set in terms of order. I've tended to be constantly suggesting things when we're together, and I'd like to leave him alone more. So that the responsibility will rest on him to amuse himself and not on me." Jeffrey's legs are crossed. He reaches over and pets the cat again. "Right now that means he's watching more TV than I personally am happy with, but I try not to complain about that. I figure sooner or later he'll get bored with TV."

Jeffrey has his briefcase parked next to his chair. It's exam time and he's anxious to get started on the many papers he has to grade. Besides teaching a full schedule at the college, Jeffrey is the chairperson of a gay fathers' group, and a gay rights group. What spare time he has beyond that he spends working for a gay newspaper. Jeffrey is an extremely busy person. During the weeks when Eric is his responsibility, Jeffrey often has Eric take the bus after school and meet him at the newspaper. Or Jeffrey will bring Eric along after dinner to one of his meetings.

"What I've noticed about other fathers," Jeffrey continues, "is that they stop hugging their sons when they get to be Eric's age, or even younger. What's happening here is not that we—that I—am teaching Eric to hug. Other parents do it too when their kids are little. It's when the kids get older that they teach them not to.

"However, there is one thing that I will not allow Eric to do with me. We do not ever play with punching. If he wants to punch me I try to transfer it over to punching pillows. I just can't deal with the punching and the fighting situation." Jeffrey is adamant. He crosses his arms in front of him. "Eric is somewhere in between a bit combative and genuinely combative. And at times I think other people get more of that than they would if he could work it out with me. But I won't have it."

The wooden chair creaks as Jeffrey leans back. He takes off his glasses and rubs his eyes. "This all came up because Eric was called to committee several times at his school for beating on kids. There was a conference in which Beth and I and Eric's teacher talked about it a great deal. I'm drawing a blank right now in terms of what was said exactly... the tone was concern, but no real worry.

"His teacher thought it was probably, in some way, anger towards Beth, or Beth and me, or me, that was being expressed. We tried to see if that was the case by raising situations where Eric could talk to us about his feelings. At any rate, that pattern of behavior disappeared not long afterwards and he hasn't been rough with other kids since then."

Eric comes down the steps. He walks into the dining room. "Hello," Jeffrey says. "I'll be a little bit longer." Eric plops down on a chair. He leans his elbows on the table. "Do you want to sit here while I talk?" Jeffrey asks.

"Yeah," Eric answers. He rests his head on his hands.

"Okay", Jeffrey tries to remember where he was. He blinks several times. "Do you want anything to eat, some fruit or cookies?" he asks. Eric gets up and goes into the kitchen. He comes back with a handful of cookies. Three of them he puts in a stack on the table. The other one he starts to eat.

Jeffrey watches Eric for a moment. He seems to have lost his train of thought. After a moment he clears his throat and continues. "I have a real need to be with gay people. But unfortunately, there are very few situations where gay people incorporate children." Eric is eating his cookie in little rabbit bites. He nibbles his way across one side of the cookie again and again. He finishes the first one and starts on a second.

"This is why I helped form the gay fathers' group. I was hoping there would be an adult meeting and a simultaneous meeting for kids. As it turned out, though, most of the fathers are not out to their children, or they don't live with their children as I do. So, it's still an adult group." Eric is watching his father as he nibbles. "Other situations of adults together with their children, as at Eric's school, tend not to be a gay setting. And I tend not to be interested, Jeffrey says." Eric reaches for the third cookie.

****

"I think the parents at Eric's school like Jeffrey a lot," Beth says, "as a parent as well as a person. The mothers and fathers of the kids are generally, quote, 'liberal-thinking people.' They know that Jeffrey is gay and they seem to accept that in him. But that doesn't mean that they would want their children to explore it, or that they would even want their children to have a greater positive image of it. They want their kids to grow up heterosexual, you know? They would feel very threatened if Jeffrey were to come in and say, 'I want to talk to these kids about what it means to be gay.' "

Beth is sitting at the kitchen table. The overhead light is on and it shines on the white walls. The cabinets in the kitchen are unpainted wood with leaded glass panels in the doors. One can see the dishes neatly stacked inside. The door to the basement is closed. Eric is already in bed downstairs, asleep. From the living room the radio can be heard playing softly.

"I know Eric has a strong desire to please. I know that he's always delighted when he does something that pleases me or Jeffrey. I'm beginning to think that it can't help but affect him if he knows that Jeffrey would rather that he be gay. I can't say whether that's good or bad. I can just say that will have an effect on him. It may cause confusion, you know? Because at some point it may become clear that I would prefer he not be gay.

"These are still fairly new feelings in me to think of him in those terms. It wasn't so long ago that he was the little kid who sat in my lap. In fact, I went to school to pick him up the other day, and he was chasing this eleven-year-old around. She's very precociously developed. She was going, 'Whooo Whooo.' And Eric was saying, 'I'm gonna rape you—I'm gonna rape you.' She screamed, 'Don't rape me—don't rape me!' Just sort of egging him on. She's very precocious, already developing and everything. Finally, in the midst of this game Eric turns to her and asks, 'hey, what does rape mean?'" Beth breaks out laughing. The laugh seems to gather all the tension from her face and release it in one sudden burst. "What does he know?" she says.

The living room where Eric was watching TV all night is a mess The cushions are off the couch, Eric's clothes and toys are on the floor Beth is not a compulsive housecleaner. She cleans, but she doesn't follow Eric around cleaning up after him. A room might stay messy for a day and it wouldn't bother her.

Beth gets up and turns the burner on under the kettle. It makes a soft "whoosh" sound. Another song comes on the radio. It's a country song, with a woman singing. Beth looks out the window.

"The thing that worries me is what will happen if I keep seeing this woman I've been spending time with? What if we really get involved permanently?" Beth turns back towards the room. "This woman is only in town temporarily. She actually lives in California. I've already been invited to move back with her when she goes. But I don't know how that would be for Eric.

"It scares me to think that I wouldn't be able to see him every two weeks. And it's just as scary to think that I would be fully responsible for him if I brought him along." Beth gives a nervous smile, a little too wide of a smile to look comfortable. "Neither Jeffrey nor I want to be a full time single parent."

The kettle starts to whistle and Beth turns the burner off. The tea bag from her last cup sits in a spoon on the stove. She puts it in her cup and pours in the water. Softly, in the next room, the man on the radio is giving the news. Beth sits back down at the table. She looks worried.

"Maybe Eric could stay here for elementary school, and then go out there for high school. Or..." Beth shakes her head. She raises her voice as she explains, "I don't know. I really don't have a sense of what could happen. It's like, right now Jeffrey and I have to take care of ourselves first. If we feel good about what we're doing, if we feel positive about how we're relating to Eric, then Eric will respond to that and he will feel good about himself.

"Admittedly it's not an arrangement that has a lot to do with Eric's needs. We want to do what's right for us right now. We figure the rest will follow." Beth stops talking as she stirs her tea. She sounds tired.

"It seems to be working," Beth says softly, "that's all I can say. But I do worry about Eric. I worry about Eric if I decide to leave."

****

Eric is watching something outside the window. He sits on the couch and his lips are moving as he talks to himself. This interview hasn't been like the others. Eric is finding himself talking about all these confusing thoughts. Although he is anxious for the interview to be over, part of him wants to continue. He wants to see if, as he talks, he can draw together and express the many different thoughts and feelings which are bothering him.

"I don't want to be married," Eric says very definitely. He has his hands folded in his lap. "And I don't want to have kids. I'd be a bad father."

Eric's brown hair falls on top of his glasses. His t-shirt is hiked up so an inch of white belly is showing.

"I know I would. If you'll ever see me at school, I-am-not-nice." Eric draws each word out. His eyes start to tear. "I might change," he says, with his voice shaking. "Probably not...but I might."

Eric sits very still. The room is quiet. Through the small window you can see that outside the sky is a cool gray and a soft wind is blowing. "I won't have kids. I'll live by myself I think," Eric says in a subdued voice. "I hope I have lots of friends... I just don't want to be a husband."

Eric is trying to contain himself. He closes his hands into little fists. "I DONT KNOW WHY!" he shouts suddenly. "I just know I don't want to be!"

****

The bus brakes to a halt and Jeffrey gets on. He finds a seat in the back. The engine revs and the bus pushes forward again. Jeffrey puts his briefcase on his lap.

"In the last year I've just had hunches that Eric might be straight," he says. "And in thinking about that I've tried quite consciously to talk more about positive images of straight people."

The bus brakes and pulls to the curb again. The doors jump open and more people get on. "Eric has an image of heterosexual relationships that... that isn't complicated enough. I think I should start complicating it somewhat." The bus pulls back into traffic. "The kind of thing that bothers me," Jeffrey says, "is, say, the mythology of heterosexual marriage. Now I'm not identifying the heterosexual structures, such as marriage and the nuclear family, with all heterosexuals. I trust that there are many who feel as oppressed by those as I do.

"The straight people I feel most comfortable with are those who are living life closer to the positive values that I find in gay culture. For example, the absence of marriage as an institution, the absence of monogamy as a virtue. The real plus that I find in gay society is that we can have many sexual and emotional partners and we don't have to be cast out. We have worked that into our society."

The bus slows down and pulls inside the subway station. Jeffrey gets off with everyone else and walks down a long corridor to the escalator. He stops to buy a paper and slips it under his arm. The escalator takes the people to a platform in between the tracks.

Jeffrey waits. The station is all white tile. The platform is crowded with people and filled with the hum of voices. Jeffrey glances through his paper. The sound of the train starts small and far away. It builds until the train bursts from the tunnel and into view. "YAT-YAT-YAT-YAT-YAT-YAT-YAT-YAT." An ugly whining sound of metal against metal comes from the brakes as it stops. The doors open and Jeffrey files in with the others. He finds a seat.

"Beth and I were together until Eric was five, he continues. "However, from the time he was maybe two years old Eric would meet my gay friends or lovers. While Beth and I were still together, I would go to the park with a lover and take him along." The train stops. The doors open and more people get on.

"It has never occurred to me that being gay would have any negative effects on being a parent. The problem that I didn't anticipate has been in the social structures. That is, how do I take my child with me into the world that I'm most comfortable with? That's what I've found difficult.

"And in terms of Eric's world—personally, I make no secret of the fact that I am gay. Anyone that knows me very well knows that I am. However, if Eric cared to, he could hide my sexuality from his classmates. But I don't think he cares to. I have a sense that there are a lot of things more important with regards to Eric making friends than my sexuality."

The train stops again. Jeffrey gets up and goes to the door. He waits for the train to start. It rattles back and forth as it picks up speed. As soon as it seems to be hitting top speed it brakes and stops again. The doors pop open and Jeffrey gets off. He takes the escalator upstairs and goes through the revolving gate into the cold. Jeffrey turns up the collar on his leather jacket. With his briefcase in one hand and the paper under his arm, he passes through the twin pillars that mark the entrance to the university.

"One time I advertised for sitters for Eric and an older woman called." Small clouds of mist punctuate Jeffrey's words as his breath hits the icy cold air. "I asked her to come by the next night a little early, so she could get used to the feel of things.

"She came over and we said hello. She seemed nice enough. I went out back where Tim and I were barbecuing and she was in the living room with Eric. It couldn't have been more than a few minutes before she came to the back door and said she had to leave. And she disappeared immediately.

"All I can think of," Jeffrey says, "is that she must have seen some gay books or newspapers lying around. Or it might have been the painting in the living room of two men hugging. I can't say for sure. But after she left Eric interpreted it as his being too—what did he say—noisy or active for her. He said, 'She was very quiet and old, and she obviously didn't want to be around a really active kid like me.'"

Jeffrey smiles. His face is stiff from the cold. "I told Eric that it probably had very little to do with him. But still, that's what he thought. He took it as a rejection of him rather than as a rejection of me, or my lifestyle."

Jeffrey cuts across the lawn to the English building. He opens the door and just as he steps inside, the bell rings. He shakes himself, trying to get the cold out of his bones. In a moment the hallway becomes crowded with students. Jeffrey decides he doesn't have time to go to his office. He starts up the steps to the class he teaches. It's one more day of rushing into class at the last minute without having time to collect his thoughts first. "Darn it," Jeffrey mutters under his breath, mad at himself for not leaving the house earlier. In a moment, he's lost in the flow of bodies.

****

"Some people just won't believe in gay people," Eric says, staring intently across the room, towards his dad's desk. "No matter what you tell them. Well... maybe they could be forced to, with a gun or something." Eric shakes his head, surprised at himself. "What am I saying?" He gives a sudden laugh. "And with a gun they might say they like you, but they wouldn't. They'd try to fool you. They wouldn't like you, but they'd pretend they did."

Eric tucks his hands under his legs again. He is getting antsy from all the talking. He's ready to go out to the park where, on Saturday afternoons, there usually are other kids playing. Eric hunches up his shoulders as he thinks. He looks around the room as if he's searching for what he wants to say.

"I would like to tell the straights, the ones who don't believe in gays, who hate gay people—" Eric takes in deep breath, "—that they're stupid. They don't think gays should exist. They think it's an awful way to live." Eric leans forward for emphasis. "Actually, it's a great life."

The furnace is burning with a soft hiss behind Eric. The room has that smell of cement that basements have. Eric's bottom lip begins to quiver. He pushes his glasses up on his nose. "I would like to say to them. 'I hope you like gay people. I hope you like your mother and father. And I hope you're not like me.' " Eric's voice cracks. He takes off his glasses and wipes his eyes.

****

In the living room the radio has gone back to playing music, softly. Beth is at the kitchen table with her cup of tea in front of her. She smiles, "One time I asked Eric who his ideal parents would be and do you know who he said? Julie Andrews from The Sound of Music, and Rhett Butler from Gone With the Wind. Eric calls him Red Butler."

Beth laughs softly. "Julie Andrews had those seven kids that she took care of, and Rhett totally adored his little Bonnie Blue. Eric doesn't have parents like that, you know? We don't measure up to that ideal by any means." Beth laughs again as she shrugs her shoulders. "And Eric has to deal with that. I mean every kid has to deal with parents who are different in some way, but I think with Eric it's more obvious."

As she thinks Beth runs her finger around the rim of her cup. Her smile slowly disappears.

"It frightens me to think of Eric as an alienated person," she says. "It was a real shock to me when I first realized he has problems making friends. I used to think, 'Oh, he's so well adjusted.' I also used to think that Eric was able to explore everything openly with me. Only recently did I get worried that he shares a limited amount with us, and there are other things that he keeps to himself and thinks through on his own. I mean, he is entitled to his own private life..." Beth's voice drifts off. There's the sound of a car passing outside. The headlights sweep across the back wall of the kitchen. Then it's gone, and the sound quickly dies away.

"I like being Eric's mother. I really do. I didn't so much when he was little, because I had trouble with the demands of a baby. But now that he's a person, with his own sense of self, I just enjoy being with him. It's like I enjoy being with a really good friend.

"For me, being a mother is something that I do that's worth something. You know? And that's important because I don't value a lot of what I do. As Eric's mother I feel that who I am is a positive thing for him. Even though I have depressions, whatever, I still feel that I am generally a positive influence on him. And that will always be there."

The news comes on the radio, in the living room. The clock above the refrigerator says twelve thirty. Beth gets up and turns the radio off. She is wearing a simple blue dress with buttons down the front. It's an old-style dress, and it moves with Beth's body as she walks. Beth is an attractive woman. However, she always seems to look tired due to the dark lines under her eyes. When she smiles, though, Beth's whole face seems to come alive.

Beth goes and sits back down at the kitchen table. The room is very still and quiet. The clock can be heard as it clicks forward every second. "The things that are important to me about Eric," Beth says, speaking softly, "are that he be sensitive, that he care about other people, that he use his capabilities, that he not put himself down, and that he have a positive, strong self-image." Beth breathes in slowly as she considers that list.

"I feel Eric is a fairly healthy child. He tends to deal with things as they happen to him. He has the emotional equipment, and the intelligence to bring to it. That's important." Beth folds her hands underneath her chin. "I mean, he's generally a kid who goes through life with a fairly positive outlook. At least I think he does. Some of the other kids at his school, well, they have a lot more anger and resentment in them than Eric does, for whatever reason that is.

"And then there's always the positive side of Eric's situation. That he's literally forced to become sensitive at an early age. He understands things that other kids will maybe understand when they're twice his age." Beth smiles, "I mean he seems pretty sophisticated now. But it wasn't that long ago that he thought gay just meant you like kissing other people. He didn't know it meant same sex, or anything else." Beth laughs as she tucks her hair back behind her ears.

Beth stretches. It's late and she has to work tomorrow. She gets up and pours her tea into the sink. The house is warm, and quiet, and still. Beth looks out the window above the sink into the darkness. After a moment, she heads to the stairway, turns off the light in the kitchen and she walks down the steps to bed.

****

"I just like fighting with little kids," Eric says. "Not all little kids, not really little kids." Eric is becoming very excited as he talks. His voice gets louder. "Sometimes when I hit people they want to hit me back. So I run away, and sometimes they run after me. Then I just have fun with people chasing me. Unless they're people faster than I am."

Eric starts bouncing up and down on the couch. His hands are on the seat cushion. He pushes up, and bounces, and pushes up again. "I wish I were an animal," he says. "I want to get REVENGE like the animals. I want to get revenge like a porcupine. I want to get their needles!

Eric laughs excitedly. "They're so lucky. When somebody attacks they can shoot out their needles." Eric holds his fists are in front of his face. He opens his fingers as if he were shooting out quills. He laughs. "If I were to get porcupine needles that would shoot out of me, that would be really tough. I'd send them out at PRE-DA-TORS!" Eric's voice is rising and his eyes open wide with excitement. "People who attack me, or people I don't like, to get revenge on them."

The wind has stopped blowing. The branches on the big tree outside the window are still. Eric is full of energy, though. "One thing I would like to become," he says, "is a bald eagle. They're like the kings of the sky. They can kill other animals." A big laugh rises out of Eric and explodes into the room. "The neat thing is that if I were a bald eagle and I were killed, the person who shot me would be put in jail. Because there's only fifteen or sixteen bald eagles left. That way at least one hunter would be arrested."

Eric jumps up off the couch. He is laughing as he moves his arms up and down. Eric runs around Jeffrey's desk. "Of course, if I were my size, I'd be a large eagle. And I'd be super strong!" Eric shows his teeth, and he puts his fingers out like claws. He scurries around the room as if he is chasing something running along the floor.

Eric collapses on the couch. His arms are at his sides like wings that are resting. He closes his eyes as he is struggles to catch his breath. Slowly his breathing calms down and he sits back up. He rubs the side of his face as he thinks.

"I don't know," he says. "I might be a trumpeter swan. Trumpeter swans—male trumpeter swans—have such STRONG wings. They can almost knock people out. With my strength I could do more than knock people out. I'd get people who attack me! People who try to clip my wings to keep me in residential parks where they want me to stay."

Eric leaps up off the couch again and he circles the desk flapping his wings. He climbs up on the big chair and yells, "Haaaa, Whoop!" Eric cranes his neck and beats his wings at invisible foes. He is laughing excitedly as he tells his stories.

Eric jumps down from the chair and flies around the room again. "Eeeeeehhh," He shouts. "They'd lose their minds when they woke up!"

Eric flies up on the couch and battles more enemies there. "Up, Up, and AWAY!" he yells. Eric jumps back to the chair and then leaps off and flies around Jeffrey's desk. He's laughing and whooping until he finally throws himself into a heap on the couch. His face is red and his breathing is like a bellows pumping.

Eric tries to talk, but he can only shake his head and smile. "I'd like—to be—a huge—animal!" he says in-between gasps for air. He takes a big breath and lets out a sigh. Eric closes his eyes. For just a moment, he is resting.

Update:

Beth Leonard

Winter, 1982

Dear Joe,

This response is late, for which I am sorry—I literally have not had a free evening in two months. My life is very busy, and I spend a lot of time during the evenings on work related to my new job, which, fortunately, I like very much.

I'm going to leap in with my bottom-line response—I'm afraid I don't feel very much like being "nice"—I think at this point "nice" is inappropriate.

I strongly feel that I do not want this chapter published, and that if it must be published, our names should be changed and sufficient details altered to make us unrecognizable, since it is no longer "us" anyway. I have read this chapter several times now, and each time I become angrier and angrier.

Basically, I feel the article is very slanted—that you have taken real people and turned them into characters of your own making—for what purpose I'm not sure. It seems to me that you decided to present us in a certain light—thus my choice of the word "slanted"—and changed facts to be consistent with your choice of how we should appear to be.

I have to say very firmly that my response goes beyond the personal, beyond concern for only myself and Jeffrey and Eric. I feel that we would be lacking in integrity if we let this be published as representative of one gay family—it's not us—it's not anyone. It's like characters out of a Chekhov (spelling?) play going through their grim rounds of interrelating and acting out their dreary lives.

At first, I responded to this chapter (in addition to the totally angry negative response) with the worry about the time and money you've put into this project—I bought into your boyish enthusiasm for doing some "good". But I feel that buying into that trip would be a cop-out on my part. Like any would-be author, you took the risks and I can't be responsible for whether you win or lose.

This has really been long-winded, speaking of bad writing, but I am so very angry and even angrier about having to spend an evening writing this letter. It would be irresponsible to do any less. Let's go to the text so you can better see what I'm talking about in regards to slanting and misinformation.

Page 25—This is the biggy. How DARE you say that Eric is not good at sports. How many laps of an olympic-sized pool can you swim—or better yet, how many could you have swum (real word?) at age 8. He taught himself to swim at age 2, now swims like an angel—or at least a good swimmer—lap after lap. Taught himself to ice skate—single runner skates, not kids' skates—before he was three. Plays tennis like a natural, etc., etc. Now he's taking ping- pong (thinking about getting into amature competition) lessons, swimming lessons; last year it was judo lessons, and before that gymnastics. They play kick-ball at his school, and he plays as well as any of them. But it's a different culture in Montreal, and the sports programs at most schools are not emphasized nearly as much as in the USA.

My whole point here is that to make a statement like that ("not good at sports") stands out like a red flag—it's like a cue to the reader, or a banner headline which totally pigeonholes Eric into a wrong pigeon coop and will affect the reader's impression of everything else the kid says or does. (Notice I do not object to you calling him pudgy—he loves pasta unfortunately—though in the summer he does slim down somewhat.)

And furthermore, every time that Eric fidgets in his seat, kicks his legs, or moves in any way, you make it sound like he's a miserable neurotic. For God's sake, man, that's the way kids move—especially boy kids—especially boy kids who are nervous about being interviewed. This kind of nonsense runs through the article wherever Eric appears.

Page 32—You and I are supposed to be talking in my kitchen. That sure as hell isn't my kitchen. I do not have double sinks, or a garbage disposal (at least not at that house)—the device of ending the section with a non-existent garbage disposal making a sound of a roaring dying gasp or whatever is really a tacky cheap-shot. Fun for you, perhaps as a writer, but really melodramatic nonsense.

Page 50—Must you always have melodramatic connotations for every simple act we performed. I got up from the table and walked down the basement stairs. Big deal. This was not a symbolic act for the whole of my life!!!

I could go on and on—I have major objections to material on pages 2, 4, 6 (cheap shot with the nail biting—I long ago learned that I have to have short nails to be a potter and I got into the habit of just biting them off at my studio, and it's become a habit—I hate long nails. I don't bite from nervousness. If my nails are so significant, why didn't you ask me about them?) Page 12, (the way you talk about Jeffrey's piano playing makes him sound like he feels like he failed or something. He doesn't practice because he doesn't have the time—that's the sadness) Page 16 (I wouldn't be caught dead working for the phone company. I was working for a department store, which is bad enough, but working for the phone company is like working for Nancy Reagan or something—ugh!!) Page 21, the inference that Eric doesn't have continuity because we're separated. Lack of continuity has never been an issue, not even now when Eric lives with Jeffrey and I'm 3,000 miles away from Montreal. Pages 26, 27, 31, 32, 35,41,—my apt. didn't have a thermostat—another cheap dramatic shot, 50, 51.

Soo

This has not been easy for me to do. I am not by nature someone who confronts easily, but I have been thoroughly aroused by this whole affair (no puns intended) and my need to speak out easily overcame my fear of doing so.

I hope you don't take this letter as speaking to your basic character. You are a perfectly decent human being like the rest of us. I just feel that, here, you were really out of your territory, trying to be the writer, and you badly missed the mark.

It seems somehow out of line to speak about what I've been doing since we last met, but suffice it to say that I have a job that I really enjoy, a great home life, a new car, and in general am happier than I have ever been. The move to California was a very good one for me in all aspects.

The only decent way I can think to end this letter is to say I hope you have some empathy for my point of view, and can understand what I'm talking about, and why I feel the way I do.

Sincerely,

Beth Leonard

In response to Beth's letter, I took out the line where I said that Eric is not athletic. I don't know if Jeffrey told me that, or if Eric said that he was not athletic, or if I came up with that on my own. And I may have made some inadvertent changes to Beth's kitchen due to visiting many kitchens as I wrote this book. However, all of the dialogue in this book comes from the transcripts. So the dialogue, which actually is mostly monologue, from Beth and Jeffrey and Eric, and all of the families, is accurate.

Joe Gantz

CHAPTER 5

The Stanley Family

Stephanie, age 15
Irene, age 19
Arliss (Stephanie and Irene's mother)
Jon (Stephanie and Irene's father)

Stephanie puts her hands underneath her hair and carefully sweeps it back away from her face. Her hair is dyed blonde and falls just below her shoulders. Stephanie touches it to make sure it is lying just right.

"Well, we were sitting at dinner and Tim, my dad's friend, brought up Judy. Judy is Tim's cousin. He brought up that maybe I could try and stay with her for the summer. See, Judy is trying to adopt someone. Tim said that maybe she would like me and at the end of the summer keep me there, adopt me or whatever. And my dad didn't say a thing against it. I got really upset."

Stephanie's face shows little emotion. As she takes a drag off her cigarette, her hands are shaking. "They were both saying, 'Oh, she could give you everything you want, she has lots of money. You won't have to ask for anything. You could go to the best of schools.' And all that crap." Stephanie is speaking softly, with her arms crossed in front of her.

"That was the last straw with Tim. I got really upset. I said, 'You don't give a damn at all, do you?' And Tim goes, 'What do you mean, I don't give a damn?' And all this other stuff. And, um..." Stephanie is staring in front of her, lost in thought. She shakes her head. "What was I talking about? What was the conversation? I get so confused..." Her voice trails off.

It's already very warm outside. It's a July morning in Milwaukee. Stephanie is sitting at the kitchen table. She has on eye liner, lipstick, rouge, all very carefully applied. Stephanie is fifteen years old and her appearance is very important to her. She is an attractive girl, with a round face, blue eyes and a full figure. Stephanie seems older than fifteen, both in the way she looks and the way she acts. She is a very serious young woman.

"I can understand my dad and Tim wanting me to go away for a while," Stephanie says. "It's like newlyweds, you know? Who wants a kid around when you're trying to work stuff out? But that was the last thing I could take from Tim. I went to my room, I was bawling my eyes out. And then the next morning I said, 'Forget it. I'm gonna leave.'

"See, I was always Daddy's little girl. And I'm not now. I could have lived with my dad forever. But I'll never forgive him for not sticking up for me and saying, 'Shut up, Tim, I don't want her going there.' He just didn't say anything. He agreed. He said he'd do everything on the list. That's his problem, he just goes along all the time.

School's out for the summer and Stephanie is sitting at home with no plans for today. Arliss, Stephanie's mother, and Stephanie have just moved into this apartment together. In fact, this is the first day that boxes haven't been all over, full of things waiting to be put away. Arliss had been renting a room from a friend since the family separated. However, when Stephanie couldn't get along living with her father and his lover, Tim, she found this place for the two of them.

"I think my dad's real mixed up right now. It used to be that everyone came before him, and now it's the opposite." Stephanie takes a drag from her cigarette. She watches the smoke as she blows it out. "My parents were never going to get a divorce. They were going to be separated, but they were never going to go through the awful legal procesures—procesures..." Stephanie giggles, embarrassed. She tries again. "—Procedures." Her laugh fades away quickly. "And Tim pushed that a lot.

"It's like the guy is so inconsiderate. I'd walk in the door and I'd say, 'Hi, Tim, how are you?' " Stephanie uses an excited voice. "He wouldn't say anything. It's weird. It's like he was so cold that I tried to be real warm, and it just didn't work.

"I hate Tim," Stephanie says with no apology in her voice. "He's cold, he's jealous... he's just everything terrible rolled up in one ball." Stephanie seems to have a lot of nervous energy that she is holding in. She shakes her head as she taps her fingers on the tabletop. Her fingernails are painted a dark red. Stephanie turns her cigarette in a circle on the edge of the ashtray. The smoke from the cigarette slowly rises towards the ceiling.

****

"I feel good right now. I feel very much in control of myself, in what I want." Jon is sitting at a picnic table. It's a hot day and his sport coat is folded across the bench beside him. "Just in the short time that Stephanie has been gone I'm thinking, 'okay, arrangements have been made. I'll go along with that. But I'm so glad that it's over. Tim and are free to be ourselves and come closer together. We don't have this pull and tug all the time from Stephanie for attention."

Jon is in a park that is commonly referred to as the "gay park." Except perhaps for having more trees than most, it's an ordinary park in downtown Milwaukee. There are the sounds of traffic, and softer, in the distance, there is the sound of music coming from a portable radio. Several men are sunning, stretched out on beach towels in the field to Jon's left. It's a good day for sunning, with no clouds and barely any breeze.

"Arliss and my relationship is through," Jon says emphatically. "I want to go on with my life and let Arliss go on with hers. But Stephanie hasn't let us do that. Stephanie has always been in the middle manipulating. She would tell Arliss something to get her mad at me, and tell me something so I'd get mad at Arliss. It was all negative attention. She really wanted both of us. She was jealous of Arliss's friend Janet, and she was jealous of whoever I was with and the time that I was spending elsewhere.

"Right now, Stephanie is feeling angry. She's blaming a lot on Tim—not that he's without blame, he isn't and he knows that. But at the same time she hasn't helped. Tim and I had Stephanie for five months, almost six, and there were times when it was hell on wheels.

"It was very simple what we wanted of her in terms of a contract. We weren't expecting perfection, but we have a nice place. When we cleaned up her room we found cigarette butts in the bookcase, in the closet, we found them underneath the bed. It was just bad news."

Jon opens a styrofoam container and takes out the hamburger he's brought with him. He takes a bite out of the sandwich and follows it with a sip of coke.

At forty-nine, Jon has brown hair sprinkled with gray. He wears his hair cut straight across in front and just over the tops of his ears on the sides. Jon has a moustache and a goatee, and wears thick, horn-rimmed glasses. He seems to always have a wide-eyed, interested expression on his face. However, this is somewhat caused by the thick lenses of his glasses.

"I got to the point where I realized that all Arliss and the kids really needed me for was financial security. And okay, they're going to get that out of me, but then leave me alone. Let me get some semblance of order in my life. Let me get my relationship, that's very meaningful, in order. Tim and I haven't had a chance to do that." Jon's voice is rising. It is a rare moment where he is showing his anger.

"This is not easy for me. It's contradictory to the way I've been brought up. I've always been the placater—seeing that things are on an even keel, seeing that everyone is taken care of. But, at this stage of the game, I can't anymore.

"I know this is going to be hard for Stephanie, but she's going to have to accept it. I mean, she's my daughter, and I'll see to it that things are taken care of. But it's going to take some cooling off time. At this point, she is better off dealing with one person, rather than trying to deal with two anymore. She needs one person to guide her."

The park is peaceful. There is the slightest breeze, and the music can be heard each time the wind blows by. The faint sound of cars comes from beyond the trees. Jon puts the wrapper from his sandwich neatly away in the bag it came in.

Jon is a somewhat formal person. He wears a sport coat to work and nice clothes at home. He's very polite when he speaks with someone. As he looks around the park, at the people sunning, he thinks to himself that it's something he probably would never do. Jon looks at his watch. He takes the bag off the table and holds it in his lap.

"You know, it isn't as if I wasn't home over the years. When they were younger I was always home. And okay, maybe I wasn't the best father in the world. But the kids always had clothes, we had a nice house, we ate well." Jon pushes his glasses up on his nose. "I did the best I could with the tools I had to work with.

"And Arliss wasn't the best mother either. She damn well better admit it. But the two of us, together, you know, I think we did pretty good to come up with those kids." Jon takes a breath and lets it out slowly.

"It's about time the kids realize they have to wake up. Things are not going to be the way they have been in the past. Stephanie is not going to be able to manipulate and get things the way she wants them, not any more. Because now I'm looking after myself for a while."

****

Irene is nineteen, four years older than Stephanie. One thing that makes her very angry is when she is mistaken for being the younger of the two sisters. And it happens often. Irene is very thin, with a boyish figure. She has short blondish-brown hair, and a thin, aquiline nose.

Irene walks quickly and talks quickly. She goes fast all day until 8:30 or 9:00 in the evening, when she falls asleep. She has a lot of energy, but few physical reserves. The reason for that is that Irene has a serious asthmatic condition. She's had it since she was very young.

"A lot of people don't realize it," Irene says, "they don't understand. Here's this person who is skinny. 'Oh God, would I love to be like you.' If they only knew what I went through to get this way. Then they wouldn't be saying it."

Irene speaks in a high voice when she's excited, as she is now. "An asthma attack," Irene says, "is like choking on a piece of food. You can't breathe. You gasp for air and you can't get it." Irene is sitting stiffly, with her hands resting on the table in front of her. "My doctor says that even if it's really small, to take my medication. Because it's better than taking it when it gets really bad.

"See, there's the possibility that the medication won't work, and I'll have to go to the hospital and have a shot of adrenalin. I don't like that to have to happen. I mean, when I get a shot of adrenalin I can feel my heart pumping. I can feel it. It's like it's jetting out of my body. The blood is rushing through my system and my whole body turns like rubber. If I were to try to stand up. I'd fall right onto the floor."

It would be hard to imagine sisters more different than Irene and Stephanie. Stephanie has long hair, Irene's is short. Stephanie is a touch on the heavy side, while Irene is skinny as a rail. Stephanie has lots of friends, boyfriends as well as girlfriends. She's always going off to meet someone, or talking on the phone. Irene has few friends her own age and is happy to spend time alone. Her normal dress is jeans and a t-shirt, and her appearance is not something she worries about. If Irene does go out, it is often with her mother, to the parties of her mother's friends.

"When I was younger I was really sick. I would go to the hospital a lot and be put in an oxygen tent. I'd be fed intravenously, and the whole bit. I went to school like all the other kids, but it put me behind because I was in the hospital so much. I ended up with a learning disability. Not a real drastic learning disability, but it was enough to keep me back a year.

"Most of the time it would happen in the middle of the night. If I had a real bad cold and I couldn't fight it any more, I'd end up with an attack. Now I don't have it as frequently as when I was, say, ten years old." Irene is speaking softly. She's leaning with her elbows on the table, and she looks worried. "Oh, sometimes I have it twice a week. It depends. It depends on what I have on my mind. If I have a lot of things on my mind, it happens more often."

****

"Jon was a shadower," Arliss says with a half smile. "There are people who I call shadow people, and they become who they are with. In fact, they are very boring because they don't have an original thought in their cotton-picking heads. And that's where Jon and I had our problems. He was forever shadowing me. It used to bug me to death. I used to say to him, 'Johnny, do what you want to do. Don't always do what I want to do.'"

It's Saturday morning and Stephanie has gone back to her room. Arliss is dressed and in the kitchen with a cup of coffee. Every weekend for the past four years Arliss has stayed at her friend Janet's house. But now that it's just she and Stephanie, it won't be possible to go off the way she could when the whole family was together. Arliss doesn't know what arrangements can be made. Things are so new, she doesn't even know what she thinks about it.

"I haven't got it thoroughly sorted out," Arliss says. "I chose to take Stephanie. I chose to do that because it's not going to be long. She'll be with me at the most for two years and I want those years to be good for her.

"But I've been through so much. I'm tired. I'm real tired. I can hear it in my voice. I'm not sure I can take much more. I hope Stephanie is sensitive to that. I hope she realizes it and doesn't ask the impossible of me."

Arliss pauses, lost in thought. She slowly stirs her coffee cup. Arliss takes a deep breath. "Right now in my life, I don't want much to do with anybody. Janet's the only person I'm really close to, and even Janet—there's a distance." Arliss shrugs. "The gals at work got me to join a pool league, and I do that once a week. But I could not go and it wouldn't mean anything.

"I find it really hard right now to go out there, muck around, and just have fun. If I were left to my own devices I would stay at home and go nowhere. I would read, and I would draw into myself. I am just in a state, right now, of semi-retirement from the world."

Arliss has always been a woman of moods. She can be very entertaining. She is witty and has a good sense of humor. But Arliss can also be sullen and withdrawn. And the other family members long ago adjusted to her temper, with its short fuse.

Arliss has brown hair that's only a couple inches long and a strong, straight nose. She's a big-boned and fairly tall woman at 5'10". But she has a presence which has nothing to do with her appearance. Just as the two girls are different, Jon and Arliss are very different as well. Arliss dresses casually, in jeans and a button down shirt. She jokes easily, talks easily. Also, Arliss is more assertive than Jon is. She is very strong-willed, and she makes it clear to people what she expects from them.

"There was a time, years ago after we had both come out, when Jon and I talked a great deal about separation." Arliss passes her hand back through her hair. "We planned at that point for Irene to live with me and for Stephanie to live with her father. But when we talked about it with the children they became very, very upset—especially Stephanie. This was, like, four years ago. So, we decided at that point that we'd stay together, at least until the kids finished high school.

"For the four years before we separated I looked on our marriage as a business relationship. Staying together was the economically sensible thing to do. Jon and I had separate rooms, as well as separate lives in many ways. I could have stayed like that forever, it was fine with me. I was happy. But, as it turned out, it just wasn't good enough for Stephanie. It just wasn't what Stephanie wanted. She had to push it."

Arliss picks her coffee cup up in both hands. She takes a sip and puts it down. "The family would still be together if it hadn't been for Stephanie, if Stephanie hadn't forced the issue. It was going to happen sooner or later, we were going to split up, that was inevitable. But Stephanie brought it to a head a lot sooner. Her running away did it."

Arliss gets up and walks to the window to turn on the air conditioner. The dull hum covers up the sounds of the traffic on the street. She sits down in the big leather chair next to the window, leans back and the footrest springs out and lifts up her feet. Arliss takes her glasses off and sets them on the coffee table. She rubs her eyes.

"It was convenience. That's what our relationship was. And we both sort of felt we had to do it that way as long as Stephanie was at home. But by running away Stephanie showed us that she didn't want that.

Her running away said to us, 'hey, you don't have to hang together for me. Don't do this for me.'"

****

"My school situation was really terrible and I wanted to get away from that." Stephanie shrugs her shoulders as she fans herself with a piece of paper. "It's kind of a stupid thing I did, because it didn't help anything. It just made people nervous and upset and mad. I don't know why I did it."

It's a hot, muggy day. Stephanie is in her bedroom sitting on her waterbed. She's leaning back against the wall, with her legs stretched out in front of her.

"See, I wasn't supposed to be seeing this guy, Larry," Stephanie says. "He was eighteen. I had met him at my Dad's work and we had gotten really close and stuff. Then one day after school he met me at the bus stop and we were walking down the street together. All of a sudden I see this green car coming. It was my Dad's car. I ducked down and Larry kept on walking, and Dad drove right past. But I figured he saw us. I knew I was gonna get in trouble when I got home, so I guess that's another reason why I ran away."

Stephanie opens her eyes wide and she sticks out her tongue to show how hot she is. It's one of those summer days where a person's clothes stick to them everywhere. Stephanie is wearing a white halter top that has a pretty lace border on it, and jeans. She's barefoot. Her toenails are painted the same dark red as her fingernails.

"What I did was, I stayed downtown with Larry. We stayed one night at a church, and then the next night at the house of some friends of his. That was kind of crummy. So we met some friends of those friends and stayed with them. And that didn't work out at all. After that we just floated around. We'd go to the 24 hour Big Boy and stay up all night." Stephanie giggles. "I wore the same clothes for two weeks," she says, hardly able to believe it still.

"I called my family a lot. I'd just say, 'I'm alright. I'll tell you when I'm gonna come home.' I wasn't gonna come back right away. But the police found me. They picked me up and put me in a jail cell." Stephanie laughs again. Then she yawns. "When my dad came to get me, he brought two sheets full of rules and regulations and things that I was not going to be able to do for a couple of months. He read them

239

in front of the police officers. I had to agree with them before I could go home. I was going, 'Dad, give me a break!' "

The sun is slanting in through Stephanie's window. It shines on the rug. Stephanie's room is very neat. There are pictures of her family on her dresser and on the wall next to the closet. On the wall next to the bed there are two framed pictures of wide-eyed little pixy girls. The girls in the pictures have on gingham dresses and gingham hats. They are staring out from the frames with big, blue, innocent eyes.

Arliss and Stephanie's new apartment is in a long brick building. It's clean and newly painted. It's carpeted and it has a small kitchen with new appliances. But it's nowhere near as big or as nice as the house the family lived in before Arliss and Jon separated. Just living in a place this small takes some getting used to.

"It was after I ran away that the whole family started going to counseling." Stephanie smiles an uncomfortable smile. "The counseling was upsetting at times, because all the bad stuff was coming out. The good stuff too," she says. Stephanie leans over and takes her cigarettes off the night table. She takes one out and lights it.

"One day we were in there and it all spilled out, everything. See, I really didn't want to tell the counselor. I didn't know if we could trust her. You know? But she knew there was some missing part. Halfway through we were talking and she said, 'There's something else, there's something that I don't understand.' "

Stephanie is uncomfortable talking about all this. It can be heard in her voice. She is speaking softly, hesitantly. "Finally, Mom says, she goes, 'Well, kids.' She said something like that and I knew it was coming. I just sat there. Mom said, 'I can't hold it back any longer.' She said, 'I'm a lesbian.' And then my dad said, 'Yes, and I'm gay.' "

Stephanie starts to laugh. The laugh bursts out of her, loud and high. She covers her mouth. Stephanie's eyes shine with an almost uncontrollable wave of emotion. "See, we had never told anyone," she says. "We'd never even talked about it at home. Never. And then it came out and everyone started crying.

"They were saying all this stuff. They were saying it's hard for the kids and things like that. That maybe I was having a difficult time." Stephanie takes a drag from her cigarette. She crosses her arms and holds herself.

"I'm the type of person who cries really easily. The slightest thing upsets me. I was crying. My mom was crying too." Stephanie gives a brief laugh, and her smile disappears almost immediately. She looks down into her lap and shakes her head. As she does, her hair falls and covers her face. "It was really something."

****

"I remember it very vividly," Irene says. "Because a couple of nights before, my mother had asked us, 'What would you think if I brought this out in the open?'

"I said, 'well, I'm not really sure I want you to.' And that was the last time it was brought up, until the next session when Mom said, 'there's something that has to come out in the open—we're gay.'"

Irene clears her throat. Her voice is high and strained with emotion. "Both Stephanie and I just fell apart," she says. "Well, Stephanie—she cried more. I just said, 'Oh, oh no, oh no. Now what's gonna happen?' Because this was the first time it came out with a stranger. You know? All of a sudden it was like a big bomb dropping on your house. All your defenses are down, and you don't know about it until it hits."

Irene is at the lakefront summer cottage of a ninety-year-old woman named Blanche, who she takes care of. Arliss got her this job after she left school. Blanche is deaf and gets around with a walker. Irene has a lot of responsibilities but also a lot of time to herself. She likes it up at the lake. Irene's happy that they're going to be staying here all summer.

"I think we would have been able to talk about it more with the counselor if the whole family would have known more in advance. If we would have had some idea when it was going to come out." Irene sits back in her chair. "That's when it ended. That's when we ended our sessions.

"See, I didn't find any need to go. I wasn't contributing to the problem, you know? We were mainly going to get ideas organized for Stephanie, to get the situation cleared up for her. We all talked it over and we said, 'no, I don't see any reason why we should go.' Everybody said that. But I was the one that brought it up. Because I thought, you know, 'why am I here?' And then everybody else thought it over, and they said the same thing."

Irene finished high school a year ago. She had respectable grades, mainly B's. Her favorite courses were horticulture and biology, and her plan was to go into forestry. The fall following high school Irene went to college in Northern Wisconsin. She was very excited about it. The school she went to was known to have good agriculture and forestry departments. Irene was also pleased with the fact that she could go to all her classes and only walk up one flight of stairs. She felt that her asthma would not be aggravated.

That fall Irene entered college, and in one semester she flunked out. She had failed or dropped almost every course. It was a shocking surprise to the whole family. In fact, the one that seemed to show their disappointment the least was Irene.

"In the beginning," Irene says, looking out the big bay window towards the lake, "I thought we had the traditional family. You know, your basic husband loves wife, wife loves husband—that kind of thing. The husband and wife love the kids, and the kids love Mom and Dad." Irene smiles as she slowly bobs her head up and down. "And then, as we grew up, things were changing. They were still talking to each other, but they were starting to get further and further apart.

"When I first noticed that something was different, I didn't know what gay was. At that point, Dad was seeing someone in Madison, and Mother was seeing Janet on weekends. But, I didn't know what the word was, what term they used for man and man, and woman and woman together."

Being four years older, Irene remembers more of what the family used to be like than Stephanie does. Things changed dramatically when Arliss and Jon "came out" to their homosexuality. (At the time, Irene was 13 and Stephanie was 9.) They had never been a close, sharing couple, especially not physically. But at the time that they "came out" they started having two very separate lives. Two years later, Jon moved into his own room and the distance between him and Arliss became even clearer.

"In some ways, it really didn't affect me because, okay, see I was old enough to know about it. My parents brought home books. And well, they really weren't on homosexuality, but they were on sex. I read the books and stuff. So, I was informed that way."

Irene speaks with a sincerity that is almost childlike. "I knew, up to a point, what was going on," she says. "But, in a way, I thought, 'well, it really isn't my business what they're doing. It's their life. I'm going to let them live it their way.'" Irene crosses her arms. She shrugs. "And besides, one major reason that they moved into different rooms is that my Dad snores a lot. You know? My mom would have to be in bed before he was, in order for her to get to sleep."

The next door neighbor lets her dogs out. She ties them up outside the door. Irene looks out the side window. Two tiny longhaired dogs are pulling at their ropes and barking. Irene gets up and closes the window. She watches the dogs and shakes her head.

The lake is calm. The sun, which is low in the sky, sparkles on the surface of the water. Irene likes to fish. There's a dock in the backyard that she fishes from, almost every day. Irene knows where the fish feed, and at what times of the day they do. She knows what type of bait the different fish like. She's very patient too. It isn't every day that Irene catches a fish, but it's often enough so that there is more than one stored away in the freezer at the moment.

"Okay, my parents are gay. But even though they are, that didn't interfere with our family. Because it was a part time thing. During the week my dad would go out and my mom would take care of the family. And then on weekends my dad would be around, and Mom would go live with her friend Janet.

"The thing is that we've grown up, okay? Stephanie and I know that our parents spent a lot of time with us when we were little. When we got older, we were able to stay home by ourselves, and we wanted to give them a chance to do what they wanted to do. So, we let them have their time alone in return, their free time.

"At one point it was really bothering me that Mom wasn't home a lot, and that Dad wasn't home a lot. You know? Dad would go out and he wouldn't give me a phone number or anything. If it was getting real late that would upset me."

Irene is sitting up straight in her chair. She smiles as she struggles to keep her voice even. "If someone wasn't home all the time, it would just get really frustrating. Because when I'm home alone, it acts up on my nerves. And then it gets to my asthma. Everything else just comes in and piles up on me." Irene's eyes start to tear up. There is just a trace of a smile, as if she's trying to hold onto it. "And then I don't know what to do," she says. "I don't know how to dig myself out."

****

"How I came out to my children was certainly not calculated," Arliss says. "We never really discussed it with the kids. And that might have been because it was too difficult for me, so I chose not to. But I don't know that it was a mistake, they did find out about it eventually.

"I guess the reason that I didn't tell them was because I didn't want to garbage up their lives with it. I want them to live their life the way they want to live it. What I do is immaterial." Arliss looks around the room as she remembers that time. "I'm not ashamed of what I am," she says, "but I'm not proud of it either. And I certainly don't want to lay anything on the kids."

Arliss and Jon never actually told their children that they are gay. They never sat them down for a discussion. At the same time, they didn't hide their lifestyles. In fact, they assumed, rightly, that Stephanie and Irene understood the situation. But by not openly announcing it, they effectively deprived the girls of the opportunity to ask questions. There was no forum for Irene and Stephanie to discuss things they didn't understand, or to talk about anything that bothered or confused them.

Arliss has come over to Janet's house to get some privacy. Janet is still at work. Arliss is sitting on the couch. Except for the two cats, the house is quiet and empty. Arliss leans back and rests her chin in her hand.

"When the kids did find out, Irene sort of took it as a matter of course. She thought, 'well, that's okay.' Irene is an asexual person. She really is not..." Arliss shrugs. "I don't know, you'll have to talk to her about it.

"Stephanie, on the other hand, was very uncomfortable with the situation. She didn't like it. This definitely—" Arliss is shaking her head slowly from side to side, "—this definitely brought me out. Mother was definitely weird." Arliss laughs a soft laugh. "Stephanie still thinks that. She still thinks that it's sick. And that's okay, I can understand that. I try to cooperate and be as low key as possible."

For years there was something of a standoff between Stephanie and Arliss. Irene always got along much better with her mother, and Stephanie with her father. Stephanie never seemed comfortable with her parents' homosexuality, but she was less comfortable with her mother being gay. It seemed to bother her less to be around her father and his lover, than her mother and Janet. And Arliss was critical of Stephanie in many ways as well. There were certain topics, such as Stephanie's make-up and boyfriends, that seemed to always cause arguments between the two of them. So it was a surprise to the whole family that after Stephanie moved out from her father and Tim's place, when Arliss found an apartment for the two of them. No one in the family really expected it.

"I tried giving up my homosexuality," Arliss says. "After high school, when I was nineteen, I broke with this woman I was having an affair with. I decided that I couldn't handle it, that I was going to start anew." Arliss holds her hand over her mouth as she takes a slow, deep breath. "I decided I was going to go into religious life, and I was going to make reparation for all the sins of homosexuality that I had committed.

"I picked Roman Catholicism. I joined a religious order and took the vows of celibacy. I became a zealot." Arliss pauses. She partially closes one eye in a cynical expression of hers. Arliss is good at telling stories. She can't help but put a pregnant pause in a story at an opportune moment. "For two and a half years I did that. Until, towards the end of that time the altar boys started looking very good to me. I thought, 'Honest to God, I think I've made it. I think I've made the whole jump. I think I want to get married—by golly, I do!' "

One of the cats jumps up on the couch. Arliss pets it. It tries to get on her lap and she pushes it away. "Go on kitty. Go play with your little kitty friend there." The cat sits down and watches Arliss. "Go on shoo," Arliss says as she waves the cat away. It jumps off the couch. Arliss tries to remember where she was. She continues.

"I came back to Milwaukee and got a job in a publishing house. Jon was an editor there. I worked on a lot of his texts, so we spent a lot of time together.

"Jon never dated any women," Arliss says, smiling. "He never had anything to do with women. He was one of those pure fellows who got up at four in the morning and read history, and then went to church and served mass. And I thought he was great.

"I thought, 'By golly, this is a very sensitive man. I think I could make it with him. I think I could do it.' " Arliss laughs softly to herself. The other cat is watching her from the chair underneath the lamp. It stares at her with bright green eyes.

"And so I pursued Jon. I worked very hard. I worked two years for him. And I finally got him. Finally, he got off the bench, and we got married."

****

"As a matter of fact," Jon says, "our wedding night experience was very traumatic for both of us. Arliss really didn't know how to handle it. She broke down. In terms of our sleeping together, we were not able to consummate that night."

The sunbathers start to gather up their towels. One man takes his clothes out of a bag and puts them on over his swimsuit. Jon watches the man. Then he looks at his watch.

"In the four years between the two children, I can count on one hand the number of times Arliss and I had sex." Jon rubs his forehead. He gives an almost apologetic look. "One of the things that got in the way in the early years of marriage, is that I knew so damn little about women and anatomy. Arliss kept saying, 'Do something! Find out who I am.' But I had no desire to do so. I did nothing about it. I felt badly, but I always seemed to say to myself, 'Oh, what the heck.' "

The park is nearly empty now. The music plays softly, far away. The man who was sunning walks past the picnic table on his way to his car. He smiles at Jon and Jon says hello. Jon brushes his hair to the side. He picks his sport coat off the bench and lays it across his lap.

"I went to college at Marquette. After that I joined the Paulist Fathers and went into the Novitiate. I did that for two years before I decided that religious life was not for me. That's when I came to Milwaukee and started working for the publishing house. At that time, except for acting out some of my voyeurism regarding young men at the Novitiate, I had had no sexual experiences. None at all. In fact, I wasn't a sexual person.

"Arliss's and my relationship was somewhat societally induced," Jon says. He pushes his glasses up on his nose. "Instead of making a conscious decision on my part to get married, I just sort of fell into it. It was the same thing with becoming a parent, she just happened to get pregnant.

"I think to answer if I really like being a father—I would have to say no. The kids were here. They were a fact, and I wasn't going to just abandon them. I realize, too, that the family did fulfill certain needs of mine. I had never really had a close relationship with anyone up until the time I was married. I was an isolate. By being married and having a family, I was not alone anymore."

Jon is speaking in an unemotional, detached voice. For the past sixteen years Jon has made his living as a social worker. As he sits and discusses this all so clearly and rationally, with his even, unruffled manner, it sounds as if he is speaking of a client's family and their history, rather than his own.

Absently, as Jon thinks to himself, he runs his finger and thumb down his moustache and over his goatee. Jon's the only one left in this section of the park. A soft breeze blows the leaves on the trees in front of him. They flutter weakly and then stop. They remain still, shining green in the sunlight, until another puff of wind comes and they flutter again.

"For the first fourteen years we were married," Jon says, "I had no notion about Arliss' orientation." Jon clears his throat. He smiles slightly. "We had sex very rarely, and I knew she didn't enjoy it. I thought I was a poor lover. Yet I had no desire to do anything about it, not really. For all those years we just raised our family in a very conventional way.

"Then finally, how it came about was, well—Arliss at one point almost had a nervous breakdown." Jon blinks several times. There is real concern in his voice. He puts his finger to his lips, and some of the worry he felt at the time shows in his eyes.

"Arliss realized that the reason she was going through all that confusion was that she was struggling with her sexuality. She had a very hard time for quite a while. Finally, she started coming to grips with the fact that she was gay and that's when she came out to me." Jon puts out his hands. "Before that I had no inkling of it," he says. Jon is lost in thought.

A cloud comes in front of the sun. The shadow of the cloud moves across the park. As it passes over Jon it seems to wake him up. He looks at his watch, and then gathers up his coat and the trash from his lunch. He walks quickly to the car and throws everything in the front seat. Jon starts the engine, which is loud from many miles of use. His blinker clicks on and off as he turns onto the road and joins the flow of traffic.

****

(We are now going back two years earlier, when everyone still lived together at the house on Grayson Street, before Jon and Arliss formally separated.)

"When I was little," Irene says, "the girls were supposed to dress up in dresses to go to church. We wore hats and little white gloves. But now that we're more grown up we don't have to go to church if we don't want to. We include God in our lives but... right now we're so busy, we just don't have the time. You know, Mom has her way of living, and Dad has his."

Irene is upstairs in her small, messy bedroom in the house on Grayson Street. The family is still living together. Irene is seventeen, with long hair that she wears in two pigtails. Her room is full of books on birds, and hiking equipment. There's a pair of binoculars on the wall and a camera on the shelf.

It's Saturday, so Arliss is at her friend Janet's house. Jon is downstairs and Stephanie is shopping with her girlfriend. It's a crisp, fall day in Milwaukee. The leaves have changed colors and are falling from the trees with each gust of wind. Irene is lying on her side on her unmade bed.

"Originally my parents figured, 'Oh, well. We have to go with the church. This has to be done. It's this way or no way at all.' You know? It wasn't until they broke away from the church that they realized there was another side to the story.

"Now, they've found other friends," Irene says, "and there is more openness now. I think they feel more free. They don't feel as controlled." Irene has her head resting on her hand. She speaks in a high voice. "They don't feel like they're mice in an experiment. Because when you're in the church you feel like there's no getting out of it. You feel like there's no escaping from the church or from the experiment."

As the kids were growing up, Jon and Arliss continued their involvement with the church. The family went to services every week. But it was more than that. Much of their social life, and all of their friends, revolved around the church and church activities.

The church provided a structure that Jon and Arliss needed. Although they weren't admitting to themselves that they were homosexual when the kids were younger, they weren't really heterosexual either. In the process of trying to stifle any trace of them being gay, Jon and Arliss had cut themselves off from any sexuality at all. They had also cut themselves off from their emotions. Jon and Arliss were living lives separate from each other. They were unhappy parents, leading a regimented, isolated life.

"My parents said, 'THE HECK WITH THE CHURCH. We're not going to go with the church because the church makes us unhappy.' You know? They were able to pick new friends," Irene continues. "And okay, maybe they were the same sex, whatever. But the church was against that. The church was just one obstacle that they couldn't jump, they couldn't get over for a long time. And once they did get over it, they said, 'why couldn't we just do this before?'"

Irene sits up and swings her feet over the edge of her bed. She is wearing beige corduroys, a white turtleneck and gym shoes. The sun is shining outside and a fall wind is blowing the leaves around the yard. Irene looks out the window. She watches the birds eating out of the two feeders she's set up. If there were any birds that she didn't recognize, Irene would get the binoculars off the wall and take a closer look. But the birds feeding now are the same ones that feed in the backyard all the time.

"I think as we grew up our parents saw what was happening. They realized, you know, 'this is really tearing us up. This is not how we planned our family.'" Irene brings one foot up onto the edge of the bed and hugs her leg to her chest.

"I think our parents thought that they weren't really giving us the love that they felt they should. And I think that once they broke away from the church they figured, 'well, geez, now we can give them the love and tenderness, and the hugging and kissing, and the talking that we wanted to in the beginning.'

"At that point we said, 'well, this is togetherness. Now that they've cleared the air and their minds with the church, this makes the family more open. And now that the family's more open, more feelings come out. We've got God, but we've also got more freedom.'" Irene stretches. She gives a big yawn and leans back against her headboard. "So that's what we're forming," she says, "we're forming togetherness. But not with the church, we're forming togetherness our own way."

The doorbell rings. Irene doesn't move. She knows it's Mitch, her dad's lover. He comes in every weekend from Madison. Lately, though, things have been pretty much on the rocks. It's really over, her dad tells her. Irene doesn't mind Mitch, but she does get the feeling that he would rather she and Stephanie weren't around most of the time.

Irene takes one of her books off the shelf and starts paging through it. It's got beautiful pictures of birds from all over the world. The sounds of Jon and Mitch laughing come up from downstairs. Irene doesn't pay attention to the noise. Her heels are tucked into the railing underneath her bed, and the book is open across her lap.

"Lately our family started going to this certain church in town," Irene explains. "It's a gay church. I really have been going more than the rest of the family." Irene looks at the pictures in the book as she speaks softly.

"At this church they showed us that God accepts you, even if you're gay. They said that God accepts us for what we do, no matter what it is. And he forgives us for whatever we do as well. So, in this day and age," she says, "there really is no wrong, you know, against God. God likes us all, no matter what. And he always forgives us."

****

"We do our own thing," Jon says, "and yet we're also here as a unit. We're concerned about one another, but we're not parents who deprive ourselves of a lot of things for the sake of our kids." Jon is in his bedroom. Mitch has come and gone. The visit was organized around exchanging things that had been left at one another's places. "There was a time when we did, when the children were smaller. We never went out, we never did anything. We were totally child oriented. We lived a whole different lifestyle at that time."

Jon is sitting in his reading chair, an unopened book in his lap. The shade on the window behind Jon is down, and the floor lamp is turned on. The house is peaceful and still. Arliss is at Janet's for the weekend, Stephanie is at a movie with her boyfriend, and Irene has left the house to walk around the neighborhood taking pictures. It is one of those rare moments where Jon finds himself alone in his own home. The quiet feels too good to be true.

This room used to be the library until Jon moved out of the room he shared with Arliss. The same books still line two walls. One or another member of the family often comes knocking on Jon's door looking for a book. The intrusions bother Jon, but he makes every effort to endure them quietly.

"I'm realizing that I have very strong affectional needs, much more than I ever realized," Jon says, leaning back in his chair. "But in spite of that, I don't have the energy to fight Stephanie in her need for all my attention. In fact, I said to Stephanie just recently, 'Look, you had nothing to worry about as you were growing up. You never had to worry that you didn't have decent food, or clothes. You lived in a decent home, and in a good neighborhood. So get off my back about what you want!'

"I've done a lot of things for a lot of people over the years. And I realize, okay, I've done it of my own free will. I've gotten my bennies, you might say, out of doing that, out of being the good guy. But along the way there have been people who have taken me for granted. 'Good old Jon, he's always there.'" Jon is slowly getting angry, like a candle that is sputtering before it lights. "And in the midst of that I am finally saying to myself, 'Hey, what about my needs? I'm a human being, too!'"

Jon crosses his arms. He is scowling out through his thick glasses. The screen door slams. Irene is back. She knocks on her dad's door on her way up the steps. "It's just me, Dad," she calls out.

Footsteps can be heard through the ceiling over Jon's head. Irene's room is directly above his own. Jon takes off his glasses. He looks older without them. There are deep wrinkles around his eyes. Jon is nearing fifty. However, because he spends so much time going out during the week to bars and other places where gay men gather, he often speaks of himself as being in a second adolescence.

"I can't remember the exact context of the conversation, but Irene and I were doing something together and talking a while back," Jon says. "I asked her how she was feeling, about her sexual propensities, if you will. I asked her if she felt more attracted to women than she did to men.

"I can't remember how it came up, it was a natural flow in a conversation we were having. Tears kind of welled up in her eyes and she said, 'yes,' she was. I told her, 'well, it's not uncommon at your age for that to be true. In fact, boys will do the same thing.'

"I said, 'if that's what you feel you need to be, in terms of expressing yourself, that's okay.' I told her, 'Of course, if I had done the same thing at your age, you wouldn't be here now. But in spite of that fact I will back you in making your choice.'"

Jon sits forward in his chair and he lowers his voice. "It's interesting but Irene is not by nature a very affectionate person. She doesn't quite know how to handle close affection, even by me. When I hold her and give her a kiss, she's somewhat, well—" Jon hunches up his shoulders into a closed-off posture. "She's like this," he says, "held back."

Jon's bedroom consists of a double bed, the chair he's sitting in, a dresser, a closet, and the minimum amount of space needed to walk from one to the other. It's cramped, but it's a private place where he can go to be alone. The few quiet moments he has to relax here, he greatly appreciates.

Jon opens his book and pages through it to find his place. He puts his glasses back on. Before he begins reading, though, he looks up to make one last comment.

"I think one thing that's true in this family," he says, "is that we're all very independent people. Arliss and I have encouraged that. I think that partly our lifestyle has fostered it." Jon chuckles. "Of course, when Stephanie makes up her mind, we often wind up at loggerheads. She's determined to go off and do her own thing." He gives a tight smile.

Creaking can be heard through the ceiling as Irene moves about in her room. Jon continues, "I think Arliss and I have given the kids an appreciation of what it is to be human. In spite of the fact that we might like things to be cut and dry, to be in their own little compartments, it doesn't always work out that way. Human beings are subject to change."

Jon looks very intent on what he is saying. "And that's not necessarily to say that families have to be adaptable like a chameleon, so you don't know which way your head's screwed on. But there has to be some flexibility. There has to be a willingness to change."

The phone rings. Jon listens until Irene picks it up. He starts to turn back to his book.

Irene calls down loudly from upstairs, "Dad! Stephanie's on the phone."

Jon doesn't answer immediately.

"She wants you to pick her up!"

Jon clears his throat, "Tell her I'll—" He stops, wondering if he should give himself a little more time alone or just leave right away. It seems every time he opens a book there's an interruption. Irene is waiting at the top of the stairs. "Tell her I'll leave here shortly," Jon yells to Irene. The tap of footsteps can be heard as Irene goes back to the phone. She gives Stephanie the message.

****

The biggest bedroom in the house belongs to Stephanie. It's three times the size of Irene's little room. Stephanie's bedroom is on the back of the house. The windows start just above the floor because the slope of the roof cuts into the wall halfway up along either side.

Stephanie is very neat and her room is always straightened. A big bed, which used to be her parents' bed, is in the center of the back wall. There is a dresser on one side of the room, and her desk is on the other. Two pictures of smiling pixy girls in old fashioned dresses are hanging next to the door. On Stephanie's desk in a brown metal frame is a snapshot of her boyfriend. Stephanie is thirteen years old.

"My parents," Stephanie says, "are two very different people. The way they live is different. Their lifestyle—well, not really their lifestyle. But the things they do, they're just different."

Stephanie is speaking so softly it's difficult to understand her. She's not at all sure she even wants to talk about this. It wasn't her idea to be interviewed in the first place and, in the second place, she almost doesn't know how to talk about all this because she never has. She's never discussed her parents' homosexuality, not with her sister, not with her parents—not with anyone.

"Um, just the fact that my mom is very close to Janet, and my dad was close to Mitch—but not anymore. They respect each other and love each other. But they have things that they want to do and when they're together," Stephanie is sitting on her bed with her hands in her lap, "it just doesn't work, I guess."

Stephanie is wearing a delicate pink shirt and jeans. She has on three bracelets, several rings, and silver hoop earrings. She is wearing dark eye makeup and flesh colored pimple medicine. Her hair is pulled back in a ponytail.

Stephanie looks worried. She thinks for a moment, and then she takes a deep breath and lets it out with a sigh. "My parents wouldn't be living together if it weren't for us kids. They are going to get separated after I get out of high school," she says. "I know that for a fact. They told us that." Stephanie clears her throat. "See, my mom wants to wait until I get out of school because she thinks I should have a mother, and because she doesn't like the idea of being one parent, I guess.

"But my mom wants to go live with Janet, because they're close. And my dad probably wants to live with someone else too, who he'll probably get to know. So, it's kind of hard. It's hard working it out like this."

A new addition to the family pushes herself in through the crack in Stephanie's door. It's a grey-striped kitten named Tinkerbell. Standing next to the door, Tinkerbell looks around the room in all directions. Satisfied, she darts across the open space and jumps onto Stephanie's bed. Stephanie picks the kitten up. Tinkerbell whines and struggles to get free. But Stephanie holds onto her, cradling her in her arms.

"My dad and I are very close," Stephanie says. "I could do very well with my father alone. I mean, I still love my mother and I want her to stay, but if they would separate, I'd get along well with my father. Like my mom says, I'm his little girl and Irene's my mom's little girl. My dad and I, we just get along really good, on almost everything."

Tinkerbell has now relaxed. Her eyes are closed, and Stephanie is stroking her tummy. "My dad is the one who's always home on weekends, usually," Stephanie says. "And every weekend he takes me over to the south side, either to a disco or to a movie, so I can see my boyfriend Ken. See, my dad knows that Ken is special to me. He told me. He said, I'm doing this because I know you like to see him.' " Stephanie gives a big smile. "I thought that was a pretty neat thing," she says. "When my dad said that I knew he cared about me."

Tinkerbell suddenly arches her back and wiggles out of Stephanie's arms. She jumps off the bed and runs halfway across the room. In mid-leap she stops, sits down, and quietly begins licking herself. Tinkerbell's back foot is pointed straight up. With her eyes closed she is calmly licking the fur on her leg.

Stephanie has many friends, and when she is with them she is very outgoing. She is always talking and laughing and joking. But inside the house she's different, she's much more serious. Each day Stephanie comes home after school and cleans the entire house. She spends two hours vacuuming, dusting and straightening all the rooms. She wants to do her part to make the house run smoothly. She wants very much for things to work out, although she is afraid sometimes that they won't.

"Me and my mom, well, last year we weren't getting along at all. We were always fighting. She was always yelling at me for something I did, and I was always angry with her." Stephanie gives a sad smile. "Like in the morning when I was getting ready to go to school, I would be putting on my makeup, and she was always crabby about that. So, we would just start fighting, like cats and dogs. I tried to do my best and she tried to do her best, but something would go wrong during the day and then everything would start happening."

Stephanie pushes her bangs out of her eyes. She feels a strand of stray hair and she carefully tucks it behind her ear. "But we're getting along better now, my mom and I. Like if I ask her for a favor, to go somewhere, or if I want to buy clothes or something, my mother understands. You know? If I need something, she gets it for me." Stephanie shakes her head. "Not to be spoiled, whatever I want I get. That's not it. But..." Stephanie's voice drifts off.

Tinkerbell jumps back up onto the bed. The kitten crawls into Stephanie's lap. "Now you want to cuddle," Stephanie says. "When I wanted to hold you, then you didn't want to." Tinkerbell curls up into a little ball of gray fur. She closes her eyes. "Silly kitty".

The sun is going down. Stephanie looks out her window. The clouds are a pink color. Tinkerbell is purring softly. With one hand Stephanie is cradling Tinkerbell's little head.

Stephanie picks up the kitten and holds it to the side of her face. Tinkerbell looks at Stephanie through sleepy eyes. She meows a protest and struggles to get free.

"Okay, okay," Stephanie says as she puts Tinkerbell back in her lap. In no time at all the puff of gray fur has her eyes closed and is sleeping again.

"I guess it's nice when the whole family is together," Stephanie says, "because we aren't together all that often. But then sometimes, sometimes when the whole family is together, we don't get along that well." Stephanie shrugs. She looks confused. "So it seems better the other way, where we get along. I don't know," she says.

****

"In my own way I love Jon," Arliss says of her husband, "but it's my own way. And in his way he loves me, too. Believe me, if something happened to me, he'd be the first one there. He'd beat Janet there, he'd beat everybody." Arliss leans back in her chair. "And sometimes something will come up, say an argument between Jon and I, and the kids will look at me. They'll give me this look. I'll just say to them, 'I'm here, aren't I? I'm here.'"

The family is still together, living on Grayson Street. Dinner is over, and since this is a week night Jon is out for the evening. The kitchen has been cleaned up. The girls are upstairs studying. Arliss is in the kitchen, sitting at the dining room table. The portable dishwasher has been rolled in front of the sink and plugged into the faucet. It's noisily chugging away as it cleans the dishes.

"Maybe I love Jon as a brother, I don't know. We are good business partners. What I lack in faith, he has, and I temper his inclination to believe in everyone." Arliss puts her hand over her cup of coffee. "Jon's a good man," she says, "and I value that. But because I care that much about Jon I will criticize him, where no one else will. I want him to be the best that he can be. However, he sometimes gets threatened by the fact that I'm very articulate and I don't mince words."

Arliss is wearing a yellow button-down shirt and blue pants. As usual, she is wearing her tinted glasses. The kitchen table is set for breakfast. The table is in a little alcove with a large window that looks out on the street. Mealtime is the one time when the family is together. And the kitchen table is the one place where both parents and both kids are sure to see each other in a given day.

"There was a time when I did everything in this house," Arliss says, speaking loudly in order to be heard over the washing machine. "I did all the laundry, I did all the ironing, I did all the cooking. Now Jon probably does more than I do. It all changed some years ago."

Arliss pauses and clears her throat. She purses her lips together. "I did have a nervous breakdown, okay? I spent three weeks in the hospital. The whole family realized that this was serious, and that's when they started helping. I just sort of played it cool for a while." Arliss sits very still. The washing machine is making it hard to hear Arliss. It sounds like a car that won't start.

"At that time I wasn't out with my homosexuality. I was having a relationship with this woman, and I was confused about that. I had gone back to graduate school. I was trying to be the perfect wife, the perfect mother, keep a beautiful home, and get all A's as well. It was too much, too much pressure on me, obviously, because I broke.

"I didn't talk to my doctor about it in the hospital, I didn't think he would understand. But I arrived at a private decision at that time to come out about my homosexuality. So, after fourteen years of marriage, and twenty years of keeping this secret, I finally told Jon." Arliss lets out a sigh. She gives a half smile. "There wasn't a great deal of probing on his part, it was more like a total acceptance. 'Yes, understand. Yes, we'll work this out.' That was four years ago," Arlis says, "that's when Jon and I sat down and proceeded to redefine ourselves."

The dishwasher turns off, and suddenly the room is quiet. Arlis looks up confused. Stephanie's music can be heard softly coming from upstairs.

"I knew I couldn't live with the secret any more. I tried for many years and just about killed myself in the process." Arliss shakes her head. "There's nothing wrong with me. I'm a perfectly good person. don't do anything to hurt anybody.

"I am who I am, and if that causes problems for the children, then I feel for them. But you see, I'd rather have my children see me as a complete and utter foolish human being, with all the warmth, the anger, the mistakes, and happiness that that entails, than the way I was Now the children have the choice either to emulate me or say, 'now that is something that I never want to do.' But I want them to see me as a human being, and as I really am." Arliss sits quietly again. The kitchen is warm, and it still smells of the pot roast Jon made for dinner Arliss bites on one nail as she thinks about that period of time, and all the changes the family has gone through since then.

"The thing is," Arliss says, her voice much softer now, "after Jon and I came out our home life became much easier. Because the kids knew where we stood. And the problems we had, well, they knew i wasn't them."

Stephanie comes downstairs. There is the sound of the TV switching on in Arliss's room. The moon is visible through the bay window. It's almost full. The few clouds are small and low in the sky They are nearly as white as in the daytime. Arliss runs her hand back through her short hair.

"Now I may not be sexually mad for Jon. But I think it's very easy to be sexually involved with someone, and attracted to them, and ou of your skull. That's romantic, whatever. I don't give a damn abou that. But I care about him deeply. I care about his humanness, and don't want him to screw up his life." Arliss pauses a moment, and then continues. "I think that is of far more substance than someone who is mad for someone else's body.

"I think we've gone through the crisis of the separation," Arliss says "I'm not sure I'll separate from him. He may want to, and I car

257

understand that, if he does. But we've worked together for so long and relied on one another for so long, that it's very conceivable that we'll just stay together." Arliss stretches. She yawns. "Besides, it wouldn't be economically feasible to separate," she says. "And I'm certainly not going to the poorhouse over this, okay?"

****

(Returning to the present. Two years later.)

"My friends' parents don't understand a lot of things that my parents do," Stephanie says. "When I tell my parents some things, right from the heart, they understand it. Like if something happens in school and I get in trouble with the teachers. My friends' parents would probably ground them. They wouldn't even want to hear what happened. But my parents would talk to me about it. They would want to discuss it with me.

After Stephanie graduates from high school she wants to become a beautician. Her three-step plan is to first go to a beauty college, then to work for someone else, and finally to open her own shop. Stephanie is very focused when it comes to her future. She knows she wants to make a good living, and she is already making plans for her life in a way that doesn't leave that to chance.

That's one reason why the new apartment her mom found is so perfect. There are two businesses on the first floor facing the street, and one of them is a beauty parlor. With all the unpacking and chaos of the last week, Stephanie still hasn't gotten around to talking to the ladies who work there. But she plans to get to know them and learn what she can from watching them.

The second reason why the apartment is so perfect is the other business. It's a weight-lifting room. Very well-built guys go in and out of that doorway all day long. They drive up in their cars, or on motorcycles, wearing tank tops that show off their muscles. And Stephanie's bedroom window overlooks the entrance to the gym. As far as Stephanie is concerned, when her mom went to find an apartment, she couldn't have found a better one.

"My parents are just like regular parents. They love my sister and me. I mean, whatever they do, it's their life. They're not harming us in any way. I don't know if people get that idea." Stephanie is sitting on the windowsill waiting for her hair to dry. The window is open. It's quite hot out for eleven in the morning. The only saving grace is that there is a bit of a breeze blowing. The wind feels nice as it blows through Stephanie's hair.

"I really don't know why people have a hard time with it," Stephanie says. "I guess they think God didn't mean for men to be with men, and women to be with women. I don't know." Stephanie shakes her head. "I can't explain that about people. But, if they think gays are terrible, rotten people, they're all wet. You know? Because they're not."

From where she sits on the windowsill, Stephanie can watch the traffic and people go by on the street. This is just another hot summer day with nothing to do. Stephanie feels her hair to see how dry it is. She takes her bangs and parts them down the middle.

"I don't know a whole lot about homosexuality, and I don't really want to know. It's my parents' business. I don't need to know, because I'm not gay. Whatever they do, it's their life, and I don't think I care right now. I know what it is, but—" Stephanie stops to think. "—what I know is fine. It's fine. I think I know enough."

Stephanie is impatient to explain this. In fact, she would love to explain this and then have the discussion over with. Speaking about her parents' homosexuality makes Stephanie very uncomfortable. She crosses her arms in front of her. "I don't really care, you know? I don't care if they're gay. I wouldn't care if they were black. I just don't care. It's the idea. Not the idea of being gay, it's the situation. It's having their friends over and all the arrangements, and all the stories I have to come up with. It's just the fact that I have to hide things. I have to make a lot of adjustments, you know, to cover things up. That's the hardest thing for me."

A car pulls into the parking lot and parks directly under Stephanie's window. It's a beat-up old car with rust spots that have been sanded down but not repainted. The engine shuts off and three big, muscular guys get out. They all look like they've been lifting weights since they were babies.

Stephanie watches them from above. She's not more than twenty feet away but they don't see her, they don't look up. She watches them as they slam the doors and slowly lumber down the sidewalk and around the corner of the building. Stephanie smiles, she can't get over it. It's like being invisible, or looking through a one-way mirror.

It takes a while for Stephanie to get back to what she was talking about. She's been mesmerized by the passing of the muscle men. Finally, she snaps out of it, takes a deep breath and begins again.

"When we lived over at the old house," she says, "there would be all kinds of dad's friends over there. How could I explain that? All my friends were having slumber parties. But I never did. I wouldn't bring my friends over to the house. And then when Dad first met Tim, and he used to stay with us on weekends, I used to tell everyone that Tim was my uncle. I used to tell people that Tim was lonely. So he would stay with us and we would help him and stuff on weekends."

Stephanie looks out the window. The sun is shining on the brick building across the parking lot. "Mom's relationship was easier to explain, because she went to Janet's house instead of Janet coming to ours. But if someone asked, I would never tell them that my mother was staying over at a friend's house. That would be kind of weird." Stephanie wrinkles up her nose. "There's no suburban wife that does that.

"I just said that she was at a convention." Stephanie snickers like it's a private joke. "I always said the same thing, 'Mom's at a convention.' I probably told that to the same person three weeks in a row." Stephanie shakes her head. "I have no idea what they thought."

Stephanie jumps up and goes into the bathroom. She takes her blow dryer off the shelf and plugs it in. Looking in the mirror Stephanie proceeds to comb and dry her hair. She is wearing a blue bathrobe with green paisleys on it. The bathrobe is made out of a velour material. She gives her hair the proper attention, until she is satisfied it is dry and is lying just right.

Stephanie unplugs the dryer and puts it away. There doesn't seem to be much reason to fix her hair, since there's no place really to go. But at this point it's more of a habit with Stephanie. She does it every morning. Stephanie goes back to the window and sits down.

"I think that people don't accept it, maybe, because they're scared for themselves, scared that they'll be approached by someone gay." Stephanie looks out the window. "Irene goes to my mother's and Janet's parties, but I don't. I don't enjoy them. I'm not comfortable around—" Stephanie pauses, "—around pronounced gay people." Stephanie bites on her lip. "I don't know why. I guess, I don't want them to think I'm that way."

A motorcycle pulls up loudly into the parking lot. The man who gets off is thin, but he still looks very strong. He parks his bike and disappears around the corner. Stephanie watches him but her mind is somewhere else. She stares at the corner of the building.

"I do feel very different from the rest of the family," she says after a while. "And I have a feeling that it's going to bother me someday, you know?" Stephanie is speaking softly. She looks worried as she stares out the window. "Well, if my sister turns gay, and everybody else is—I don't know," Stephanie closes her eyes and rubs her forehead. "It's just, it's just—odd."

****

"Aaam Naa Aangry." It sounds like a foghorn without the volume. "Aaam Naa Angry," Blanche repeats in her monotone voice. Irene is impatiently standing in front of Blanche's big chair trying to figure out what it is that she is trying to say.

Finally it comes to her. She shakes her head and waves her hand so Blanche won't go through it again.

"Aaam Naa Aangry," Blanche says anyway.

"YOU'RE NOT HUNGRY RIGHT NOW," Irene mouths to the deaf woman. She speaks each word slowly so Blanche can read her lips. Blanche nods. "OK, WE WILL EAT IN ONE HOUR."

Blanche nods again. "liine," she says.

Irene goes into the kitchen. There are two small fillets on the counter wrapped in plastic. It's a fish that Irene caught two days ago. The fillets have been thawing out all afternoon. Irene puts the fish in the refrigerator and goes back to the table. Sometimes Irene would rather not listen to Blanche repeat things in that deaf voice of hers. She would rather just tell Blanche what is happening and leave it at that. But that is usually not possible.

"After I left college," Irene says, sitting with her back to Blanche, "I went to the local technical school to take this aptitude test. We wanted to see what occupation I should go into. On one form I had to finish a sentence and I wrote, 'men take advantage of me because I'm a woman.'" Irene shrugs. "That really hasn't happened to me, but it's happened to my mom.

"My counselor, he's a man, he read that sentence and he said to me, 'are you a lesbian?'" Irene's eyes open wide. "I just said, 'now wait a minute!' " Irene raises her voice. "I couldn't believe he said that!"

Irene's hands are in front of her on the table, balled up into fists. She's holding her body very straight. She smiles nervously. "He'd read the sentence and he kept bringing up the lesbian thing. I thought, 'what is he bringing this up for? I don't believe this!' And then he asked me flat out. So I said, 'I'm not sure. I'm not sure if I am, and I'm not sure if I'm not.'"

Irene and Blanche are practically back to back. Blanche is reading with a magnifying glass in the big chair facing the lake. Irene, who doesn't talk about this with anyone, not even her family, is speaking in a loud voice two feet from Blanche. But as far as Irene is concerned, Blanche doesn't hear a thing.

"I had a boyfriend my last year in high school. We were not really dating-dating, but we went out on the weekend a couple of times to a movie." Irene brushes her hair out of her face with her hand. "His name was Thad," she says. "I didn't like what he was doing. He would drink beer in his car. He smoked marijuana. We went to dinner one night and he reached over and said to me, 'hey, how would you like to smoke some marijuana?' I said, 'wait a minute—this is crazy!'

"I went home that night and talked to my mom about it. She said, 'that's the worst thing you could do being asthmatic.' Well, I called him up that very night and left a message with one of his family members. I thought that was the best way to do it," Irene explains. "Go through a family member, so they all know what's happening. I said, 'Tell Thad that I don't want to see him anymore,' and they said, 'okay.' And that was the end of that."

Irene's leg is moving up and down under the table. "I still think, okay, personally I like dating. I like going out with the opposite sex. But I still enjoy staying, you know, with the girls. I think, also, as I've become older I've become more like my mom. I don't mean that I'm a lesbian. I mean I've become a feminist.

"I'm a full-fledged member of NOW," Irene says. "I've helped out with the newsletter. I went on the walk to take back the night. I get involved in all the feminist activities I can get into. And Stephanie is always saying, 'oh, you're just like Mom.' But I've decided, 'well, geez, this is really neat. I really like what they're doing.'"

Blanche's magnifying glass rests on her book. Her eyes are closed. Blanche was very sick when Irene first moved in with her. It is Irene's care that has produced such a change. Irene is not a nurse, she's had no medical training. But Blanche was drinking. She was drinking a nip at a time, for most of the day. And Blanche could hardly get out of bed, she was so sick. The first thing Irene did when she moved in with Blanche was throw out all her liquor bottles. Blanche was furious. But Irene wouldn't give in. Within a month Blanche went from being a bedridden woman without much time left, to being able to get around with a walker, and doing quite well.

Irene crosses her arms. She smiles nervously. "Okay, first of all, I've said this a lot. I've said, 'we're all gay no matter what. Because boys hang out with boys, and girls hang out with girls. So, in some parts of you, you're gay.' " Irene looks out towards the water as she tries to put together what she is thinking.

"Okay, there are a lot of women who say, 'I think I can handle it. My body says it's time to go with the opposite sex.' Then others don't find the right guy, or it's not the right time. So they say to themselves 'well, I don't fit in. I'm going to go back to my old life. I feel more comfortable with the girls than I do with the boys.' And still others are sort of stuck in the middle. They think, 'well, maybe if I'm independent for a while, then I'll figure it out.' "

Blanche wakes up. She picks up her book and starts to read again. She holds her big magnifying glass an inch above the page. Irene looks out towards the lake. It's very still. There is barely a ripple on the surface.

"My parents' situation didn't shove it in my face and say, 'this is the way it is.' But it introduced me to quite a few people. There were a lot of people that I was able to meet and get to know well. I said to myself 'hey, I really like this. I have a chance to be with someone I like, besides a family member.' Okay? And in that way, I guess I could say yes to almost everything dealing with being a lesbian.

"You know? I hang around women more than I do men," Irene says, with her eyes opened wide. "But I've always thought of it as just friend to friend. I've never thought about it as physical or anything like that. And I haven't felt that way towards a boy either."

Irene gets up and goes into the kitchen to start dinner. She opens a can of corn and puts that into a pan. She slices two carrots and puts them in another. Irene is no fancy cook. She never really cooked a home. She's even had some disasters putting together easy meals. Blanche doesn't complain, though. She doesn't have much money. For room and board she gets a live-in cook, housekeeper, and nurse.

Irene sets the table with the red and white china plates. She gets down the cast iron frying pan and puts it on the stove. Irene pours oil from a large bottle into the pan. More oil pours out than Irene wanted, more than she should use. Irene just spreads it around. She takes the two pieces of fish and sets them in the oil and turns on the gas.

"Stephanie thinks about that stuff," Irene continues. "Stephanie goes, 'look at that guy's body!' But I never do. That's something that, as far as I'm concerned, is not important." Irene takes the spatula out of the drawer.

"If I'm going to live out there, I have to have a diploma in my hand saying I'm qualified to do a certain job. If I don't have that diploma, I can stand on the employment line for the rest of my life. So, education is more important to me than seeing someone walk down the street and saying, 'boy, he's sexy, or she's sexy,' or whatever," Irene says. She shakes the pan with a stiff, quick motion.

"That part I don't worry about. You could say, the hell with it." Irene is uncomfortable talking about this. She looks to be making an effort to keep smiling. "And this woman, Kathy, sometimes I'll have dinner with her, or go to a movie. But I don't want to hop in bed with her—that kind of thing. I don't go for that. I never have."

The fish is getting brown. Irene turns both pieces over and goes into the other room. She taps Blanche on the shoulder to get her attention. Blanche looks up. "Din-ner," Irene mouths. Blanche looks confused. "DIN-NER," Irene says louder.

****

"If you're not heterosexually oriented, don't get married," Arliss says. "I made a big mistake. I shouldn't have done it." Arliss is on the couch in Janet's living room. She's in a low mood, speaking without any enthusiasm in her voice.

"I knew I was gay, but I tried to overcome it. I did everything. It doesn't work, and don't let anyone tell you that it does. The sexual act is no place for play acting. If it doesn't happen, say 'we're not compatible'." Arliss shakes her head. She runs her hands back through her hair. "I'm not saying you can build a relationship on sex either.

That won't hold it together. But it's important. I thought maybe it wasn't and I was wrong. It's absolutely important."

One lamp is on, across the room, casting a soft light. Headlights sweep across the front window as a car pulls into the driveway next door. Soon the engine turns off, and a car door slams. Arliss leans forward and rests her weight on her knees.

"The hardest thing for me," Arliss says, "was that I was no longer living with the family. I was no longer living in a group situation, and I missed that. I mean Jon was a friend of mine, I could always talk to Jon. And although Janet and I have a good relationship, and she does try to reach out to me, it's not her strong suit." Arliss pauses, lost in thought. After a moment she continues. "A lot of people thought we had an ideal family. In the beginning I even thought we did. But there was still that thing that was missing."

One of the cats runs across the room. The other cat, lying on the chair, watches it. Arliss is sitting hunched over, looking down at the floor.

"What I feel badly about is that I have brought two children into the world who have to somehow deal with the fact that they are the fruit of a relationship that didn't work very well. I hope that it won't interfere with their concept of who they are, but I'm afraid that it will. Because I'm the fruit of a relationship that didn't work very well, and it certainly had an effect on me." Arliss looks up, squinting into the light. "And here I am repeating that sad story again."

Arliss is wearing black pants, a blue shirt and sandals. There are lines under her eyes from not sleeping well. She leans back on the couch.

"Stephanie is not relaxed," she says in a tired voice. "Everything is imperative. Irene, on the other hand, is almost too relaxed, too low key." Arliss throws up her hands. "I don't know, maybe I'm looking for things that can't be. But I find it almost inconceivable that Irene flunked out of college. I mean, I went to school, I played around a lot. But I never failed. I suppose I have to realize that she has a learning disability, and that frightens me. I just hope that she can find something that she will be able to master.

"I'm also concerned that people will take advantage of Irene. She doesn't have the street smarts of Stephanie. She's so... trusting, naive. Irene may get married, but it's gonna be some kind of guy that gets her turned on." Arliss laughs to herself. "I don't know," she says, "Jon was a late bloomer. He was definitely a late bloomer." She laughs again, a sad laugh. "In fact, by the time Jon bloomed, everyone else had died."

The cat jumps on the windowsill and looks through the glass. "I just hope it works out with Stephanie and I," Arliss says speaking softly. "I guess it has to, there isn't anywhere else for her to go." Arliss stares at the cat. Her gaze is full of worry. "Stephanie seems to always be wanting to press this issue and press that issue. Why is she so demanding?

"Stephanie has needs that are so great. She's always been like that. She's less like that now than she used to be. I give in to it more, and she asks less. I think that's my theory. I'm gonna try to go on like that." Arliss rubs her hand across her forehead. "She's got to get filled up sooner or later, doesn't she? Surely it can't be a bottomless, neurotic pit?"

Arliss chuckles softly. But as her smile fades away she looks sad, sad and tired. "I think we'll be okay," she says in a low voice. "But, really, I have no answers. It seems that everything came so suddenly. And yet, maybe it wasn't fast at all. It did take so long for us to finally..." Arliss's voice trails off. She sits and stares for the longest time. An occasional car passes on the street and the headlights sweep across the far wall. "We'll see... we'll see.

****

"I thought I was doing okay in school. In botany class I thought I was doing really good," Irene says. "Then the teacher told me, 'I recommend that you drop this course.'" Irene shakes her head. "I said, 'well fine, if that's the way you look at it, okay.' So I dropped it.

"See, I made a big mistake. I took about three—well, two hard courses at once. I shouldn't have done that. But you learn." Irene shrugs her shoulders.

"Now I'm going into printing and publishing. I'm gonna learn how to run the machines. My parents met in publishing. My mother always crossed out everything on my dad's page and sent it back to him to redo." Irene covers her mouth as she laughs.

After dinner Irene helped Blanche to bed. She finished the dishes and sat down in Blanche's chair facing the picture window. At that point it was still light outside, even though the sun had set. Irene was debating whether or not to fish from the dock until dark. She sat in the big chair and watched the lake. But her mind kept jumping from one thought to another, until the next thing she knew, the stars were out.

"I never thought of having a family," Irene says. "I've always thought of just being by myself—of not having kids, not having a husband, that kind of thing." Irene sits forward in the chair. "I've always been very independent. I've always thought, 'okay, I might know somebody and everything else, but it just wouldn't work. Because I hold so many jobs, and I hold, umm,' " Irene stumbles looking for the words. "I've never really had the feeling that I'd like to, you know, I've never..."

Irene's voice trails off. When Irene is talking about something and she gets confused, she doesn't like to stop. It makes her feel like she doesn't know what she's saying. She'll talk on and on, rather than pause for just a moment to compose her thoughts.

"See, my mom is very independent, and my dad is very dependent." Irene is speaking fast. "My mother can go out and strive for what she wants and get it. But my dad needs someone to back him up. There's no getting around it." Irene nods her head, like she's on the right track. "See, I'm more like my mom, and Stephanie is more like my dad.

"For instance, with dad and Tim. Now dad's relating just to Tim. Tim's the head honcho, you know, of dad's brain. It's, 'Oh, Jon, you should do this', 'oh, Jon, you shouldn't do that.' You know, dad's letting Tim walk all over him."

Irene looks out the window. The next door neighbor's boat is tied to his dock. One time he took her out fishing, and Irene caught the only fish that day. As they were tying up the boat afterwards, he muttered that it was bad luck fishing with a woman. And he hasn't invited her out since then.

Irene spends a lot of time alone, fishing or reading. She didn't have a lot of friends when she lived at home, but at least every day she could talk with the family. Up at the lake she doesn't know the neighbors, and she can't have much of a talk with Blanche. They talk, but Irene can hardly understand what Blanche is saying. And Irene has to repeat everything she says three of four times.

"The way it is now, my mother is more interested in my feelings than my father is. I mean, I have to call my dad if I want to talk to him. He won't call me, very rarely does he call me. But my mother. I'm in constant touch with her.

"And I think Stephanie realizes that Mom is sticking up for her. I think she sees the way things are and says, 'Wow, I was really wrong. I was wrong about Mom.' " Irene pushes her hair out of her face.

"See, my mom and Stephanie used to always argue. It was the way Stephanie treated herself. She wore all kinds of makeup, and big tight pants. Stephanie went out and socked it to those guys, you know? I think that was the main reason she and Mom had a big gap between them. It was just the way they—well, see, their ideas were different."

Suddenly Irene sees a shooting star. It floats halfway across the sky. Her mouth drops open. Without even grabbing a jacket she runs outside, just wearing a t-shirt and jeans, no shoes even. The dogs next door are tied up. They start barking.

Irene is in a funny mood. She's usually in bed by now. Besides, it's cool by the lake. It's not like her to go outside without dressing warmly. If she catches a cold it's dangerous for her asthma. But it's a beautiful night, and she wants to think about these things.

The stars are out like crazy. Crickets are everywhere, and the water is lap-lapping against the side of the dock. Irene is already swatting the mosquitoes on her arms. She sits with her arms wrapped tightly against her body, covering as much skin as she can, watching the lake. As she gently rocks back and forth in Blanche's metal chair, there's a feeling of excitement going through her.

****

"I knew they were going to separate," Stephanie says. "I knew it when they talked about selling the house. That was it, you know? Then they were really going to do it because they weren't going to get another place together." Stephanie wipes the sweat off her upper lip. "It wasn't a shock to me, though. If they were real close and everything, it would have been. But they weren't. I think it's better that they separated."

Stephanie is at the kitchen table. She has on white shorts and a pink tube top. Stephanie has just turned on the air conditioner for about the tenth time. When she turns it on it gets too cold, then when she turns it off it gets too hot. The air conditioner is purring loudly. Stephanie takes a deep drag on her cigarette and blows out the smoke in a thin stream.

"If I think about it, my parents didn't have much to do with each other even when we were younger. But, I don't know, I guess that seemed kind of normal to me. Because a lot of my friends' parents were like that too. Still, when my friends came over, I always expected them to ask, 'why aren't your parents sleeping together?' You know? Separate bedrooms seemed kind of weird to me."

Stephanie takes a last drag off her cigarette and crushes it out. "I'm not going to tell any of my friends that my parents are gay until I'm much older. It wouldn't go over very well. I know, I hear them talking." She makes a face. "You just don't see a lot of kids with parents who are gay."

Stephanie looks bored. She's bored from talking about her family so much, and bored from sitting around all day. Reaching behind her chair, Stephanie opens the refrigerator and takes out a bowl of macaroni. Stephanie is, as usual, on a diet. Her method of dieting consists of eating nothing for most of the day, then when she can't stand it anymore, to eat whatever snacks and fattening foods she can find. Consequently, she never seems to lose weight. Stephanie takes a fork and starts stabbing noodles. She eats them carefully, so as not to disturb her makeup.

"My mom and I, we've gotten pretty close," Stephanie says. "When I was living with my dad, every time I saw her we'd have the greatest time. We'd just laugh, or window shop, or something like that. Mom's changed, she's more easygoing. She's got a short temper, but she controls it more now." There is a "ting-ting" sound as Stephanie's fork strikes the metal bowl. "Mom likes my idea of things, and she likes my boyfriend. She cares a lot about me, and I never felt that before."

Stephanie puts the bowl down. She licks the corners of her mouth with the tip of her tongue. "I'm the one who's really changed though. I've changed a lot. I used to snoop in everyone's room when I was cleaning the house. And when they found out they were really mad. I wouldn't do that anymore. I have more respect for other people's things, for other people.

"I'm more conservative now, too. Before I was seeing all these guys and always going out. Now I've been going with Michael for ten months," Stephanie has a big smile on her face. She looks to be very proud of herself. "That's the kind of thing I like, you know."

It's cold in the apartment again. Stephanie gets up and turns the air conditioner off. She puts her bowl in the sink and starts the water so she can do the dishes before her mom gets home. While the water is running, she looks in the mirror and adjusts her hair.

Another boring day of watching "soaps" and smoking cigarettes is nearing the end. Stephanie hasn't done much of anything all day. But Arliss isn't pushing her. Arliss feels Stephanie needs a rest from all the confusion of the separation, and moving twice—besides all the fighting that went on at her dad and Tim's place before she left there. Stephanie doesn't plan to do this forever. She wants to get a job. But for the moment, sitting around the apartment seems to be all she can handle.

"I suppose I'm like my dad," Stephanie says, speaking softly. "I'm pretty dependent. I want to have a family—two kids, a neat husband, a big house, a big yard." Stephanie laughs, embarrassed. "I mean, I'm sure I'll be like my parents in some ways. I'll be stern like they were. But sometimes I think I'll be more like this family I babysit for.

"This family I babysit for is really a neat family. They have two little girls that are real special to them. And the parents, they're best friends. They both work and when they get home it's like 'God, am I glad to see you!' Every day they have a big reunion. I really love to watch it."

Stephanie's face lights up as she thinks about it. "My parents used to be like that," she says. "Well, not exactly, but they used to come home and say, 'how was your day? Let's sit down at the table and talk about it', and stuff like that. But it just faded, I guess."

Stephanie stacks the dishes in the dishrack to dry. She's antsy, from being inside all day. She takes out her last cigarette and lights it.

A car pulls into the parking lot. Stephanie watches as two guys get out. One of them is short with blond hair and a striped tennis shirt. The other is taller with brown hair. He's wearing a pair of green army pants. They're younger than most of the men who go in and out of the weight room. They look to be of high school age. The two of them are kidding each other loudly and laughing. Stephanie watches the one in the army pants. As he walks beneath her window she catches his eye and he smiles at her.

Stephanie jumps up and puts on her shoes. She checks her hair and her makeup quickly. With both hands she pulls up her tube top. Stephanie runs to get a dollar from her bedroom to finance her excuse for going out, a pack of cigarettes. She leaves a short message for her mom on a piece of paper by the sink. "Gone for a walk, be back soon. Your loving daughter, Stephanie."

Stephanie puts the dollar in the pocket of her shorts as she hurries down the steps. As she opens the door and walks out into the parking lot she's struck by a wave of bright sunshine. Stephanie stops on the stoop for a second, a little dizzy. She squints into the sunlight. After a moment her eyes adjust and she continues down the sidewalk. Her heart starts to beat quickly as she looks tentatively around the corner of the building. And then she takes a deep breath and walks past the big window at the entrance of the weight room.

Update:

Stephanie Stanley

Summer, 1982

Dear Joe,

Well, I'm sorry it's been such a long time since you've heard from us. We've had a very busy year, and not all good. The chapter on our family brought back a lot of mixed feelings for me. I must say it was mighty depressing—for me. It all sounds really good though. It turned out pretty well considering all the chasing you had to do to squeeze information out of me. Sorry.

I am not sure what else I can say about the chapter. I've had mixed emotions about it from the start, as you well know. But it's a touching biography on our family, and I'm glad everyone went through with doing it. Maybe it will help others through tough times to know they're not alone. And it may open minds of other people who aren't sure what this lifestyle is all about. They can see that our family is basically a "normal" family—maybe not normal, but can you understand what I'm trying to say? It's not one of my stronger points, expressing feelings. I guess I got that from my dad!?! So good luck on it. I hope a lot of people read it. I hope your average American family situation takes the time to pick it up so that maybe they can understand this more. Anyway, I have almost a whole year to tell you about.

First, the biggest news around is that I finished High School this year! I am very pleased. I felt I'd never see the day, and I feel now I can start over on a clean slate. I am going to be starting Beauty School Sept. 23, which I am very excited about. It's been my dream for as long as I can remember. Father is forking the bill... which he isn't too pleased about!

I haven't seen Dad much. He took me out for my birthday back in June. But otherwise he doesn't bother with us girls a great deal. Oh well!

I don't think his life is all together myself. I feel the vibes when I speak with him. Every once in a while I call him up at work. He has never called me up to just say, "hey, how are you, how's stuff going?" I'm getting used to that, but someday he'll wish he had. And when that day comes I probably won't want to bother with him, which is very, very, sad.

He and Tim are still together, I guess. I'm sure things aren't Honky Dorry with them. I can't tell you any more about him because I have no other info. He hardly ever brings up his personal life to me, which is fine. I am not terribly interested in the first place. But he asks plenty about Mom and her life.

Anyway about Mom, she's had a few hard knocks this summer. For one, she was asked to leave her job. It was not by any means because of the quality of her work. It was always done to a tee, she's a perfectionist. It was because of her relationship with her boss. I guess they just couldn't seem to work together. So, Mom is looking for employment. She's not desperate for a job, she's got money set aside that we're using. She wants to make sure she finds something that really interests her, so we shall see. She's a multitalented lady who knows how to do just about anything you put in front of her. Right now, she's doing a lot of painting for Janet on her house, and some other friends of hers want some work done too. But Janet is another story...

That's another blow my mom has had to handle. Seems Janet has found someone else she's quite interested in. She went down to Texas to visit a lady, another "intellectual." She had been writing to this woman but never met her, and I gather they hit it off well. So that has hurt Mom a great deal. Anyway, this lady is going to be moving up into Janet's house!! Oh my!! That's made it all the worse.

I must explain that Mom and Janet have formed a sister relationship, non-physical type bond, which seems to be working out okay. But it's still going to be hard when this lady moves here. Everything will change. All of us aren't sure it will last. It's probably just a physical attraction. So Mom is playing the field you could say, keeping her eyes and ears open. She feels very sad, first the divorce and now this. The parting from the relationship with Janet is worse than the divorce and everything else put together. But they're still close, in a different kind of a way now. So, we'll see where things end up.

Now to Irene. She's doing well, still taking care of the man in Reedley. Oh dear, maybe you don't know about that either. Things didn't work out with her and Blanche, so she found a job taking care of a 47-year-old quadriplegic. He can't move his legs or arms. They have a very special relationship, I don't exactly know what it is. But she's very happy there.

She's awful busy, never a minute to sit down. They have a very nice apartment, and have everything they need and want!! So she's fine. I don't see her too much either. We all have our own lives which we're trying to arrange. And most of the time she has to stick around there, in case he needs cathing or whatever.

I don't exactly agree with how she's chosen to live and support herself. He's very dependent on her and she is on him. But he's not always going to be around, and I think she'd fall apart if anything ever happened to him. She'd be left without any source of money! I wish she'd go to nursing school. She'd be a darn good nurse! But she's doing what she loves and that counts too!

Well, what else can I catch you up on? The apartment is really cute. It's just big enough for mother and I. My Grandma put her house up for sale, since Grandpa passed away last Nov., and she is planning on moving back here. It looks like we'll probably move in with her. Well, Mom will. And I will for the short time I'll need to be supported. Hopefully I'll find a job after getting out of school and can get an efficiency or a room somewhere. I am really looking forward to being on my own.

Well, my hand feels like it's going to fall off, so I'll let you go. Thanks for everything, lots of luck. I'll write again, you write too.

Lots of love, Stephanie.

2022 update to the Stanley family

Joe - Okay, so let's talk about you and your family. Let's jump in.

Stephanie - 40 years is a long time to squeeze into an hour. But I'll let you lead the way.

Joe - Well, if we need to we can talk again in a week... So, as everything was taking place in your family, it's interesting because no one was talking about it. As your mom came out as lesbian, and then your father came out as gay, no one was bringing it up. No one was sitting you down and saying, "Stephanie, this is what's happening", so that you could ask questions or have a discussion.

Stephanie - Well, to this day, my adolescence is kind of a blur. I remember that in the book, you know, I was kind of an angry teenager. And it was a very troubling time for me. There was very little that I understood about what really was going on in our house. As far as I remember, my mother was home during the week. And my father was gone with his relationships during the week, and then he was home on the weekend. And I was doing the best I could to understand everything and kind of make some normality out of life, to integrate my teenage years and carry on. But it wasn't working very well. Joe, you know, I wish I could say it was wonderful. But for me, it was a struggle.

Joe - I think any child that has to absorb that much change is going to have a lot to deal with. But your parents, for whatever reason, they never really sat you down and said, "look, this is what we're doing. This is what it means." And so, you and your sister had to figure it out on your own.

Stephanie - I do recall that at one time they brought us into a family counseling session. But it was kind of-- it was kind of a train wreck of a session. That didn't go very well. And I'm not sure at what juncture that was. I don't remember. But for having such highly educated parents, and both being very good communicators, in our home life that was not the case. I guess we all muddled through and made the best of it.

Joe - Somebody talked about that therapy session in the book, where your parents brought up the fact that they were gay for the first time. It was after you ran away that the family decided to go to therapy. And the way it was described in the book was that your mom brought up that she was gay, and then you father said that he was as well. But you were all sitting in therapy and your family had never spoken about it. Never. And then all of a sudden she brought it up.

Stephanie - Thank you for bringing me back there. Okay. Yes, yes!

Joe - What was that like?

Stephanie - As I remember, it was a pretty profound moment. It was a sad moment. You know, there was a lot of anger in the room, and a lot of confusion. And I don't think there were a lot of follow up sessions, like there probably would be nowadays. From my recollection, I think it was just a comfortable place for my parents to come out with all of us there. And then that was that.

Joe - After the session your sister said that she didn't need to go again. And then both your parents agreed that there was no need to go again. So, after that bombshell was dropped, your family never went back to therapy. And maybe your family still didn't discuss the fact that your parents had "come out" as gay.

Stephanie - Yeah, it's kind of like we were just expected to deal with it. And honestly, Joe, it's kind of the way my mom is to this day. I love her dearly, but you know, we just kind of deal with things and that's it. And kids don't always have those natural coping mechanisms. I certainly didn't, when it came to those kind of intense family dynamics. Maybe my sister was a little bit more flexible with everything. But I wasn't.

Joe - The family was going through all those changes. There were so many changes going on at once. First of all, your parents were separating. Although they remained in the same house for a couple years, they were separating. And they were both discovering their sexuality, or finally admitting it to themselves. And I think your parents were kind of becoming more selfish, in a way, because they wanted to take the time to find someone new. I think it was your dad who said, "it was like going through a second adolescence". It's like they had never really explored their sexuality.

So, they were intent on doing that.

Stephanie - I'm sure that was the case. You know, now that I'm older and I've gone through a divorce myself, and different things have happened to me, I can now say that I understand how they felt. And I hate to say it, but I suppose that having kids at that time when they wanted to explore their sexuality, we were kind of underfoot, maybe. I hate to say that. It sounds so dismissive. But it was difficult. And my mother has confided in me and said, "I wasn't a real natural Mom, I wasn't real good at it." In my mom's situation, being a mother didn't come naturally to her. That's very different from how I am. I am the mother. So yeah, I wouldn't want to go back there.

Joe - Your dad says in the book, "I was a doting father and I was there for them when they were younger. So now that they're older they need to give me my space to be myself." But older, in your case, was like 13, 14 years old. That's not very old. That's, that's--

Stephanie - Not older. Yeah, that was very hard for me, for many years. It took me a long time to forgive. But I did because, as I got older, I feel that forgiveness is a gift. And I couldn't begin to heal myself until I forgave. But it took me a long time. Because I felt like they expected way too much out of me as a young person, to just kind of raise myself at an early age, and not lean on them. As much as I really needed to. And I'm sure that even when I talk right now, it's sounds scattered. Because that was such a scattered time in my life. It was just, yeah, it took me a long time to really forgive my parents, for a lot of things. And my mom is aware of that.

Joe - It had to be difficult to be 13, 14, 15 years old, and you weren't told what the situation was in your family, but you were expected to figure it out on your own.

Stephanie - I wonder if that was because my parents really didn't understand totally themselves. I mean, they were at that point of exploration. And some of it was pretty wild stuff that I was exposed to, to be honest with you. They're lucky that I stayed on a pretty safe path, throughout my life. Because some of the things that I saw back then weren't safe practices that I was exposed to.

Joe - Such as what?

Stephanie - Well, I mean, my father went to the baths in downtown Milwaukee, not that I went along to that. But there were some, I would say, some unsafe sexual practices probably going on, you know. It was not so much with my mother, but my dad. I was brought along to a couple of those events where, you know, the men were just acting kind of really wild out in public. And I would imagine what was going on behind closed doors. So, it was definitely a time of exploration for my dad.

Joe - Well, back then there was so much negativity and guilt directed towards gays and lesbians. Perhaps part of the reason your parents didn't come out for all those years, and the reason that they weren't able to be true to who they were earlier, is because they felt guilty about it.

Stephanie - Absolutely. And their religious background had a lot to do with it. Just think, my dad was in the seminary to be a priest. And my mother, I don't know if that ever came up. But mom was in New York, in a convent. And my father's family pushed for him to go in the seminary. Now, I was never told that it was because my father told his family that he had those feelings, that his family pushed for a religious life. But anyway, he was in the seminary in Michigan to be a priest. And my mother was a nun for a while. And by Gosh, that's just astounding to me that they found each other and got married. My dad, he came from a very well to do, well known, family.

Joe - Maybe they chose each other partly because they sensed that the other person wouldn't put many sexual expectations on them.

Stephanie - Yeah, a comfortableness about it. There's a lot of things I've wondered. But of course, with it being your parents, you don't want to broach those questions.

Joe - Do you remember that period of time when your family was just starting to separate, and they're just starting to be open about their interest in the same sex, but they hadn't explained anything to you? Do you remember that period where you're like, what's going on here? And no one was filling in the blanks for you.

Stephanie - I can just remember secluding myself. Isolation was comfortable for me as a teenager. I do remember it starting to happen that my mom had her friend Sharon, and mom was gone on the weekends. And daddy had a whole host of different friends. No one consistent, really, but a lot of different partners that would kind of come and go. And that was uncomfortable for me. I remember all that starting and we lived in suburbia, so you couldn't tell anybody. And, of course, I kept all my friends at arm's length. After school, you know, they would want to go do things and I wouldn't do anything with them. Because I didn't want them to come over and then have to explain what the situation was. Where is your father? What's going on? And, of course, there were different books around the house which I didn't want them to see. It was just all consuming.

Joe - I think most every child from the book dealt with the feeling that no friend their age would be able to be understanding and supportive of their situation. They felt like, eventually, if I tell anybody, it's going to bite me in the ass.

Stephanie - Oh boy, yeah, that's so true. Everyone will ditch me. And one of the things that I always thought about, I thought for sure that because both of my parents were gay, that I was going to grow up to be gay And I remember one time when I was very, very young, after I found out about my parents, I thought for sure I was gay. Because when I was very, very young, you know how little kids are. Well this friend and I, when I was very little, we were dancing naked. And this is probably when I was about five. So of course after I found out about my parents, years later when I was a teenager I thought back to that. And I thought, well, I must be gay because that happened, you know? And another thing, after I got that worry, I thought I'll never be able to get married because I will never be able to tell this to my potential partner, or his family. So, I'm going to be alone the rest of my life.

Joe - That must have been stressful.

Stephanie - Well, I really did think that. And I wanted children so bad. I had my first baby when I was 20. I was married, not that that matters. But I got married for the first time when I turned 19, which was pretty young to get married. Yeah, there was a lot of concern. I'm never gonna have a normal life like everybody else. I have this huge secret, and it will hang over my head forever.

Joe - Do you remember telling your husband, your first husband, about your family?

Stephanie - I do. I do. We have remained friends even after we got divorced. And I really have to give a lot of credit for my ability to stay friends with him, to my parents. Because even though I had a very tumultuous adolescence, my parents really did teach me a lot of good qualities about being a good human. My first husband was a very kind person. I think I picked him initially, looking for those qualities. I needed someone that I could tell all sorts of things to. Unfortunately, we did grow apart. We were very young when we married. But yes, I do remember telling him, and it wasn't a big deal.

Joe - Do you remember telling your girlfriends about your parents when you were young?

Stephanie - I'll be honest with you. I didn't have a lot of friends, and I still don't. It's kind of sad, isn't it? But, you know, I'm very cautious about who I allow into my life. And I have always chosen not to have a big circle of friends. It's kind of been my life partner and my kids. I've kept it very simple. I see all these people and they have all these friends. And that's really great. But I'm just comfortable with simplicity. I guess it's my soul.

Joe - It could be partly that you don't want to deal with people's reaction if you tell them something personal, and they aren't open to that.

Stephanie - Well, I don't like a lot of drama. I don't do good with a lot of drama. I guess I look back on my adolescence and I say that was a lot of drama. You know, my life was a little dramatic.

Joe - You were seen as the one causing a lot of the turmoil in your family.

Stephanie - You know, my dad always tried to make me out to be someone that was very demanding, and kind of high maintenance. I'm not sure that that was entirely accurate, but okay. That's how they felt.

Joe - Your parents sort of lived out a second adolescence after they separated. Your dad was gone during the week, and your mom was gone on the weekends. And you were still pretty young at the time.

282

Stephanie - I agree. When I had kids, my two kids were my entire focus. Yes, we got divorced and I got remarried. So, of course there was that transition into a new relationship and everything. But I made it perfectly clear the second time around that my kids were my entire life and my focus, and there was no misunderstanding about that. I didn't want my kids to ever feel like they weren't the most important.

Joe - Did you have a conversation at some point with your kids? Did you sit them down and say, now I want to explain that your grandfather and your grandmother, are gay and lesbian?

Stephanie - I did. We've raised kids that are quite broad minded.

Joe - Did you say the words, my dad is gay, my mom is lesbian? Because your parents talked around actually spelling things out.

Stephanie - I don't know if I did, Joe. I probably said gay. I have over time had a harder time with my mom's situation than I did with my dad's. It's hard for me to admit that. And it shouldn't be the case. But I think I'm-- I'm not sure really where that stems from. If it's just because I'm a female, and I wasn't sure about my own sexuality at one time. Or if it's because I really wanted my mother to be somebody different than who she was as a mother. But for a time, I had an issue with saying that.

Joe - Your mom said that after they came out, her relationship with your dad was almost like a business relationship. Your parents went from what you thought was a loving couple, to a new situation where they're living together in this very practical way. Was that a difficult adjustment for you to make?

Stephanie - You know, I got some counseling when I was older because of some different things that I went through. After going through a divorce, and with all the different things I was dealing with throughout my life, I felt like I had a rotten childhood. I would go to a therapist and they'd say, "okay, well tell me about your childhood." I was 30 some years old and I'm feeling like, do we really need to bring all that up again?

Joe - It might have been harder for you to bring all that back up because you'd never been given the framework to deal with it at the time. If they had sat you down and discussed the situation so that you could understand it, it might have been easier for you both at the time, and easier to rehash it again later.

Stephanie - It just felt like a whole ton of work. It felt like going through a cornfield.

Joe - What do you mean, going through a cornfield?

Stephanie - Like, you can get lost in a cornfield very easily. Right? But isn't that our life journey? I mean, we were never promised a clear path in life.

Joe – No, I guess we're not. How old are your kids?

Stephanie - Abby is 34 and Jacob is 31. I started early, huh?

Joe - I actually have a copy of your wedding invitation. You sent it to me.

Stephanie - Do you? Well, I have very fond memories of you staying with the family, and it's very special for us to connect up again, Joe. I appreciate you doing the follow up for the book, because it's going to be very profound to see the difference between 40 years ago and how society has evolved over the years. It's amazing. So, and I hope that you get in touch with all the other people as well.

Joe - Well, I really appreciated that as much as you were struggling with understanding what was going on in your family back then, to the extent that you could make sense of it, you were very straightforward about telling me what you were feeling. And it was helpful to have that perspective.

Stephanie – My present husband and I actually worked side by side. He was in law enforcement and I was the confidential admin for the department. And so I would process all the cases for the department. I did a lot of the training with the officers and I worked with the district attorney's office in the courts. So, there was a lot of secrets to be kept when you're away from work, and I was the perfect girl for that. I guess my personal background helped me there. And then I went into behavioral health. I went into taking care of very special need clients, a lot of them came from mental health institutions that we would try to re integrate into society.

Joe - Have you told any of those folks about your family?

Stephanie – yes, I've talked a lot about it, because some of the clients that I work with have struggled with it. I can't really talk a whole lot about my personal life. But I sense that talking about it has brought comfort to certain clients. And I'm really glad about that. I don't really care so much anymore about keeping that secret, and that's really liberating. But yet, even though it's liberating, I still keep people at arm's length. I still do.

Joe - When you moved in with your dad he was in a place where he was feeling like, I gave you this many years so now I get to live my life. Did he ever come back to a place where he was calling you and seeing you more?

Stephanie - Let's see... I lived with Dad and Tim, and you know they were together up until dad died, just as a caveat there. And then I went to live with mom. During that time when I was with Mom, I didn't have a phone number for dad. And that was very hurtful. But then, yes, he did come around. I got married and had a little baby, Abby. He was around, but he wasn't what I would call a doting grandfather. Which is fine. But to this day, I do look after Tim. And sometimes I think he could be a perfect candidate for me to be really angry at about the whole thing. But I just, I let go of that. I love my dad so much. And I know he did a lot of things that, you know, weren't right. But I try to remember all the wonderful things he was as a dad when I was little. Because my mom went through so many hard times. And without my dad, I don't know how we all would have made it when I was little, when she was so sick. So, I try to always remember that my dad was really everything to me. I'm able to just forgive and forget.

Joe - Because you focus on the good times when he was a doting father?

Stephanie - Yes, that's helpful. Does that make sense?

Joe - Sure. I imagine that it's easier for you to get peace about the relationship by focusing on the good times.

Stephanie - There's certainly a lot there that I could be angry about. But, you know, I always try see the positive. That's my own little tidbit to offer as far as life. And I went back to see my mother in April. My mother went back to the church. She's almost 90. What really was strange, was when I had to deal with her and her partner, Katie's, medical issues. The nurses would ask the relationship between Katie and mother, and there was a big difference in how they answered it. They would question mother's name on the paperwork and Katie would say, that's my partner. My mother would say, that's my friend. You know? My mom's gone back to the church and she considers herself a celibate. And so here we go.

Joe - It's been a wonderful opportunity to be able to have this follow up conversation after all these years.

Stephanie - Well, I'm really happy for you. And it was just like old times.

Joe - Great talking with you.

Stephanie - You too, Joe.

§

ABOUT THE AUTHOR

Joe Gantz is a writer and documentary filmmaker known for examining personal stories with honesty, humor, and depth. He is the producer of Taxicab Confessions, which was on HBO for 16 years, as well as many feature length documentaries, including American Winter, Ending Disease and The Race to Save the World. Over his long career his goal has been to capture "life in progress", showing authentic and relatable stories that allow viewers to see controversial issues with compassion and understanding.

Made in United States
North Haven, CT
11 February 2023